A Call to Spiritual Reformation

A Call to
Spiritual
Reformation

Priorities from Paul and His Prayers

D. A. Carson

BakerBooks

A Division of Baker Book House Co.
Grand Rapids, Michigan 49516

© 1992 by Baker Books

Published by Baker Books
a division of Baker Book House Company
P.O. box 6287, Grand Rapids, MI 49516-6287

and

Inter-Varsity Press
Norton Street
Nottingham NG3 3HR
United Kingdom

Ninth printing, July 2002

Printed in the United States of America

Library of Congress Cataloging-in-Publication Data

Carson, D. A.
    A call to spiritual reformation: priorities from Paul and his prayers / D. A. Carson
        p.   cm.
    Includes bibliographical references.
    ISBN 0-8010-2569-9
    1. Prayer—Biblical teaching. 2. Bible. N.T. Epistles of Paul—Criticism, interpretation, etc. I. Title.
    BS2655.P73C365
    248.3'2—dc20   92-11392

British Library of Congress Cataloguing-in-Publication Data
A catalogue record for this book is available from the British Library.
ISBN: 0-85110-976-4

For current information about all releases from Baker Book House, visit our web site:
http://www.bakerbooks.com

This book is gratefully dedicated to

Paul and Anke Miller

Contents

Preface

I doubt if there is any Christian who has not sometimes found it difficult to pray. In itself this is neither surprising nor depressing: it is not surprising, because we are still pilgrims with many lessons to learn; it is not depressing, because struggling with such matters is part of the way we learn.

What is both surprising and depressing is the sheer prayerlessness that characterizes so much of the Western church. It is surprising, because it is out of step with the Bible that portrays what Christian living should be; it is depressing, because it frequently coexists with abounding Christian activity that somehow seems hollow, frivolous, and superficial. Scarcely less disturbing is the enthusiastic praying in some circles that overflows with emotional release but is utterly uncontrolled by any thoughtful reflection on the prayers of Scripture.

I wish I could say I always avoid these pitfalls. The truth is that I am a part of what I condemn. But if we are to make any headway in reforming our personal and corporate praying then we shall have to begin by listening afresh to Scripture and seeking God's help in understanding how to apply Scripture to our lives, our homes, and our churches.

This book is not a comprehensive theology of prayer, set against the background of modern debate on the nature of spirituality. Elsewhere I have been involved in a project that attempted something along those lines.[1] Here the aim is far simpler: to work through several of Paul's prayers in such a way that we hear God speak to us today, and to find strength and direction to improve our praying, both for God's glory and for our good.

This book began its life as a series of seven sermons preached in various settings. The sequence of seven was delivered in only one place: the Church Missionary Society "summer school" in New South Wales, in early January 1990. Humanly speaking, the timing was inauspicious: my mother had died on New Year's Eve. Yet taking that wrenching step to fulfill my previous commitment served only to demonstrate once again that God's strength is displayed in our weakness, for the meetings in New South Wales were full of the presence and power of the Lord. I am grateful to my father and brother for urging me to continue with the meetings, and to Rev. Peter and Joan Tasker and to Archdeacon Victor and Delle Roberts and their colleagues for their warmth and encouragement. I am grateful, too, to Baker Book House for their interest in this expository study, and for their practical suggestions as to how best to turn seven rather lengthy sermons into shorter chapters for the printed page. Preachers interested in how these chapters were originally configured might want to look at the "extended note" that concludes the "Notes" section of this book.

The content of these pages is substantially what was given in oral form, but the style has been modified for the printed page. Because of the anticipated readership, I have not included bibliography except where I actually cite a source. To facilitate the use of this book in group study and in Sunday school classes, I have included questions at the end of each chapter. The questions sometimes require factual answers (and are therefore useful for review), and sometimes require reflection, debate, or further study; they might be most helpful, therefore, to a group led by someone a little further down the path of Christian discipleship than the casual reader might be.

Soli Deo gloria.

D. A. Carson
Trinity Evangelical Divinity School

Introduction:
The Urgent Need of the Church

W hat is the most urgent need in the church of the Western world today? Many different responses are given to that question. Just as in the political arena single-issue groups have sometimes captured the limelight and temporarily controlled national discussion, so also in the arena of the church there are groups with a single focus and a single answer to all questions.

Some in the church say that what we need is purity in sexual and reproductive matters. Certainly the facts are alarming. A few years ago *Christianity Today* published the results of a poll showing that in several church singles groups in California—groups of unmarried and divorced people, usually between the ages of twenty and thirty-five—more than 90 percent of both men and women had engaged or were then engaged in illicit sexual affairs. Ah, you say, that is California: what can you expect? But a more recent poll published by *Leadership* is scarcely more encouraging. A study of teenagers from evangelical churches across America revealed that more than 40 percent of such churched young people eighteen years of age or younger had engaged in premarital sex (over against a national base of about 54 percent). Within a twenty-five-mile radius of my home, at least four pastors have ruined their ministry in recent years because of moral failures. The directors of several mission boards in North America and in Europe have quietly mentioned to me that they have had to deal with more problems of sexual immorality among missionaries during the past five years than during the previous thirty, forty, or fifty years.

Although a frog dropped into hot water will immediately jump out, that same frog can be quietly cooked to death if the temperature of the water in which it is already lying rises slowly. Like this proverbial frog, our culture is slowly heating up and destroying us. Technicolor celebration of lust and violence invades our homes through magazines, radio, newspapers, and television. Pornography that would not be admitted into *any* neighborhood cinema three decades ago is now readily available. The invention of the video recorder and the widespread availability of both cable and pay-television have exposed millions of people to soft and hard pornography that even today could not be shown in public cinemas. A glance at the magazine rack at the checkout of any grocery store shows we belong to a culture obsessed with sex.

But that is not all. The World Health Organization estimates that no fewer than ten million people will die of AIDS, no matter what discoveries are made in the near future. Doubtless a small percentage of AIDS sufferers are entirely innocent of any sexual misconduct: hemophiliacs have contracted the disease, and so also innocent spouses, children born of infected mothers, and drug addicts who have shared dirty needles. But there is little doubt that the disease is driven by promiscuity, both homosexual and heterosexual. If promiscuity were miraculously barred, the disease would die out.

Others locate the most urgent problem of the church less in personal morality than in larger policy issues connected with reproduction. Christian outrage at the continued tolerance of abortion-on-demand is steady: not a few see this issue as the most urgent challenge before the contemporary Western church.

God knows we need purity in sexual and reproductive matters. But let us be frank: some societies experience high degrees of sexual rectitude without much knowledge of God, without eternal life. Many Muslim nations, for instance, exhibit a far higher degree of sexual purity and a far lower abortion rate than any Western nation. Surely this cannot be our greatest need.

Others say the church's most urgent need is a combination of integrity and generosity in the financial arena. It might be embarrassing to discover how many people who read this page have at some time cheated on their income tax forms. There was a time in many Western nations when what a business person promised was as binding as a written contract, but no longer. Large-scale corruption has rocked financial houses whose names once symbolized utter reliability.

One of the most frightening characteristics of the return to a more conservative lifestyle in the eighties and nineties is the sheer greed in which it is wrapped. The conservatism of the fifties arose out of the Depression of the thirties and the world war of the forties: parents worked hard to build a better world for their children than they had known themselves. But the new conservatism devotes little thought to the future, and still less to children. We want to get our own little nest-egg together, and spend it; we want the government to do as much as possible for us, but to defer the taxes until the time our children will have to pay for our excesses. Marketing techniques conspire to make us think that happiness is bound up with acquisition—people in business know of the number of credit cards at their limits; rank in society is heavily tied to perceived wealth.

In some measure, of course, greed characterizes every culture in this fallen world. But the raw worship of Mammon has become so bold, so outrageous, so pervasive in the Western world during the last ten years that many of us are willing to do almost anything—including sacrificing our children—provided we can buy more. So what we need, then, is integrity coupled with generosity, a new freedom from this miserable enslavement to wealth, an enslavement that is corroding our resolve and corrupting our direction.

God knows we need to be released from our rampant materialism. But candor forces us to recognize that there are societies far less devoted to the creed of "More!" than we are, but whose people do not know God. How can this be our greatest need?

Well, then, someone might say, what we need in this hour of spiritual declension is evangelism and church planting. World population figures are escalating. Also, "missions" can no longer be thought of as something that takes place "over there." Most Western nations are growing in ethnic diversity. In America, we are told, by the year 2000 WASPs (white, Anglo-Saxon Protestants) will make up only 47 percent of the population. If we ask how much effective evangelism has been done among Hispanics in Chicago, Greeks in Sydney, Arabs in London, or Asians in Vancouver, we must hang our heads in shame. World-class cities continue to draw in the bulk of the world's population, while in most Western countries the church at its strength (however weak that "strength" may be) is rural and suburban, not urban. Although there are some wonderful bright spots, evangelicalism is not proving very zealous or very effective in obeying the Lord's mandate to evangelize.

Yes, we urgently need more and better evangelism. But we must candidly come to grips with several alarming facts. To what extent do those who profess faith at world-class evangelistic meetings actually persevere, over a period of five years from their initial profession of faith? When careful studies have been undertaken, the most commonly agreed range is 2 percent to 4 percent; that is, between 2 percent and 4 percent of those who make a profession of faith at such meetings are actually persevering in the faith five years later, as measured by such external criteria as attendance at church, regular Bible reading, or the like.

Even such frightening statistics do not disclose the immensity of the problem. Many who profess faith seem to think that Christianity is something to add to their already busy lives, not something that controls, constrains, and shapes their vision and all of their goals. The Princeton Religion Research Center, which studies religion in America, has demonstrated that the slight increase during the last ten years in Americans attending church must be set against the marked decline in professing American Christians who think that there is an essential connection between Christianity and morality. The sad truth is that much American Christianity is returning to raw paganism: the ordinary pagan can be ever so religious without any necessary entailment in ethics, morality, self-sacrifice, or integrity.

A CALL TO SPIRITUAL REFORMATION

In short, evangelism—at least the evangelism that has dominated much of the Western world—does not seem powerful enough to address our declension.

Perhaps what we most urgently need, then, is disciplined, biblical thinking. We need more Bible colleges and seminaries, more theologians, more lay training, more expository preaching. How else are we going to train a whole generation of Christians to think God's thoughts after him, other than by teaching them to think through Scripture, to learn the Scriptures well?

I am scarcely in a position to criticize expository preaching and seminaries: I have given my life to such ministry. Yet I would be among the first to acknowledge that some students at the institution where I teach, and some faculty too, can devote thousands of hours to the diligent study of Scripture and yet still somehow display an extraordinarily shallow knowledge of God. Biblical knowledge can be merely academic and rigorous, but somehow not edifying, not life-giving, not devout, not guileless.

Time fails to list other urgent needs that various groups espouse. Some groups point to the desperate need for real, vital corporate worship; others focus on trends in the nation and therefore the need to become involved in politics and policies.

Clearly all of these things are important. I would not want anything I have said to be taken as disparagement of evangelism and worship, a diminishing of the importance of purity and integrity, a carelessness about disciplined Bible study. But there is a sense in which these urgent needs are merely symptomatic of a far more serious lack. The one thing we most urgently need in Western Christendom is a deeper knowledge of God. We need to know God better.

When it comes to knowing God, we are a culture of the spiritually stunted. So much of our religion is packaged to address our felt needs—and these are almost uniformly anchored in our pursuit of our own happiness and fulfillment. God simply becomes the Great Being who, potentially at least, meets our needs and fulfills our aspirations. We think rather little of what he is like, what he expects of us, what he seeks in us. We are not captured by his holiness and his love; his thoughts and words capture too little of our imagination, too little of our discourse, too few of our priorities.

In the biblical view of things, a deeper knowledge of God brings with it massive improvement in the other areas mentioned: purity, integrity, evangelistic effectiveness, better study of Scripture, improved private and corporate worship, and much more. But if we seek these things without passionately desiring a deeper knowledge of God, we are selfishly running after God's blessings without running after him. We are even worse than the man who wants his wife's services—someone to come home to, someone to cook and clean, someone to sleep with—without ever making the effort really to know and love his wife and discover what she wants and needs; we are worse than such a man, I say, because God is more than any wife, more than the best of wives: he is perfect in his love, he has made us for himself, and we are answerable to him.

Even so, this is not a book that directly meets the challenge to know God better. Rather, it addresses one small but vital part of that challenge. One of the foundational steps in knowing God, and one of the basic demonstrations that we do know God, is prayer—spiritual, persistent, biblically minded prayer. Writing a century and a half ago, Robert Murray M'Cheyne declared, "What a man is alone on his knees before God, that he is, and no more." But we have ignored this truism. We have learned to organize, build institutions, publish books, insert ourselves into the media, develop evangelistic strategies, and administer discipleship programs, but we have forgotten how to pray.

Most pastors testify to the decline in personal, family, and corporate prayer across the nation. Even the recently organized "concerts of prayer" are fairly discouraging from an historical perspective: some of them, at least, are so blatantly manipulative that they are light-years away from prayer meetings held in parts of the world that have tasted a breath of heaven-sent revival. Moreover, it is far from clear that they are changing the prayer habits of our churches, or the private discipline of significant numbers of believers.

Two years ago at a major North American seminary, fifty students who were offering themselves for overseas ministry during the summer holidays were carefully interviewed so that their suitability could be assessed. Only three of these fifty—6 percent!—could testify to regular quiet times, times of reading the Scriptures, of devoting themselves to prayer. It would be painful and embarrassing to uncover the prayer life of many thousands of evangelical pastors.

But we may probe more deeply. Where is our delight in praying? Where is our sense that we are meeting with the living God, that we are doing business with God, that we are interceding with genuine unction before the throne of grace? When was the last time we came away from a period of intercession feeling that, like Jacob or Moses, we had prevailed with God? How much of our praying is largely formulaic, liberally larded with clichés that remind us, uncomfortably, of the hypocrites Jesus excoriated?

I do not write these things to manipulate you or to be engendering guilty feelings. But what shall we *do*? Have not many of us tried at one point or another to improve our praying, and floundered so badly that we are more discouraged than we ever were? Do you not sense, with me, the severity of the problem? Granted that most of us know some individuals who are remarkable prayer warriors, is it not nevertheless true that by and large we are better at organizing than agonizing? Better at administering than interceding? Better at fellowship than fasting? Better at entertainment than worship? Better at theological articulation than spiritual adoration? Better—God help us!—at preaching than at praying?

What is wrong? Is not this sad state of affairs some sort of index of our knowledge of God? Shall we not agree with J. I. Packer when he writes, "I believe that prayer is the measure of the man, spiritually, in a way that nothing else is, so that how we pray is as important a question as we can ever face"?[1] Can we profitably meet the other challenges that confront the Western church if prayer is ignored as much as it has been?

My aim, then, in this series of meditations, is to examine the foundations again. Many different approaches might have been chosen, but the one adopted here is simple. Just as God's Word must reform our theology, our ethics, and our practices, so also must it reform our praying. The purpose of this book, then, is to think through some of Paul's prayers, so that we may align our

18

prayer habits with his. We want to learn what to pray for, what arguments to use, what priorities we should adopt, what beliefs should shape our prayers, and much more. We might have examined the prayers of Moses, or of David, or of Jeremiah. But here we focus on Paul, and especially on Paul's petitions, acknowledging that the focus is limited. We shall constantly try to grasp not only the rudiments of Paul's prayers but also how Christians can adopt Paul's theology of prayer in their own attempts to pray. And since lasting renewal, genuine revival, and true reformation spring from the work of the Holy Spirit as he takes the Word and applies it to our lives, it is important for me as I write this, and for you as you read it, to pause frequently and ask that the Holy Spirit will take whatever is biblically faithful and useful in these meditations and so apply it to our lives that our praying will be permanently transformed.

Questions for Review and Reflection

1. What is the most pressing need in the contemporary church of the Western world? Defend your view.
2. List as many of the church's needs mentioned in this chapter as you can remember. Add to this list. How do these things relate to the fundamental question of how well we know God?
3. Although this book is concerned to encourage biblical praying, quite obviously it is possible to pray without any real knowledge of the living God. How can this be so? Is there a certain kind of prayer that should be avoided? If so, what kind?

1

Lessons from the School of Prayer

Throughout my spiritual pilgrimage, two sources have largely shaped, and continue to shape, my own prayer life: the Scriptures and more mature Christians.

The less authoritative of these two has been the advice, wisdom, and example of senior saints. I confess I am not a very good student in the school of prayer. Still, devoting a few pages to their advice and values may be worthwhile before I turn to the more important and more authoritative of the two sources that have taught me to pray.

Among the lessons more mature Christians have taught me, then, are these.

1. Much praying is not done because we do not plan to pray. We do not drift into spiritual life; we do not drift into disciplined prayer. We will not grow in prayer unless we plan to pray. That means we must self-consciously set aside time to do nothing but pray.

What we actually do reflects our highest priorities. That means we can proclaim our commitment to prayer until the cows come home, but unless we actually pray, our actions disown our words.

19

This is the fundamental reason why set times for prayer are important: they ensure that vague desires for prayer are concretized in regular practice. Paul's many references to his "prayers" (e.g., Rom. 1:10; Eph. 1:16; 1 Thess. 1:2) suggest that he set aside specific times for prayer—as apparently Jesus himself did (Luke 5:16). Of course, mere regularity in such matters does not ensure that effective praying takes place: genuine godliness is so easily aped, its place usurped by its barren cousin, formal religion. It is also true that different lifestyles demand different patterns: a shift worker, for instance, will have to keep changing the scheduled prayer times, while a mother of twin two-year-olds will enjoy neither the energy nor the leisure of someone living in less constrained circumstances. But after all the difficulties have been duly recognized and all the dangers of legalism properly acknowledged, the fact remains that unless we plan to pray we will not pray. The reason we pray so little is that we do not plan to pray. Wise planning will ensure that we devote ourselves to prayer often, even if for brief periods: it is better to pray often with brevity than rarely but at length. But the worst option is simply not to pray—and that will be the controlling pattern unless we plan to pray. If we intend to change our habits, we must start here.[1]

2. Adopt practical ways to impede mental drift. Anyone who has been on the Christian way for a while knows there are times when our private prayers run something like this: "Dear Lord, I thank you for the opportunity of coming into your presence by the merits of Jesus. It is a wonderful blessing to call you Father. . . . I wonder where I left my car keys? [No, no! Back to business.] Heavenly Father, I began by asking that you will watch over my family—not just in the physical sphere, but in the moral and spiritual dimensions of our lives. . . . Boy, last Sunday's sermon was sure bad. I wonder if I'll get that report written on time? [No, no!] Father, give real fruitfulness to that missionary couple we support, whatever their name is. . . . Oh, my! I had almost forgotten I promised to fix my son's bike today. . . ." Or am I the only Christian who has ever had problems with mental drift?

But you can do many things to stamp out daydreaming, to stifle reveries. One of the most useful things is to vocalize your prayers.

This does not mean they have to be so loud that they become a distraction to others, or worse, a kind of pious showing off. It simply means you articulate your prayers, moving your lips perhaps; the energy devoted to expressing your thoughts in words and sentences will order and discipline your mind, and help deter meandering.

Another thing you can do is pray over the Scriptures. Christians just setting out on the path of prayer sometimes pray for everything they can think of, glance at their watches, and discover they have been at it for all of three or four minutes. This experience sometimes generates feelings of defeat, discouragement, even despair. A great way to begin to overcome this problem is to pray through various biblical passages.

In other words, it is entirely appropriate to tie your praying to your Bible reading. The reading schemes you may adopt are legion. Some Christians read a chapter a day. Others advocate three chapters a day, with five on Sunday: this will get you through the Bible in a year. I am currently following a pattern set out by Robert Murray M'Cheyne in the last century: it will take me through the Psalms and the New Testament twice during this calendar year, and the rest of the Old Testament once. Whatever the reading scheme, it is essential to read the passage slowly and thoughtfully so as to retrieve at least some of its meaning and bearing on your life. Those truths and entailments can be the basis of a great deal of reflective praying.

A slight variation of this plan is to adopt as models several biblical prayers. Read them carefully, think through what they are saying, and pray analogous prayers for yourself, your family, your church, and for many others beyond your immediate circle.

Similarly, praying through the worship sections of the better hymnals can prove immensely edifying and will certainly help you to focus your mind and heart in one direction for a while.

Some pastors pace as they pray. One senior saint I know has long made it his practice to pray through the Lord's Prayer, thinking through the implications of each petition as he goes, and organizing his prayers around those implications.[2] Many others make prayer lists of various sorts, a practice that will be discussed in more detail later.

This may be part of the discipline of what has come to be called "journaling." At many periods in the history of the church, spiritually mature and disciplined Christians have kept what might be called spiritual journals. What such journals contain varies enormously. The Puritans often used them to record their experiences with God, their thoughts and prayers, their triumphs and failures. Bill Hybels, the senior pastor of Willow Creek Community Church, takes a page to record what he did and thought the day before, and then to write out some prayers for the day ahead of him.[3] At least one seminary now requires that their students keep such a journal throughout their years of study.

The real value of journaling, I think, is several-fold: (a) It enforces a change of pace, a slowing down. It ensures time for prayer. If you are writing your prayers, you are not daydreaming. (b) It fosters self-examination. It is an old truism that only the examined life is worth living. If you do not take time to examine your own heart, mind, and conscience from time to time, in the light of God's Word, and deal with what you find, you will become encrusted with the barnacles of destructive self-righteousness. (c) It ensures quiet articulation both of your spiritual direction and of your prayers, and this in turn fosters self-examination and therefore growth. Thus, journaling impedes mental drift.

But this is only one of many spiritual disciplines. The danger in this one, as in all of them, is that the person who is formally conforming to such a régime may delude himself or herself into thinking that the discipline is an end in itself, or ensures one of an exalted place in the heavenlies. That is why I rather oppose the imposition of such a discipline on a body of seminary students (however much I might encourage journaling): true spirituality can never be coerced.

Such dangers aside, you can greatly improve your prayer life if you combine these first two principles: set apart time for praying, and then use practical ways to impede mental drift.

3. At various periods in your life, develop, if possible, a prayer-partner relationship. Incidentally, if you are not married,

make sure your prayer partner is someone of your own sex. If you are married and choose a prayer partner of the opposite sex, make sure that partner is your spouse. The reason is that real praying is an immensely intimate business—and intimacy in one area frequently leads to intimacy in other areas. There is good evidence that after some of the Kentucky revivals in the last century, there was actually an *increase* in sexual promiscuity. But whatever the hurdles that must be crossed in the pursuit of rectitude, try to develop an appropriate prayer-partner relationship.

In this connection I have been extremely fortunate. While I was still an undergraduate, in one summer vacation a single pastor took me aside and invited me to pray with him. We met once a week, on Monday nights, for the next three months. Sometimes we prayed for an hour or so, sometimes for much longer. But there is no doubt that he taught me more of the rudiments of prayer than anyone else. One or two of his lessons I shall detail later; for the moment, it is simply the importance of this one-on-one discipleship that I want to stress.

At various periods of my life, other such opportunities have come my way. For the last year or so of my doctoral study, another graduate student and I set aside time one evening a week to pray. Eventually (I was rather slow on this front), I got married. Like most couples, we have found that sustained time for prayer together is not easy to maintain. Not only do we live at a hectic pace, but each stage of life has its peculiar pressures. When you have two or three preschool-age children, for instance, you are up early and exhausted by the evening. Still, we have tried to follow a set pattern. Quite apart from grace at meals, which may extend beyond the expected "thank you" to larger concerns, and quite apart from individual times for prayer and Bible reading, as a family we daily seek God's face. About half the time my wife or I leads the family in prayer; the rest of the time, the children join us in prayer. We have discovered the importance of injecting freshness and innovation into such times, but that is another subject. Before we retire at night, my wife and I invariably pray together, usually quite briefly. But in addition, at various points in our life together we have tried to set aside some time one evening a week to pray. Usually we achieve this for a few weeks, and then something breaks it up for a while. But we have tried to return to it, and we use those times to pray for family, church, students, pressing concerns of various sorts, our children, our life's direction and values, impending ministry, and much more.

If you know how to pray, consider seeking out someone else and teaching him or her how to pray. By teaching I do not mean set lessons so much as personal example communicated in a prayer-partner relationship. Such modeling and partnership will lead to the sorts of questions that will invite further sharing and discipleship. After all, it was because Jesus' disciples observed his prayer life that they sought his instruction in prayer (Luke 11:1).

If you know little about praying, then consider seeking out someone more mature in these matters and setting up a prayer-partner relationship for a period of time. If you cannot find a person like that, then foster such a relationship with someone who is at your own level of Christian growth. Together you may discover many useful truths. Prayer-partner relationships are as valuable for the discipline, accountability, and regularity they engender as for the lessons that are shared.

There are many variations on this sort of relationship. I know a few pastors who seek out a handful of people who will meet, perhaps early in the morning, to give themselves for an hour or more to intercessory prayer. The ground rules vary quite a bit from group to group. In some suburban churches, an early morning prayer meeting may be quite open and public, simply a good slot in the day to hold a public prayer meeting, granted the scheduling difficulties of suburbanites. But I am primarily thinking of more private groups of carefully selected prayer warriors. The ground rules for such groups may include the following: (1) Those who agree to participate must do so every week, without fail and without complaint, for a set period of time (six months?), barring, of course, unforeseen circumstances such as illness. (2) They must be Christians without any shadow of partisanship, bitterness, nurtured resentments, or affectation in their lives. In other words, they must be stamped with integrity and with genuine love for other believers, not least the obstreperous ones. (3) They must not be gossips.

Such clusters of prayer partners have been used by God again and again to spearhead powerful ministry and extravagant blessing. They may continue unnoticed for years, except in the courts of heaven. Some little groups grow and become large prayer meetings; others multiply and divide, maintaining the same principles.

But whatever the precise pattern, there is a great deal to be said for developing godly prayer-partner relationships.

4. Choose models—but choose them well. Most of us can improve our praying by carefully, thoughtfully listening to others pray. This does not mean we should copy everything we hear. Some people use an informal and chatty style in prayer that reflects their own personality and perhaps the context in which they were converted; others intone their prayers before God with genuine erudition coupled with solemn formality, deploying vocabulary and forms of English considered idiomatic 350 years ago. Neither extreme is an intrinsically good model; both might be good models, but not because of relatively external habits, and certainly not because of merely cultural or personal idiosyncrasy. When we find good models, we will study their content and urgency, but we will not ape their idiom.

Not every good model provides us with exactly the same prescription for good praying, exactly the same balance. All of them pray with great seriousness; all of them use arguments and seek goals that are already portrayed in Scripture. Some of them seem to carry you with them into the very throne room of the Almighty; others are particularly faithful in intercession, despite the most difficult circumstances in life and ministry; still others are noteworthy because of the breadth of their vision. All are characterized by a wonderful mixture of contrition and boldness in prayer.

Once again, my life has been blessed by some influential models. I must begin by mentioning my own parents. I remember how, even when we children were quite young, each morning my mother would withdraw from the hurly-burly of life to read her Bible and pray. In the years that I was growing up, my father, a Baptist minister, had his study in our home. Every morning we could hear him praying in that study. My father vocalized when he prayed—loudly enough that we knew he was praying, but not loudly enough that we could hear what he was saying. Every day he prayed, usually for about forty-five minutes. Perhaps there were times when he failed to do so, but I cannot think of one.

My father was a church planter in Québec, in the difficult years when there was strong opposition, some of it brutal. Baptist ministers alone spent a total of eight years in jail between 1950 and 1952. Dad's congregations were not large; they were usually at the lower end of the two-digit range. On Sunday mornings after the eleven o'clock service, Dad would often play the piano and call his three children to join him in singing, while Mum completed the preparations for dinner. But one Sunday morning in the late fifties, I recall, Dad was not at the piano, and was not to be found. I finally tracked him down. The door of his study was ajar. I pushed it open, and there he was, kneeling in front of his big chair, praying and quietly weeping. This time I could hear what he was saying. He was interceding with God on behalf of the handful of people to whom he had preached, and in particular for the conversion of a few who regularly attended but who had never trusted Christ Jesus.

In the ranks of ecclesiastical hierarchies, my father is not a great man. He has never served a large church, never written a book, never discharged the duties of high denominational office. Doubtless his praying, too, embraces idioms and stylistic idiosyncrasies that should not be copied. But with great gratitude to God, I testify that my parents were not hypocrites. That is the worst possible heritage to leave with children: high spiritual pretensions and low performance. My parents were the opposite: few pretensions, and disciplined performance. What they prayed for were the important things, the things that congregate around the prayers of Scripture. And sometimes when I look at my own children, I wonder if, should the Lord give us another thirty years, they will remember their father as a man of prayer, or think of him as someone distant who was away from home rather a lot and who wrote a number of obscure books. That quiet reflection often helps me to order my days.

There have been many other models since the days of my youth. I can think of two women who in church prayer meetings invariably prayed with a great breadth of vision and a sense of utter reality, and above all with compelling compassion. They prayed in line with the truth of Scripture, but they prayed because they loved people. I remember the prayers of some of the Christian leaders I have met through the World Evangelical Fellowship.

I remember some of the public prayers of Dr. Martyn Lloyd-Jones. In particular, I recall how shamed I was when one of Lloyd-Jones's daughters told me some months before he died that her father had asked her to tell me that he prayed for me regularly. It was not as if I were within his inner circle of friends—and so I suddenly realized how extensive his prayer ministry must be and how deep his commitment to intercede for ministers of the gospel.

Choose models, but choose them well. Study their content, their breadth, their passion, their unction—but do not ape their idiom.

5. Develop a system for your prayer lists. It is difficult to pray faithfully for a large spread of people and concerns without developing prayer lists that help you remember them. These lists come in a variety of forms. Many denominations and mission agencies and even some large local churches publish their own prayer lists. These can be a considerable help to those with large interest in the particular organization; otherwise, they may seem a trifle remote. Despite its remoteness, there is one prayer list that offers a tremendous compensating advantage. The list to which I am referring is the publication *Operation World*,[4] which over the course of a year takes you around the world to country after country and region after region, and provides you with succinct, intelligent information to assist you in your prayers. Its value lies in its ability to enlarge your horizons, to expand your interest in the world church and the world's needs.

Many Christians who give themselves to prayer, however, find that, in addition to such published information, it is wise and fruitful to prepare their own lists. These come in many forms. Some are really a subset of journaling, briefly described earlier in this chapter. One approach to journaling involves writing down prayer requests on the left-hand side of a notebook, along with a date and relevant Scriptures, and answers on the right-hand side. This approach has the advantage of encouraging thoughtful, *specific* requests. General intercession, as important as it may be, cannot so easily be linked to specific answers.

Although I have sometimes adopted this and other forms for my prayer lists, the prayer-list pattern I have followed in recent years I adapted from J. Herbert Kane, a veteran missionary to China (1935–1950) and then a productive teacher of world mission. Apart from any printed guides I may use, I keep a manila folder in my study, where I pray, and usually I take it with me when I am traveling. The first sheet in that folder is a list of people for whom I ought to pray regularly: they are bound up with me, with who I am. My wife heads the list, followed by my children and a number of relatives, followed in turn by a number of close friends in various parts of the world. The two institutional names on that sheet are the local church of which we are a part, and the seminary where I now teach. Of course, exactly what I pray for these people and institutions will vary from time to time as my perception of their needs changes (as my children grow older, for instance, or as a close friend faces a particular challenge in life or ministry), but the heart of my burden for these people is shaped, so far as I am able to shape it, by my grasp of what Scripture wants of us.

The second sheet in my folder lists short-range and intermediate-range concerns that will not remain there indefinitely. They include forthcoming responsibilities in ministry and various crises or opportunities that I have heard about, often among Christians I scarcely know. Either they are the sort of thing that will soon pass into history (like the project of writing this book!), or they concern people or situations too remote for me to remember indefinitely. In other words, the first sheet focuses on people for whom I pray constantly; the second includes people and situations for whom I may pray for a short or an extended period of time, but probably not indefinitely. The entries on the first sheet do not change, but their particular needs often do; the entries on the second sheet are largely shaped by short-term needs, and names and concerns are being added and deleted often.

The next item in my manila folder is the list of my advisees—the students for whom I am particularly responsible. This list includes some notes on their background, academic program, families, personal concerns and the like, and of course this list changes from year to year.

The rest of the folder is filled with letters—prayer letters, personal letters, occasionally independent notes with someone's name at the top. These are filed in alphabetical order. When a new letter comes in, I highlight any matters in it that ought to be the subject of prayer, and then file it in the appropriate place in the folder. The letter it replaces is pulled out at the same time, with the result that the prayer folder is always up to date. I try to set aside time to intercede with God on behalf of the people and situations represented by these letters, taking the one on the top, then the next one, and the next one, and so forth, putting the top ones, as I finish with them, on the bottom of the pile. Thus although the list is alphabetized, on any day a different letter of the alphabet may confront me. As I write these lines, I see that names beginning with "F" are next in the folder.

I am not suggesting that this is the best system. It suits me, and I am happy with it. I need to use it more, not enlarge it more. But the system is flexible, always up-to-date, expandable; above all, it helps me pray. I tell my students that if they want me to pray for them regularly after they graduate, they need to write regular letters to me. Otherwise I shall certainly forget most of them.

Whatever the system, use prayer lists. All of us would be wiser if we would resolve never to put people down, except on our prayer lists.

6. Mingle praise, confession, and intercession; but when you intercede, try to tie as many requests as possible to Scripture. Both theoretical and practical considerations underlie this advice.

The theoretical considerations can best be set out by mentally conjuring up two extremes. The first judges it inappropriate to ask God for things. Surely he is sovereign: he does not need our counsel. If he is the one "who works out everything in conformity with the purpose of his will" (Eph. 1:11), surely it is a bit cheeky to badger him for things. He does not change the course of the universe because some finite, ignorant, and sinful human being asks him to. The appropriate response to him, surely, is worship. We should worship him for what he is and does. Because we so frequently skirt his ways, we should be ready to confess our sin. But to bring him our petitions is surely to misrepresent where true piety lies. Godliness rests in submission to the Almighty's will, not in intercession that seeks to change that will. Petitionary prayer can therefore be dismissed as at best an impertinence, at worst a desperate insult to the sovereign and holy God. Besides, if God is really sovereign, he is going to do whatever he wants to do, whether or not he is asked to do it. Of course, if a Christian adopts this line, he or she is thinking in much the same way as a Muslim: the right approach to God binds you to a kind of theological determinism, not to say fatalism.

The second extreme begins with the slogan, "Prayer changes things." Petitionary prayer is everything. This means that if people die and go to hell, it is because you or I or someone has neglected to pray. Does not Scripture say, "You do not have, because you do not ask God" (James 4:2)? Worship and confession must of course be allotted an appropriate part, but they can reduce to mere self-gratification: it can be fun to worship, a relief to confess your sins. Real work for God, however, demands that we wrestle with God, and cry, with Jacob, "I will not let you go unless you bless me" (Gen. 32:26). Not to intercede is to flee from your responsibilities as a Christian. Far from being an insult to God, petitionary prayer honors him because he is a God who likes to give his blessings in response to the intercession of his people. In fact, if you agonize in your prayers, fast much, plead the name of Jesus, and spend untold hours at this business of intercession, you cannot help but call down from heaven a vast array of blessings. Of course, if a Christian adopts this line, he or she is in danger of treating prayer much like magic: the right incantations produce the desired effect.

On the face of it, neither of these extremes captures the balance of biblical prayers, and both of them are reductionistic in their treatment of God. I shall return to this question at greater length in chapters 9 and 10. Anticipating the argument there, we must remember that the Bible simultaneously pictures God as utterly sovereign, and as a prayer-hearing and prayer-answering God. Unless we perceive this, and learn how to act on these simultaneous truths, not only will our views of God be distorted, but our praying is likely to wobble back and forth between a resigned fatalism that asks for nothing and a badgering desperation that exhibits little real trust.

Even a little reflective acquaintance with the God of the Bible acknowledges that he is not less than utterly sovereign, and not less than personal and responsive. Correspondingly, the Bible boasts many examples of praise and adoration, and no fewer examples of intercession. Indeed, "Christian prayer is marked decisively by petition, because this form of prayer discloses the true state of affairs. It reminds the believer that God is the source of all good, and that human beings are utterly dependent and stand in need of everything."[5]

Of the various models that usefully capture both of these poles, the model of a personal relationship with a father is as helpful as any. If a boy asks his father for several things, all within the father's power to give, the father may give him one of them right away, delay giving him another, decline to give him a third, set up a condition for a fourth. The child is not assured of receiving something because he has used the right incantation: that would be magic. The father may decline to give something because he knows it is not in the child's best interests. He may delay giving something else because he knows that so many requests from his young son are temporary and whimsical. He may also withhold something that he knows the child needs until the child asks for it in an appropriate way. But above all, the wise father is more interested in a relationship with his son than in merely giving him things. Giving him things constitutes part of that relationship but certainly not all of it. The father and son may enjoy simply going out for walks together. Often the son will talk with his father not to obtain something, or even to find out something, but simply because he likes to be with him.

Lessons from the School of Prayer

None of these analogies is perfect, of course. But it is exceedingly important to remember that prayer is not magic and that God is personal as well as sovereign. There is more to praying than asking, but any sustained prayer to the God of the Bible will certainly include asking. And because we slide so easily into sinful self-centeredness, we must approach this holy God with contrition and confession of our sins. On other occasions we will focus on his love and forbearance, on the sheer splendor of his being, and approach him with joy and exuberant praise. The rich mixture of approaches to God mirrored in Scripture must be taken over into our own lives. This rich mixture is, finally, nothing more than a reflection of the many different components of the kind of relationship we ought to have with the God of the Bible.

In addition to these "theoretical" considerations (as I have called them), there are some intensely practical questions. If the one to whom we pray is the sort of God I have just portrayed, then when we ask him for things, when we intercede with him, we must not think either in fatalistic terms or in terms of magic. Rather, we must think in personal and relational categories. We ask our heavenly Father for things because he has determined that many blessings will come to us only through prayer. Prayer is his ordained means of conveying his blessings to his people. That means we must pray according to his will, in line with his values, in conformity with his own character and purposes, claiming his own promises. Practically speaking, *how do we do that?*

Where shall we learn the will of God, the values of God, the character and purposes of God, the promises of God? We shall learn such things in the Scriptures he has graciously given us. But that means that when we pray, when we ask God for things, we must try to tie as many requests as possible to Scripture. That is an immensely *practical* step.

Elsewhere I have told of my first hesitant experiences along these lines.[6] They began with that pastor who took me aside on Monday nights and began to teach me to pray. I shall not repeat the account of those first experiences here. From him, however, I learned that one of the most important elements in intercession is to think through, in the light of Scripture, what it is God wants us to ask for.

That is not a superficial question, and the answers are rarely easy to come by. Thoughtful, balanced answers depend on a growing grasp of just what the Bible says in its parts, and as a whole. For example, what, precisely, should we be praying for with respect to each member of our family—and why? Someone close to us contracts a terminal disease: what should we pray for, and why? For healing? For freedom from pain? For faith and perseverance? For acceptance of what has befallen? And would it make a difference if the person in question were seventy-five years of age, as opposed to twenty-nine? Why, or why not? Are there some things we may humbly request from God, and others we should boldly claim? If so, what kinds of things fall into each category?

A very useful book could be written on this subject, provided it were written by someone not only learned in the Scriptures but also schooled in years of prayer. No matter how well done, such a book would have a lot of loose ends, precisely because effective prayer is the fruit of a relationship with God, not a technique for acquiring blessings. Besides, there are countless situations in which we simply do not know what to pray for. Then the Christian who is diligent at prayer learns what Paul means when he writes that "the Spirit helps us in our weakness. We do not know what we ought to pray, but the Spirit himself intercedes for us with groans that words cannot express. And he who searches our hearts knows the mind of the Spirit, because the spirit intercedes for the saints in accordance with God's will" (Rom. 8:26–27). When we pray, our intercessions may be off the mark; on many matters we do not know the Scriptures well enough, we do not know God well enough, to be confident about what we should be praying. But the Holy Spirit helps us by interceding for us with unuttered groanings offered to the Father while we Christians are praying.[7]

We must frankly admit that the task of tying as many petitions as possible to the Scriptures is challenging. Christians who grow in their ability to do this will learn that there are countless situations in prayer where we must simply rely on the Holy Spirit to intercede on our behalf. But having conceded these points—

Lessons from the School of Prayer

34

indeed, having insisted upon them—it is essential to pursue this discipline. How else shall we learn what our heavenly Father wants, what he expects us to ask for, and why, and how to approach him?

7. If you are in any form of spiritual leadership, work at your public prayers. It does not matter whether the form of spiritual leadership you exercise is the teaching of a Sunday school class, pastoral ministry, small-group evangelism, or anything else: if at any point you pray in public as a leader, then work at your public prayers.

Some people think this advice distinctly corrupt. It smells too much of public relations, of concern for public image. After all, whether we are praying in private or in public, we are praying to God: Surely he is the one we should be thinking about, no one else.

This objection misses the point. Certainly if we must choose between trying to please God in prayer, and trying to please our fellow creatures, we must unhesitatingly opt for the former. But that is not the issue. It is not a question of pleasing our human hearers, but of instructing them and edifying them.

The ultimate sanction for this approach is none less than Jesus himself. At the tomb of Lazarus, after the stone has been removed, Jesus looks to heaven and prays, "Father, I thank you that you have heard me. I knew that you always hear me, but I said this for the benefit of the people standing here, that they may believe that you sent me" (John 11:41–42). Here, then, is a prayer of Jesus himself that is shaped in part by his awareness of what his human hearers need to hear.

The point is that although public prayer is addressed to God, it is addressed to God while others are overhearing it. Of course, if the one who is praying is more concerned to impress these human hearers than to pray to God, then rank hypocrisy takes over. That is why Jesus so roundly condemns much of the public praying of his day and insists on the primacy of private prayer (Matt. 6:5–8). But that does not mean there is no place at all for public prayer. Rather, it means that public prayer ought to be the overflow of one's private praying. And then, judging by the example of Jesus at the tomb of Lazarus, there is ample reason to reflect on just what my prayer, rightly directed to God, is saying to the people who hear me.

In brief, public praying is a pedagogical opportunity. It provides the one who is praying with an opportunity to instruct or encourage or edify all who hear the prayer. In liturgical churches, many of the prayers are well-crafted, but to some ears they lack spontaneity. In nonliturgical churches, many of the prayers are so predictable that they are scarcely any more spontaneous than written prayers, and most of them are not nearly as well-crafted. The answer to both situations is to provide more prayers that are carefully and freshly prepared. That does not necessarily mean writing them out verbatim (though that can be a good thing to do). At the least, it means thinking through in advance and in some detail just where the prayer is going, preparing, perhaps, some notes, and memorizing them.

Public praying is a responsibility as well as a privilege. In the last century the great English preacher Charles Spurgeon did not mind sharing his pulpit: others sometimes preached in his home church even when he was present. But when he came to the "pastoral prayer," if he was present, he reserved that part of the service for himself. This decision did not arise out of any priestly conviction that his prayers were more efficacious than those of others. Rather, it arose from his love for his people, his high view of prayer, his conviction that public praying should not only intercede with God but also instruct and edify and encourage the saints.

Many facets of Christian discipleship, not least prayer, are rather more effectively passed on by modeling than by formal teaching. Good praying is more easily caught than taught. If it is right to say that we should choose models from whom we can learn, then the obverse truth is that we ourselves become responsible to become models for others. So whether you are leading a service or family prayers, whether you are praying in a small-group Bible study or at a convention, work at your public prayers.

8. Pray until you pray. That is Puritan advice. It does not simply mean that persistence should mark much of our praying— though admittedly that is a point the Scriptures repeatedly make.

Lessons from the School of Prayer

Even though he was praying in line with God's promises, Elijah prayed for rain seven times before the first cloud appeared in the heavens. The Lord Jesus could tell parables urging persistence in prayer (Luke 11:5–13). If some generations need to learn that God is not particularly impressed by long-winded prayers, and is not more disposed to help us just because we are garrulous, our generation needs to learn that God is not impressed by the kind of brevity that is nothing other than culpable negligence. He is not more disposed to help us because our insincerity and spiritual flightiness conspire to keep our prayers brief. Our generation certainly needs to learn something more about persistence in prayer, and to that point I shall return in a later chapter. Even so, that is not quite what the Puritans meant when they exhorted one another to "pray until you pray."

What they meant is that Christians should pray long enough and honestly enough, at a single session, to get past the feeling of formalism and unreality that attends not a little praying. We are especially prone to such feelings when we pray for only a few minutes, rushing to be done with a mere duty. To enter the spirit of prayer, we must stick to it for a while. If we "pray until we pray," eventually we come to delight in God's presence, to rest in his love, to cherish his will. Even in dark or agonized praying, we somehow know we are doing business with God. In short, we discover a little of what Jude means when he exhorts his readers to "pray in the Holy Spirit" (Jude 20)—which presumably means it is treacherously possible to pray *not* in the Spirit.

Something of the same perspective is presupposed in an anonymous poem that C. S. Lewis quotes:

> They tell me, Lord, that when I seem
>   To be in speech with you,
> Since but one voice is heard, it's all a dream
>   One talker aping two.
>
> Sometimes it is, yet not as they
>   Conceive. Rather, I
> Seek in myself the things I hoped to say,
>   But lo!, my wells are dry.

A CALL TO SPIRITUAL REFORMATION

> Then, seeing me empty, you forsake
>   The listener's role and through
> My dumb lips breathe and into utterance wake
>   The thoughts I never knew.
>
> And thus you neither need reply
>   Nor can; thus, while we seem
> Two talkers, thou art One forever, and I
>   No dreamer, but thy dream.[8]

As Lewis comments, this "dream" language smacks rather too much of pantheism "and was perhaps dragged in for the rhyme."[9] Doubtless the anonymous author is a better poet than theologian. But there is something important here just the same. If God is the one "who works in you to will and to act according to his good purpose" (Phil. 2:13), then of course he is the God who by his Spirit helps us in our praying. Every Christian who has learned the rudiments of praying knows by experience at least a little of what this means. The Puritans knew a great deal of it. That is why they exhorted one another to "pray until you pray." Such advice is not to become an excuse for a new legalism: there are startling examples of very short, rapid prayers in the Bible (e.g., Neh. 2:4). But in the Western world we urgently need this advice, for many of us in our praying are like nasty little boys who ring front door bells and run away before anyone answers.

Pray until you pray.

These, then, are some of the lessons I have learned from other Christians. But I would not for a moment want to leave the impression that they constitute a rule, a litmus test, still less a "how-to" manual. The words of Packer in this regard are worth pondering:[10]

> I start with the truism that each Christian's prayer life, like every good marriage, has in it common factors about which one can generalize and also uniquenesses which no other Christian's prayer life will quite match. You are you, and I am I, and we must each find our own way with God, and there is no recipe for prayer that can work for us like a handyman's do-it-yourself

Lessons from the School of Prayer

manual or a cookery book, where the claim is that if you follow the instructions you can't go wrong. Praying is not like carpentry or cookery; it is the active exercise of a personal relationship, a kind of friendship, with the living God and his Son Jesus Christ, and the way it goes is more under divine control than under ours. Books on praying, like marriage manuals, are not to be treated with slavish superstition, as if perfection of technique is the answer to all difficulties; their purpose, rather, is to suggest things to try. But as in other close relationships, so in prayer: you have to find out by trial and error what is right for you, and you learn to pray by praying. Some of us talk more, others less; some are constantly vocal, others cultivate silence before God as their way of adoration; some slip into glossolalia, others make a point of not slipping into it; yet we may all be praying as God means us to do. The only rules are, stay within biblical guidelines and within those guidelines, as John Chapman puts it, "pray as you can and don't try to pray as you can't."

Questions for Review and Reflection

1. List the positive and negative things you have learned about praying by listening to others pray.
2. List practical ways in which you will commit yourself to improve your prayer life during the next six months.
3. What do Christian preachers and teachers mean when they encourage us to "meditate prayerfully on the Word of God"?

2

The Framework of Prayer

(2 Thessalonians 1:3–12)

Before thinking our way through the petitions of Paul's prayer in 2 Thessalonians 1:11–12, we must pause to reflect on the foundations the apostle himself lays. After all, Paul begins his petitions with the words: "With this in mind, we constantly pray for you" (v. 11).[1] With what in mind? Paul can only be referring to everything that has preceded in this chapter, excluding, perhaps, the salutation (vv. 1–2). In common with many letter writers of his day, Paul usually begins his letters, after the initial salutation, with a paragraph of thanksgiving. These segments of thanksgiving usually are carefully crafted to address his readers. But in this instance, the thanksgiving that begins in verse 3 ("We ought always to thank God for you, brothers . . ."), and the entire line of thought that flows from it (through v. 10), constitutes what Paul has in mind as he begins his prayer in verses 11–12.

In other words, verses 3–10 provide us with a framework of thought that Paul keeps in mind as he prays, a framework that largely controls what Paul prays for, and why. This is not the place

40

A Prayer of Paul for the Thessalonians

¹Paul, Silas and Timothy, to the church of the Thessalonians in God our Father and the Lord Jesus Christ:
²Grace and peace to you from God the Father and the Lord Jesus Christ.
³We ought always to thank God for you, brothers, and rightly so, because your faith is growing more and more, and the love every one of you has for each other is increasing. ⁴Therefore, among God's churches we boast about your perseverance and faith in all the persecutions and trials you are enduring.
⁵All this is evidence that God's judgment is right, and as a result you will be counted worthy of the kingdom of God, for which you are suffering. ⁶God is just: He will pay back trouble to those who trouble you ⁷and give relief to you who are troubled, and to us as well. This will happen when the Lord Jesus is revealed from

---

to unpack verses 3–10 in great detail, but we must pause to observe two dominant features of this framework for Paul's prayer, if we are to understand the prayer itself.

Thankfulness for Signs of Grace

"We ought always to thank God for you, brothers, and rightly so, because your faith is growing more and more, and the love every one of you has for each other is increasing. Therefore, among God's churches we boast about your perseverance and faith in all the persecutions and trials you are enduring" (vv. 3–4). Clearly, thanksgiving is a fundamental component of the mental framework that largely controls Paul's intercession. But for what does Paul offer thanks?

For what do we commonly give thanks? We say grace at meals, thanking God for our food; we give thanks when we receive material blessings—when the mortgage we've applied for comes through, or when we first turn on the ignition in a car we've just purchased. We may sigh a prayer of sweaty thanks after a near

A CALL TO SPIRITUAL REFORMATION

> heaven in blazing fire with his powerful angels. [8]He will punish those who do not know God and do not obey the gospel of our Lord Jesus. [9]They will be punished with everlasting destruction and shut out from the presence of the Lord and from the majesty of his power [10]on the day he comes to be glorified in his holy people and to be marveled at among all those who have believed. This includes you, because you believed our testimony to you
>
> [11]With this in mind, we constantly pray for you, that our God may count you worthy of his calling, and that by his power he may fulfill every good purpose of yours and every act prompted by your faith. [12]We pray this so that the name of our Lord Jesus may be glorified in you, and you in him, according to the grace of our God and the Lord Jesus Christ.
>
> (2 Thess. 1:1–12)

miss on the highway; we may utter a prayer of sincere and fervent thanks when we recover from serious illness. We may actually offer brief thanksgiving when we hear that someone we know has recently been converted. But by and large, our thanksgiving seems to be tied rather tightly to our material well-being and comfort. The unvarnished truth is that what we most frequently give thanks for betrays what we most highly value. If a large percentage of our thanksgiving is for material prosperity, it is because we value material prosperity proportionately.

That is why, when we first turn to Paul's thanksgivings, they may startle us; they may even seem alien, for they do not focus on what many of us habitually cherish. Paul gives thanks for signs of grace among Christians, among the Christians whom he is addressing.

1. Paul gives thanks that his readers' faith is growing. "We . . . thank God for you," he says, ". . . because your faith is growing more and more" (v. 3). Since he speaks of their growing faith, he cannot be referring to their initial conversion, but to their increasing reliance upon the Lord. Indeed, the word *faith* (Gk. *pistis*) can also

The Framework of Prayer

42

mean "fidelity" or "faithfulness," and in this context "fidelity" and "trust" are not far apart. Growing fidelity to the Lord and his gospel is inevitably stamped by increasing trust in the Lord and his gospel; increasing trust breeds reliability. The Thessalonians are growing in their faith, not satisfied by yesterday's attainments but stretching upward in spiritual maturity, and for this Paul gives thanks.

2. Paul gives thanks that their love is increasing. What he has in mind in this context is not their love toward God (though he presupposes that love for God is increasing too), still less some mawkish or merely sentimental feeling, but the practical "love every one of you has for each other." If their love for one another is growing, it can only be because they are Jesus' disciples: did not Jesus himself say that such love would be the distinguishing mark of his followers (John 13:34–35)?

It is worth probing this line of thought a little further. A close-knit society with shared ideals and goals frequently finds it relatively easy to foster love, tolerance, and inner cohesion. Whether we think of the local rock-climbing club, the regional football team, or a socially cohesive local church, a certain amount of fraternal depth is common enough. Of course, such groups may run into terrible division over power politics or a disruptive member or a nasty bit of nepotism, but some measure of transparent love is not all that unusual in such groups.

Ideally the church is different. It is made up of people who are as varied as can be: rich and poor, learned and unlearned, practical and impractical, sophisticated and unsophisticated, aristocratic and plebeian, disciplined and flighty, intense and carefree, extrovert and introvert—and everything in between. The *only* thing that holds such people together is their shared allegiance to Jesus Christ, their devotion to him, stemming from his indescribable love for them.

That is why it is always wretchedly pathetic when a local church becomes a cauldron of resentments and nurtured bitterness. This pitiful state of affairs may erupt simply because there is very little at the social, economic, temperamental, educational, or other levels to hold people together. Therefore, when Christians lose sight of their first and primary allegiance, they will squabble. When social or racial or economic or temperamental uniformity seems more important than basking in the love of God in Christ Jesus, idolatry has reared its blasphemous head. When protestations of profound love for Jesus Christ are not mirrored in love for others who profess to love the same Jesus Christ, we may legitimately ask how seriously we should take these protestations.

But we may put this positively. When Christians do grow in their love for each other, for no other reason than because they are loved by Jesus Christ and love him in return, that growing love is an infallible sign of grace in their lives. As Paul hears reports of the Thessalonians, he is struck by their growing love. Such love must be the work of God, and so it is to God that Paul directs his thanks. Most emphatically is this particular display of love a signal demonstration of grace: "every one" of the Thessalonian believers has been caught up in it, not some small, spiritual elite. This is the stuff of revival, and Paul is grateful.

3. Paul gives thanks that they are persevering under trial. Formally, of course, this particular aspect of his thanksgiving is cast in slightly different form from the other two. Still, it is unmistakable enough if we follow his line of argument.

The crucial element to notice is that Paul's gratitude to God is not exclusively private, as if it were restricted to his prayer closet. Because the faith and love of the Thessalonians had increased, they were spiritually strong enough to persevere under the persecutions and trials they were even then enduring. Their steady perseverance was so outstanding that Paul boasts about it "among God's churches" (v. 4). This does not mean that Paul is saying, "See what a great church I've planted!" What he is saying is certainly not boasting of that order, for that would be boasting about himself, not boasting about them. Rather, he is saying something like this: "Have you noticed how powerfully the grace of God is operating in the lives of the Thessalonian believers? The way they withstand the pressures of persecution and of assorted trials is truly remarkable, a compelling testimony to the grace of God. Fortified by their growing faith and love, they just press on and on. What an example! What an encouragement! What an incentive for the rest of us!" Thus, his boasting is nothing other than more

The Framework of Prayer

44

praise and thanksgiving to God, uttered in the presence of other churches.

So what do we thank God for? Elsewhere, Paul tells us to set our hearts on things above (Col. 3:1). If what we highly cherish belongs to the realm of heaven, our hearts and minds will incline to heaven and all its values; but if what we highly cherish belongs to the realm of earth and the merely transitory, our hearts and minds will incline to the merely transitory. After all, the Master himself taught us that our hearts will run to where our treasure lies (Matt. 6:19–21).

So what does this have to do with our praying?

If in our prayers we are to develop a mental framework analogous to Paul's, we must look for signs of grace in the lives of Christians, and give God thanks for them. It is not simply that Paul gives thanks for whatever measure of maturity some group of Christians has achieved, before he goes on to ask for yet more maturity (though in part that is what he is doing). Rather, the specific elements in his thanksgiving show the framework of values he brings to his intercession—and we urgently need to develop the same framework.

For what have we thanked God recently? Have we gone over a list of members at our local church, say, or over a list of Christian workers, and quietly thanked God for signs of grace in their lives? Do we make it a matter of praise to God when we observe evidence in one another of growing conformity to Christ, exemplified in trust, reliability, love, and genuine spiritual stamina?

But, read on, there is a second dominant feature in Paul's framework.

Confidence in the Prospect of Vindication

The faithfulness of the Thessalonians under trial, the faithfulness for which Paul has just given thanks, itself constitutes "evidence that God's judgment is right" (v. 5), and "as a result," Paul tells them, "you will be counted worthy of the kingdom of God" (v. 5). This does not mean that the Thessalonians somehow earn the right to enter the kingdom, simply by displaying adequate perseverance. Rather, perseverance demonstrates their right to enter the kingdom; that is, it is the evidence of their right to enter the kingdom, the reason for which they are "counted worthy" to enter the kingdom. The critical turning point in their lives came when they believed the gospel: "you believed our testimony to you" (v. 10). Beyond their conversion, however, Paul assumes that real Christians will ultimately persevere. The assumption is common in Scripture (e.g., Matt. 24:13; John 8:31; Heb. 3:14; 1 John 2:18–19). Christians may stumble and fall, doubt like Thomas, and disown their Lord like Peter, but they ultimately will utter their "Amen" to Thomas's confession (John 20:28) and weep with Peter (Matt. 26:75).

This is not the place to embark on a detailed exposition of verses 5–10. We need merely note the two themes Paul has just introduced, which drive him toward the next step in the argument. (1) The "kingdom of God" in this context is the ultimate kingdom, the consummated kingdom, the reign of God without contention, the final triumph of God in the new heaven and the new earth. Similarly, (2) the perseverance displayed by the Thessalonians is not mere stamina without purpose, but steadfast endurance, squarely aimed for that final glorious kingdom. Christians are not masochists: they do not want to suffer out of some forlorn but stupid belief that suffering is intrinsically good. They are prepared to suffer and to endure because they keep their eye on the goal. Thus, both themes drive us toward the Christian's goal.

That goal is what Paul talks about in these verses. Not that he focuses on "heaven" per se: rather, Paul focuses on what the onset of the new heaven and the new earth means for believers and for those who oppose them.

1. For believers, there will be vindication. "God is just: He will . . . give relief to you who are troubled, and to us as well . . . on the day he comes to be marveled at among all those who have believed. This includes you, because you believed our testimony to you" (vv. 6, 10).

Here is a real sense of expectancy that is increasingly lacking in many evangelical circles in the West. Not many years ago we fought over eschatology, over what we thought would take place at the end. Many Christians were willing to divide over the finest details of

The Framework of Prayer

46

their speculative schemes. Today few of us are willing to fight over such niceties. There has been a commendable gain in tolerance. But we have lost something as well. Succumbing to overreaction to too much emphasis on eschatology, many of us have jettisoned not only divisiveness over details, but interest in what is central.

We are losing our anticipation of the Lord's return, the antici-pation that Paul shows is basic to his thought. Even though we do not disavow central truths, for many of us their power has been eviscerated. The prospect of the Lord's return in glory, the antici-pation of the wrap-up of the universe as we know it, the confidence that there will be a final and irrevocable division between the just and the unjust—these have become merely credal points for us, instead of ultimate realities that even now are life-transforming.

The loss is great. It means that instead of investing in the bank of heaven, where "moth and rust do not destroy, and where thieves do not break in and steal" (Matt. 6:20), we may be seduced into devoting almost all of our time, energy, and money to the merely temporal and ephemeral.

When was the last time you heard a profoundly biblical and telling sermon on the second coming? Where are the congrega-tions who sing with understanding and fervor, and not mere for-malism, such truths as the following?

> Lo! He comes, with clouds descending,
>   Once for favoured sinners slain:
> Thousand thousand saints attending
>   Swell the triumph of His train:
>   Hallelujah!
> Jesus now shall ever reign.

> Every eye shall now behold Him
>   Robed in dreadful majesty;
> Those who set at nought and sold Him,
>   Pierced, and nailed Him to the tree,
>   Deeply wailing,
> Shall the true Messiah see.

> Every island, sea, and mountain,
>   Heaven and earth, shall flee away;

All who hate Him must, confounded,
   Hear the trump proclaim the day:
      Come to judgment!
      Come to judgment! come away!

Yea, amen! let all adore Thee,
   High on Thine eternal throne:
Savior, take the power and glory,
   Claim the Kingdom for Thine own:
      O come quickly,
      Hallelujah! come, Lord, come!
        —Charles Wesley, 1707–1788
      (based on John Cennick, 1718–1755)

How many of us sing with transparent anticipation such a hymn as this?

Face to face with Christ my Saviour,
Face to face—what will it be
When with rapture I behold Him,
Jesus Christ, who died for me?

Only faintly now I see him,
With the darkling veil between;
But a better day is coming,
When His glory shall be seen.
        —Carrie E. Breck

But if on the last day there is vindication for some . . .

2. For others, there will be retribution. "God is just: He will pay back trouble to those who trouble you. . . . This will happen when the Lord Jesus is revealed from heaven in blazing fire with his powerful angels. He will punish those who do not know God and do not obey the gospel of our Lord Jesus. They will be punished with everlasting destruction and shut out from the presence of the Lord and from the majesty of his power on the day he comes to be glorified in his holy people" (vv. 6–10).

Many find the notion of retribution repugnant. This eye-for-an-eye theology, they say, does not reach the high level of the Chris-

The Framework of Prayer

48

tian gospel, where grace reigns and forgiveness displaces revenge. It is vindictive, petty, harsh, and utterly unworthy of those who follow Christ—the Christ who cries, "Father, forgive them for they know not what they do!" Surely this passage is simply an unworthy throwback to the more primitive stance of the Old Testament.

But this analysis will not do. It will not do even at the simple level of fairness. Less than a year ago, a stunning case was tried before a British court. A British soldier, in a fit of rage, shot and killed his wife and their infant. The soldier did not plead insanity; quite transparently he was crushed by the guilt and shame of his own brutality and murderous rage. The judge finally acquitted him, on the ground that he had already suffered enough.

Where is the justice in that? Where is the fairness? Where is there any flavor of what is right? Is there not something to be said for retribution?

In fact, the Christian gospel is solidly based on some elementary notions of retribution. Where evil occurs, it must be paid back, or God himself is affronted. If God forever overlooks evil, ostensibly on the ground that he is loving and forbearing, is he not also betraying the fact that he is pathetically unconcerned about injustice?

The truth is that every Christian who has thought long and hard about the cross begins to understand that God is not merely a stern dispenser of justice, nor merely a lover who lavishly forgives, but the Sovereign who is simultaneously perfect in holiness and perfect in love. His holiness demands retribution; his love sends his own Son to absorb that retribution on behalf of others. The cross simultaneously stands as the irrefutable evidence that God demands retribution, and cries out that it is the measure of God's love (see Rom. 3:21–26). That is why, in the Christian view of things, forgiveness is never detached from the cross. In other words, forgiveness is never the product of love alone, still less of mawkish sentimentality. Forgiveness is possible only because there has been a real offense, and a real sacrifice to offset that offense.

But what if men and women reject that sacrifice? What if they insist on seeing themselves as the center of the universe and utterly refuse to acknowledge God as God? What if their whole life cries out, "I'll do it my way!"

If God is God, there must still be retribution, or the entire moral order collapses. If we refuse to acknowledge that we deserve retribution, refuse to accept the forgiveness available because, out of God's indescribable love, Jesus suffered retribution in order to reconcile sinners like us to God, then we must face that retribution ourselves.

In the worst case, people may become so hardened in their vaunted independence that they pour scorn on those who have come to know the joys of God's forgiveness; they may even take it upon themselves to do as much damage to them as they can. That was the situation the Thessalonian believers faced: implacable opposition to everything they held dear. What, then, is the result? "God is just: He will pay back trouble to those who trouble you . . . " (v. 6).

The final picture is not a pretty one. Some people think of hell as a place where sinners will be crying out for another chance, begging for the opportunity to repent, with God somehow taking on a "tough guy" stance and declaring, "Sorry. You had your chance. Too late." But the reality is infinitely more sobering. There is no evidence anywhere in the Bible that there is any repentance in hell. The biblical pictures suggest that evil and self-centeredness persist and persist—and so does the judgment. Men and women wantonly refuse to acknowledge God as God; they will not confess his essential rightness; they will not own his just requirements; they will not give up their perpetual desire to be the center of the universe; they will not accept that they are guilty of rebellion; they will not accept forgiveness on the ground that God himself makes provision for sinners in the sacrifice of his own Son. "They will be punished with everlasting destruction and shut out from the presence of the Lord and from the majesty of his power" (v. 9).

In a fallen world order, these people once seemed so strong, so inevitably right, so wise. But Christians understand that the final vindication of God's revelation, of the claims of the gospel, comes at the end of the age, "on the day [Christ] comes to be glorified in his holy people and to be marveled at among all those who have believed" (v. 10).

That is what Paul understands; that is what he writes. Its importance in this context is profound. Part of what Paul has in mind, as he prays, is this fundamental orientation to the end of the age, to

The Framework of Prayer

the vindication of God's people and to God's retribution on those "who do not know God and do not obey the gospel of our Lord Jesus" (v. 8). His emphases mock so many of our own. In our pragmatic, materialistic society, where each of us seeks comfort and "fulfillment" and respect, it is hard to follow a despised, crucified Messiah—unless we fix our eyes on the end. If we do not aim for the new heaven and the new earth, many of our values and decisions in this world will be myopic, unworthy, tarnished, fundamentally wrong-headed. To put the matter bluntly: can biblical spirituality long survive where Christians are not oriented to the world to come? And, in this context, can we expect to pray aright unless we are oriented to the world to come?

"With this in mind, we constantly pray for you" (v. 11): we have seen that the "this" Paul keeps in mind is discerning gratitude for signs of grace among the people for whom he prays and simple confidence in the prospect of God's perfect vindication of his people when Jesus returns. That is the framework of his thought as he sets himself to pray for the Thessalonians.

Questions for Review and Reflection

1. For what does Paul give thanks? For what do you give thanks?
2. What kinds of things in people's lives should call forth our most profound gratitude to God? Why?
3. How does Paul's anticipation of Jesus' return shape his values and his prayers?
4. What other New Testament teaching can you think of that encourages us to live (and pray!) with eternity's values in view?

3

Worthy Petitions

If we follow Paul and adopt the kind of spiritual framework he lays out for us (the theme of chapter 2 of this book), we must nevertheless ask what kind of petitions we should present to the living God. If we are grateful for the most important things, and determined to live with our eternal destiny uppermost in mind, what kinds of things will we pray for?

Paul's Petitions

Two petitions appear in Paul's prayer for the Thessalonian Christians.

1. Paul prays that God might count these Christians worthy of their calling. "With this in mind," Paul writes, "we constantly pray for you, that our God may count you worthy of his calling" (v. 11a). This calling of which God must count Christians worthy demands some explanation. For some New Testament writers,

51

A Prayer of Paul for the Thessalonians

[1]Paul, Silas and Timothy, to the church of the Thessalonians in God our Father and the Lord Jesus Christ:
[2]Grace and peace to you from God the Father and the Lord Jesus Christ.
[3]We ought always to thank God for you, brothers, and rightly so, because your faith is growing more and more, and the love every one of you has for each other is increasing. [4]Therefore, among God's churches we boast about your perseverance and faith in all the persecutions and trials you are enduring.
[5]All this is evidence that God's judgment is right, and as a result you will be counted worthy of the kingdom of God, for which you are suffering. [6]God is just: He will pay back trouble to those who trouble you [7]and give relief to you who are troubled, and to us as well. This will happen when the Lord Jesus is revealed from

---

God's call or calling is equivalent to his invitation. For instance, in the parable of the wedding banquet (Matt. 22:1–14), many people are invited to the wedding banquet that a king prepares for his son (22:3, 8–9), but they refuse to come: the word rendered "invited" is the verb customarily translated "called." That is why the parable ends, "For many are invited [lit., called], but few are chosen" (Matt. 22:14).

In Paul's writings, however, the call or calling of God is always effective: those who are called by God are truly saved. Nowhere is this clearer than in Romans 8:29–30: "For those God foreknew he also predestined to be conformed to the likeness of his Son, that he might be the firstborn among many brothers. And those he predestined, he also *called*; those he *called*, he also justified; those he justified, he also glorified" (emphasis added). Used in this way, to be called by God means to be saved, to belong to God, to be accepted as one of his.

But Paul never thinks that we are called by God because we deserve it. How could he? He knew that it was while he was busily

heaven in blazing fire with his powerful angels. [8]He will punish those who do not know God and do not obey the gospel of our Lord Jesus. [9]They will be punished with everlasting destruction and shut out from the presence of the Lord and from the majesty of his power [10]on the day he comes to be glorified in his holy people and to be marveled at among all those who have believed. This includes you, because you believed our testimony to you

[11]With this in mind, we constantly pray for you, that our God may count you worthy of his calling, and that by his power he may fulfill every good purpose of yours and every act prompted by your faith. [12]We pray this so that the name of our Lord Jesus may be glorified in you, and you in him, according to the grace of our God and the Lord Jesus Christ.

(2 Thess. 1:1–12)

persecuting the church and trying to destroy it that God intervened and called him by his grace (Gal. 1:13–15). So Paul is not here praying that the Thessalonians might somehow become worthy enough to be called. Rather, since these Thessalonians are Christians, they have already been called, and now Paul prays that they might live up to that calling. More explicitly, Paul prays that God himself might count them worthy of his calling. That means these believers must grow in all the things that please God so that he is pleased with them, and finally judges them to be living up to the calling that they have received. In short, they are to "live a life worthy of the calling [they] have received" (Eph. 4:1).

By God's free grace we have been forgiven; by his free grace we have been made "heirs of God and co-heirs with Christ" (Rom. 8:17). By his free grace we have been justified, we have been given the Spirit, we have tasted eternal life. But Paul wants us to be worthy of this calling. Certainly none of us was worthy when we received it. Now, however, Paul wants us to become what we were not, and he prays to that end. He prays that Christians might

54

become worthy of all that it means to be a Christian, of all that it means to be a child of the living God, of all that it means to be worthy of the love that brought Jesus to the cross.

I shall tease out a little more of what this means, at the practical level, in a later chapter. But judging by this example of Paul's praying, it should already be clear that our chief concern in petition must not be that we might become successful, wealthy, popular, healthy, brilliant, triumphant, happy, or beautiful. Still less does Paul encourage us to pray that all our problems will disappear. Paul's prayer is constrained by the framework he brings to it: he prays for more signs of the grace for which he has already thanked God, and he prays with eternity's values in view.

He knows we are going to have to give an account of what we have done. On the last day, God will ask, in effect, "What have you done with the salvation I bestowed on you? How have you responded to the way I graciously called you to myself? Have you begun to live up to that calling?"

This is one of the themes to which Paul returns again and again. We are to grow up into Christian maturity. In a strange paradox, Paul is constantly telling people, in effect, to become what they are; that is, since we already are children of God because of his free grace to us in Christ, we must now become all that such children should be. God has graciously called us; now we must live up to that calling. That cannot mean less than that we should become increasingly holy, self-denying, loving, full of integrity, steeped in the knowledge of God and his Word, delighted to trust and obey our heavenly Father.

We are not strong enough or disciplined enough to take these steps ourselves. That is why Paul prays as he does. If the holy God is to count us "worthy of his calling," we must ask him for help. That is why Paul is praying: he is not simply asking the Thessalonians to try harder, he is praying for them to the end that God will count them worthy of his calling. Such a prayer is tantamount to asking that God will so work in their lives, so make them worthy, that ultimately he will count them worthy.

And so this text asks us: When was the last time you prayed this sort of prayer for your family? for your church? for your chil-

A CALL TO SPIRITUAL REFORMATION

dren? Do we not spend far more energy praying that our children will pass their exams, or get a good job, or be happy, or not stray too far, than we do praying that they may live lives worthy of what it means to be a Christian?

Many of us have had the experience of asking a parent, "How are your children doing?" only to get an answer like this: "Oh, Johnny's doing very well now. His career as a research physicist has really taken off. He is the youngest person in his company to have been appointed to the board. And Evelyn is doing very well, too. She's into computer programming and is already the head of her section."

"And how are they doing spiritually?"

A long pause.

"I'm afraid they're not really walking with the Lord at the moment. But we're hoping they'll come back some day."

Of course, the initial response of such parents may be a reflection of nothing more than privacy, a quiet and loyal concern not to disparage any family member. But too often it reflects warped priorities. I have had parents, ostensibly Christian parents, rage at me because they thought I had influenced their bright children to train for ministry, perhaps for missionary service. Others are joyous over their children's material prosperity and not terribly concerned over their children's utter indifference to the God who made them.

How will these values appear thirty years or forty billion years from now? From eternity's perspective, what should be the primary things for which we should pray for our children, for ourselves, for our fellow believers?

When was the last time we prayed for such things? When was the last time we prayed that God might count us worthy of his calling?

2. Paul prays that God by his power might bring to fruition each Christian's good, faith-prompted purposes. "With this in mind, we constantly pray for you, that . . . by his power [God] may fulfill every good purpose of yours and every act prompted by your faith" (v. 11b). Elsewhere, Paul can say that it is God himself who is at work within us, both to will and to act according to his good purpose (Phil. 2:12–13). But here he prays that God might empower us in *our* good, faith-prompted purposes.[1] What does he mean?

The idea is frankly astonishing, and very important. What Paul presupposes is that God's people have been so transformed through their conversion to Jesus Christ and his gospel that they now develop new sets of goals. Prompted and shaped by goodness and faith, they inevitably formulate new purposes, decidedly Christian plans, Christian goals.

For instance, they may start to think along such lines as these: "I wonder how I can witness to my neighbor? I wonder if I can get a Bible study going in this neighborhood. I must really sort out how I can help that rather pathetic old lady down the street who has just lost her husband and who does not seem to have any friends. What would be involved in trying to befriend the high school kids on my block? I wonder what I can do to welcome visitors coming into our church? Perhaps the local chapter of the Prison Fellowship could use me in some way."

Of course, no Christian can do everything, and none of us should try. But we can all do something, a significant something; and meanwhile, we must recognize that such plans as these have been generated by what Paul labels goodness and faith. Paul expects Christians to develop such purposes.

But Paul goes further. At this point Paul prays that God by his power may "fulfill every good purpose of yours and every act prompted by your faith." That is simply marvelous. Assuming that Christians will develop such wholesome and spiritually minded purposes, Paul now prays that God himself may take these purposes and so work them out as to bring them to fruition, to fulfillment. We may have all kinds of wonderful ideas about what we as Christians might do, yet somehow never get around to doing any of them. Alternatively, we may immediately proceed to organization and administration, and never seek, except in sporadic and accidental ways, the decisive approval and blessing of God on our Christian dreams. The truth is that unless God works in us and through us, unless God empowers these good purposes of ours, they will not engender any enduring spiritual fruit; they will not display any life-transforming, people-changing power. "Unless the LORD builds the house, its builders labor in vain. Unless the LORD watches over the city, the watchmen stand guard in vain" (Ps. 127:1). And unless the Lord fulfills our good, faith-prompted purposes, they will remain arid, fruitless—either empty dreams or frenetic activity with no life, but in either case spiritually anemic.

That means we need to go over our own agendas and priorities, and those of the people and leaders in our churches and missions, and ask again and again, "What are our goals, our purposes? What is our mission, our direction? What should we be attempting, for Christ's sake?" And as we find answers to such questions, we must intercede with God that he, by his great power, might bring these good purposes, these faith-prompted acts, to bountiful fruitfulness.

The Goal of Paul's Prayer

"We pray this so that the name of our Lord Jesus may be glorified in you, and you in him" (1:12). Having listed his petitions, Paul now discloses the two-part goal of such prayers.

1. Paul seeks the glorification of the Lord Jesus. This first part is common enough: "We pray this so that the name of our Lord Jesus may be glorified in you." For Paul, his concern that Christians might be counted worthy of their calling, and his deep desire that God might fulfill their good, faith-prompted purposes, can never be ultimate ends. True, they are valued ends, things deeply to be desired, things to be prayed for. Yet they are only proximate ends; the ultimate end is that the Lord Jesus be glorified in consequence of such growing maturity and fruitfulness on the part of believers.

The Christian's whole desire, at its best and highest, is that Jesus Christ be praised. It is always a wretched bastardization of our goals when we want to win glory for ourselves instead of for him. When we arrange flowers in the church, or serve as an usher, or preach a sermon; when we visit the sick, or run a youth group, or attend prayer meeting—when we do any of these things, and more, with the secret desire that we might be praised for our godliness and service, we have corrupted the salvation we enjoy. Its

Worthy Petitions

58

purpose is to reconcile us to God, for God must be the center of our lives, the ground and the goal of our existence. Indeed, Christ himself, the agent of God in creation, is the one of whom Paul elsewhere declares that all things were made by him and for him (Col. 1:16). Lying at the heart of all sin is the desire to be the center, to be like God. So if we take on Christian service, and think of such service as the vehicle that will make us central, we have paganized Christian service; we have domesticated Christian living and set it to servitude in a pagan cause.

Our pilgrimage as Christians need not be very far advanced before we ruefully recognize that even our best service, motivated by the highest zeal, is regularly laced with large doses of vulgar self-interest. We learn that these sins, too, we must confess and seek to overcome. Paul recognizes the problem, and articulates the proper goal in his prayer: "We pray this," he writes, not that you may be thought remarkable Christians, or so that you may gain a reputation for perseverance and spirituality and power throughout the Roman Empire, but "so that the name of our Lord Jesus may be glorified in you."

The first part of Paul's goal, then, is the glorification of the Lord Jesus. The second part is more startling.

2. Paul seeks the glorification of believers. "We pray this," Paul writes, "so that the name of our Lord Jesus may be glorified in you, *and you in him*" (v. 12). What does this mean? On first reading, it is a little strange. After making the glorification of Jesus absolutely pivotal, does Paul now soften a little and decide that we may legitimately pursue a little praise ourselves?

Certainly what Paul has in mind is not as simple, or as crass, as that. Paul is well aware of God's urgent insistence, "I am the LORD; that is my name! I will not give my glory to another" (Isa. 42:8). But there is another shading to glory that makes it entirely appropriate to talk of the Christian's glorification. Elsewhere Paul insists that all whom God calls and justifies, that is, all who are genuinely saved, will one day be glorified (Rom. 8:30). He means that one day they will be made perfect, one day they will enjoy resurrection bodies of the same order as Jesus' resurrection body, one day they will live in the splendor of the new heaven and the new earth. But even now, he insists, we "are being transformed into his likeness with ever-increasing glory" (2 Cor. 3:18).

Our final glorification will see us without taint or spot, all sin and decay purged away, enjoying the bliss of the perfection of God's unshaded presence. But even now Christians are being transformed "from glory to glory." It is as if the most monumental cultural shock, that entailed by the jump from this world to the next, is being reduced by the preparation of those who will make the leap. Thus the final transformation, as wonderful as it is, is prefaced by a whole series of transformations, as we become increasingly conformed to the likeness of Christ, in anticipation of the climactic glorification at the end.

When we glorify God, we are not giving him something substantial that he would not otherwise have. We are simply ascribing to him what is his. But when we are glorified, in the sense just described, we are being made more like him, we are being strengthened or empowered to exhibit characteristics that we would not otherwise display. Of course, in Paul's thought, this glorification that Christians enjoy does not take anything away from the glory that goes to Jesus Christ. Far from it: he is the one who makes our glorification possible, so that our glorification itself becomes the most spectacular means of bringing him glory. To think that rebellious, self-centered mortals become children of God, increasingly mirroring his character, and one day enjoying the unclouded bliss of a perfect existence in the presence of the Triune God—this could not possibly be the fruit of our own endeavors. Rather, Christ is glorified, he receives the praise that is his due, as we are glorified, as we are conformed to his likeness. On the last day, Jesus Christ will be glorified in us on account of what we have become by his grace, and we will be glorified in him on account of what he has done for us.

Thus Paul has returned to eschatology, that is, to his habit of looking toward the end of history, to his conviction that Christian life can be lived faithfully only if it is lived in light of the end. We have already seen that the apostle brings this perspective with him when he sets himself to pray: it is part of his mental framework (1:5–10). Here, his vision of the end, along with what that

Worthy Petitions

60

means for Christians here and now, helps to shape the ultimate goals he attaches to his petitions. He wants Christians to be glorified, not only at the end, in line with God's promises of final vindication, but now, as they prepare for the end and are progressively transformed "from glory to glory" in anticipation of all that will be.

This, then, is the twofold goal of Paul's prayer: that Christ might be glorified in us, and we in him. So I must ask you, as I ask myself: When was the last time you prayed with this twofold goal clearly before your eyes, as your obsession, your ultimate concern?

The Ground for Paul's Prayer

Paul writes, "We pray this [i.e., the petitions articulated in v. 11] so that the name of our Lord Jesus may be glorified in you, and you in him, *according to the grace of our God and the Lord Jesus Christ*" (1:12, emphasis added). In other words, Paul does not want to end his prayer by leaving the Thessalonian Christians with the impression that what he is really praying for is that they will simply try harder. At one level, of course, that is exactly what Paul wants. But Paul always recognizes that if we try harder, it is because the grace of God is powerfully at work within us.

We Christians must constantly be reminded of the fact that, just as we were saved by grace, so also are we sanctified and glorified by grace. The point is implicit in the fact that Paul is here approaching God with petitions: that is, he is asking God to do something. True, what he is asking God to accomplish—that he might count these Christians worthy of his calling, and so strengthen them by his power that their good, faith-prompted purposes will be brought to fruition—also sets forth goals for the Christians themselves to pursue. But that he asks God to perform these things shows that he is deeply aware that God's grace must be at work if these petitions are to be answered at all.

We become fruitful by grace; we persevere by grace; we mature by grace; by grace we grow to love one another the more, and by grace we cherish holiness and a deepening knowledge of God. Therefore Paul reminds his readers at the end of his prayer that everything he has asked for is available only on the basis of grace.

The Savior himself cannot be glorified in our lives, nor can we be finally glorified, apart from the grace that he provides.

It is vitally important to reflect on the extraordinarily wholistic thinking that is represented by this prayer. This prayer of the apostle is not made up of petty petitions, isolated requests that are to be answered by a God who, rather exceptionally, intervenes in our lives and does something remarkable. We are not to think of ourselves as basically independent and on the right track, but occasionally in need of a little input from the Deity, a little blessing called down by an appropriately formulated prayer. That sort of view is almost akin to pagan magic; it is only a whisker from raw animism. Paul's vision is much broader, much more wholistic. He remembers the grace we have received in the past, and thinks through the direction of our lives—our ultimate home in the new heaven and the new earth. He envisages the final consummation, the final vindication, and grasps what kind of lives we should be living in the light of the end. That vision properly places us in God's universe, which was made by and for him, answerable to him, redeemed by him, and it establishes what our priorities must be wherever that vision prevails. Paul's petitions and stated goals are perfectly aligned with this vision. Best of all, he remembers that if we are to move in that direction, we must have the grace of God at every point in our lives, answering our prayers—the answers themselves being nothing less than the progressive transformation of the people of God, and the glory of the Lord Jesus. In short, Paul's prayers embrace an entire vision.

In 1952, a young woman by the name of Florence Chadwick stepped off the beach at Catalina Island and into the water, determined to swim to the shore of mainland California. She was already an experienced long-distance swimmer: she was the first woman to swim the English Channel both ways. The weather was foggy and chilly on the day she set out; she could scarcely see the boats that would accompany her. For fifteen hours she swam. She begged to be taken out, but her trainer urged persistence, telling her again and again that she could make it, that the shore was not far away. Physically and emotionally exhausted, she finally just stopped swimming, and she was pulled out. The boats made for the shore, and she discovered it was a mere half-mile away.

The next day she gave a news conference. What she said, in effect, was this: "I do not want to make excuses for myself. I am the one who asked to be pulled out. But I think that if I could have seen the shore I would have made it."

Two months later she proved her point. On a bright and clear day, she plunged back into the sea, and swam the distance.

Brothers and sisters in Christ, at the heart of all our praying must be a biblical vision. That vision embraces who God is, what he has done, who we are, where we are going, what we must value and cherish. That vision drives us toward increasing conformity with Jesus, toward lives lived in the light of eternity, toward hearty echoing of the church's ongoing cry, "Even so, come, Lord Jesus!" That vision must shape our prayers, so that the things that most concern us in prayer are those that concern the heart of God. Then we will persevere in our praying, until we reach the goal God himself has set for us.

Questions for Review and Reflection

1. What does it mean to pray that God might count Christians we know to be worthy of God's calling? How will you incorporate such petitions in your prayers?
2. What good, faith-prompted purposes have you been developing? How much have you prayed that God will bring such purposes to fulfillment? What concrete steps can you take to improve your praying in this area?
3. What is Paul's twofold goal in this prayer for the Thessalonians? How should such a goal shape your prayers?

Praying for Others

Some of us think that the church, by and large, is quite a nice place. There is fellowship, friendship, sometimes a reasonably safe haven from the pressures of tense relationships at work or elsewhere; in the best of circumstances, there may be some sensitivity to aesthetics—perhaps even a quality pipe organ.

Yes, it is quite a nice place, the church, were it not for one thing: many of the people who belong are simply unbearable. If only we could enjoy church without people, revel in corporate worship without people! Of course, we're not thinking of *all* the people. Some of them are all right. But it would sure be a much more wonderful place if significant numbers of them would immediately find themselves transferred to Pago Pago or Qatar.

As soon as we have articulated our resentments so ludicrously, we are forced into a sickly grin that acknowledges our self-righteousness. The celebrated line from the old "Pogo" comic strip says it all: "We have met the enemy and he is us."

For the fact of the matter is that the church is people, people of whom I am a part. The church is not a building, still less a kingdom or a bishop. The church is people. Moreover, all of us are fallen people—forgiven, yes, and in process of sanctification, but

63

still a long way off from the perfection that will characterize the new heaven and the new earth. The church, in short, is us.

Indeed, mature and insightful Christian leaders will always relate every aspect of Christian life and service to people. They will not erect programs that have an abstract attractiveness on paper; still less will they defend programs that demand the devotion of people, as if the people of God exist in order to propagate programs. The best Christian leaders will constantly assess all proposals—no matter how aesthetically pleasing or academically respectable—in terms of their power to serve people, not the other way around.

Similarly, mature Christian preachers will not construct sermons whose primary purpose is to gain renown for their erudition, humor, oratorical skill, or exegetical finesse. They will construct sermons that are designed to help people—to nurture them, instruct them, admonish them, rebuke them, encourage them, challenge them.

Furthermore, our choice of leaders will not be based on "charisma," power, education, erudition, self-promotion, or the desire to advance our clique within the church. Instead we will ask the questions, "What kind of leader will best bring people to Christ? What kind of leader will best nurture the people of God and thus build the church? What is best for the people of God?"

Of course, none of this means that a program *must* be academically disreputable, or that a preacher *ought* to be exegetically irresponsible, or that our leaders *should* be lacking in erudition. Far from it: a degree of expertise in these areas may help us work through the basic question, What is best for the people of God? But the basic question must never be displaced. Sermons and programs and leaders are not ends in themselves: properly understood, they are designed to serve the people of God.

Of course, someone might object that our ultimate goal should be to serve God, not people. We are first of all servants of the living God, and our aim must be to please him. Surely this talk of serving the people of God is slightly skewed: should we not be primarily committed to serving God himself?

At one level the objection is entirely apposite. Christians are not mere humanitarians: we must never think that serving people is the ultimate good, or suppose that serving people is exactly the same as serving God. Christians will never make the fundamental mistake cleverly articulated in the poem "Abou ben Adam," once memorized by every schoolchild. In his vision, Abou ben Adam discovered that his name was not on the list of those who love God. Only slightly abashed, he instructed the recording angel to put him down "as one who loves his fellow man." The angel wrote and vanished, only to return the next night to display to Abou all "those whom love of God had blessed / And lo, ben Adam's name led all the rest." No thinking Christian will long identify with such sentimental twaddle. In the teaching of Jesus, the first command is to love God with heart and soul and mind and strength; the second is to love one's neighbor as oneself (Matt. 22:37–40). Jesus does not suggest that the two commands are identical. Far from it: he enumerates two commands and sets them out in terms of their relative priorities: first and second.

Having recognized the danger of identifying humanitarian concerns with elemental Christianity, we must squarely face the opposing danger. That is the danger of claiming high intimacy with God while fostering no intimacy with people; of testifying to deep love for Christ, while nurturing all kinds of petty jealousies and rivalries. The apostle John puts it bluntly: "We love because he [God] first loved us. If anyone says, 'I love God,' yet hates his brother, he is a liar. For anyone who does not love his brother, whom he has seen, cannot love God, whom he has not seen. And he has given us this command: Whoever loves God must also love his brother" (1 John 4:19–21).

So while love for God and love for brothers must not be equated, there is an important sense in which the former can be tested by the latter. When we live up to our calling, we remember that in God's church people do not set the agenda, they are the agenda. Our allegiance to God and his gospel will be demonstrated in our service to his people, to those who will become his people, to those made in his image.

Praying for Others

66

It is in this sense that Christians must be constantly asking what is best for the people of God. Our allegiance to Jesus Christ, our confession of him as Lord, entails a profound commitment to further his interests—and it does not take much reading of Scripture to perceive that his interests are tied to the well-being of his people. Moreover, if we joyfully confess the lordship of Christ, then when we ask what is best for people our answers will be cast in terms of what he thinks is best for people, not necessarily what people think is best for themselves.

"Wait a minute," someone may well say. "I thought this was supposed to be a series of meditations on prayer, and especially on Paul's prayers. What does all this theological reasoning about the importance of people have to do with prayer? What connection is there between this heavy-duty theology and my prayer life? For that matter, what connection is there between all this theology and Paul's prayer life?"

The connection is there all right, and it is enormously important. There is a school of thought that treats prayer as a discipline in which to excel, without consideration for the focus prayer ought to have on people. It encourages prayer because prayer is thought to do a great deal for the person who is praying and devotes little thought to those for whom the prayer is offered. Or it encourages meditative, contemplative, worshipful prayer, on the ground that prayer is rightly directed to God. However, this thinking does not consider our attitude toward people or think through the place of intercession for others.

One of the remarkable characteristics of Paul's prayers is the large proportion of space devoted to praying for others. Of course, one can find Paul offering simple praise to God and imagine Paul praying for himself; indeed, one could look farther afield—the Psalms, perhaps—and observe the considerable space given there to praise and to requests that serve the interests, in part, of the one who is praying. But Paul's prayers, on which this book focuses attention, are outstanding for the large part intercession for others and thanksgiving for others play in them.

The sheer power of these prayers, and the primacy of their focus, cannot easily be appreciated unless one takes the time to read through them in one sitting. So I have printed most of them below. Do not skim them. Take time to read them slowly, thinking them through, vocalizing them quietly if it will help you to slow down.

These prayers are varied in their form and content. Perhaps it is worth mentioning that many modern writers classify them into four groups: (1) prayers (where Paul appears to be praying as he writes); (2) prayer reports (where Paul tells his readers of his prayers); (3) prayer wishes (where Paul refers to God in the third person, often in forms such as "May the God of all peace do such-and-such"); (4) exhortations to prayer. But we need not dawdle over such nice distinctions.[1] Listen, rather, to the content and thrust of Paul's praying in these extended excerpts from his letters:[2]

First, I thank my God through Jesus Christ for all of you, because your faith is being reported all over the world. God, whom I serve with my whole heart in preaching the gospel of his Son, is my witness how constantly I remember you in my prayers at all times; and I pray that now at last by God's will the way may be opened for me to come to you. [Rom. 1:8–10]

Brothers, my heart's desire and prayer to God for the Israelites is that they may be saved. [Rom. 10:1]

Be joyful in hope, patient in affliction, faithful in prayer. [Rom. 12:12]

May the God who gives endurance and encouragement give you a spirit of unity among yourselves as you follow Christ Jesus, so that with one heart and mouth you may glorify the God and Father of our Lord Jesus Christ. [Rom. 15:5–6]

May the God of hope fill you with all joy and peace as you trust in him, so that you may overflow with hope by the power of the Holy Spirit. [Rom. 15:13]

I urge you, brothers, by our Lord Jesus Christ and by the love of the Spirit, to join me in my struggle by praying to God for me.

Praying for Others

Pray that I may be rescued from the unbelievers in Judea and that my service in Jerusalem may be acceptable to the saints there, so that by God's will I may come to you with joy and together with you be refreshed. The God of peace be with you all. Amen. [Rom. 15:30–33]

I always thank God for you because of his grace given you in Christ Jesus. For in him you have been enriched in every way— in all your speaking and in all your knowledge—because our testimony about Christ was confirmed in you. Therefore you do not lack any spiritual gift as you eagerly wait for our Lord Jesus Christ to be revealed. He will keep you strong to the end, so that you will be blameless on the day of our Lord Jesus Christ. God, who has called you into fellowship with his Son Jesus Christ our Lord, is faithful. [1 Cor. 1:4–9]

The grace of the Lord Jesus be with you. [1 Cor. 16:23]

Praise be to the God and Father of our Lord Jesus Christ, the Father of compassion and the God of all comfort, who comforts us in all our troubles, so that we can comfort those in any trouble with the comfort we ourselves have received from God. For just as the sufferings of Christ flow over into our lives, so also through Christ our comfort overflows. If we are distressed, it is for your comfort and salvation; if we are comforted, it is for your comfort, which produces in you patient endurance of the same sufferings we suffer. And our hope for you is firm, because we know that just as you share in our sufferings, so also you share in our comfort. [2 Cor. 1:3–7]

But thanks be to God, who always leads us in triumphal procession in Christ and through us spreads everywhere the fragrance of the knowledge of him. For we are to God the aroma of Christ among those who are being saved and those who are perishing. To the one we are the smell of death; to the other, the fragrance of life. And who is equal to such a task? [2 Cor. 2:14–16]

This service that you perform is not only supplying the needs of God's people but is also overflowing in many expressions of thanks to God. Because of the service by which you have proved yourselves, men will praise God for the obedience that accompanies your confession of the gospel of Christ, and for your generosity in sharing with them and with everyone else. And in their prayers for you their hearts will go out to you, because of the surpassing grace God has give you. Thanks be to God for his indescribable gift! [2 Cor. 9:12–15]

To keep me from becoming conceited because of these surpassingly great revelations, there was given me a thorn in my flesh, a messenger of Satan, to torment me. Three times I pleaded with the Lord to take it away from me. But he said to me, "My grace is sufficient for you, for my power is made perfect in weakness." [2 Cor. 12:7–9a]

Now we pray to God that you will not do anything wrong. Not that people will see that we have stood the test but that you will do what is right even though we may seem to have failed. For we cannot do anything against the truth, but only for the truth. We are glad whenever we are weak but you are strong; and our prayer is for your perfection. [2 Cor. 13:7–9]

The grace of our Lord Jesus Christ be with your spirit, brothers. [Gal. 6:18]

Praise be to the God and Father of our Lord Jesus Christ, who has blessed us in the heavenly realms with every spiritual blessing in Christ. For he chose us in him before the creation of the world to be holy and blameless in his sight. In love he predestined us to be adopted as his sons through Jesus Christ, in accordance with his pleasure and will—to the praise of his glorious grace, which he has freely given us in the One he loves. In him we have redemption through his blood, the forgiveness of sins, in accordance with the riches of God's grace that he lavished on us with all wisdom and understanding. . . . [Eph. 1:3ff.]

For this reason, ever since I heard about your faith in the Lord Jesus and your love for all the saints, I have not stopped giving thanks for you, remembering you in my prayers. I keep asking that the God of our Lord Jesus Christ, the glorious Father, may give you the Spirit of wisdom and revelation, so that

70

you may know him better. I pray also that the eyes of your heart may be enlightened in order that you may know the hope to which he has called you, the riches of his glorious inheritance in the saints, and his incomparably great power for us who believe. That power is like the working of his mighty strength, which he exerted in Christ when he raised him from the dead and seated him at his right hand in the heavenly realms, far above all rule and authority, power and dominion, and every title that can be given, not only in the present age but also in the one to come. And God placed all things under his feet and appointed him to be head over everything for the church, which is his body, the fullness of him who fills everything in every way. [Eph. 1:15–23]

For this reason, I kneel before the Father, from whom his whole family in heaven and on earth derives its name. I pray that out of his glorious riches he may strengthen you with power through his Spirit in your inner being, so that Christ may dwell in your hearts through faith. And I pray that you, being rooted and established in love, may have power, together with all the saints, to grasp how wide and long and high and deep is the love of Christ, and to know this love that surpasses knowledge—that you may be filled to the measure of all the fullness of God.

Now to him who is able to do immeasurably more than all we ask or imagine, according to his power that is at work within us, to him be glory in the church and in Christ Jesus throughout all generations, for ever and ever! Amen. [Eph. 3:14–21]

Pray also for me, that whenever I open my mouth, words may be given me so that I will fearlessly make known the mystery of the gospel, for which I am an ambassador in chains. Pray that I may declare it fearlessly, as I should. [Eph. 6:19–20]

I thank my God every time I remember you. In all my prayers for all of you, I always pray with joy because of your partnership in the gospel from the first day until now, being confident of this, that he who began a good work in you will carry it on to completion until the day of Christ Jesus. [Phil. 1:3–6]

And this is my prayer: that your love may abound more and more in knowledge and depth of insight, so that you may be able to discern what is best and may be pure and blameless until the

day of Christ, filled with the fruit of righteousness that comes
through Jesus Christ—to the glory and praise of God. [Phil.
1:9–11]

Do not be anxious about anything, but in everything, by
prayer and petition, with thanksgiving, present your requests
to God. And the peace of God, which transcends all
understanding, will guard your hearts and your minds in
Christ Jesus. [Phil. 4:6–7]

The grace of the Lord Jesus Christ be with your spirit. Amen.
[Phil. 4:23]

We always thank God the Father of our Lord Jesus Christ,
when we pray for you, because we have heard of your faith in
Christ Jesus and of the love you have for all the saints—the
faith and love that spring from the hope that is stored up for you
in heaven and that you have already heard about in the word of
truth, the gospel that has come to you. All over the world this
gospel is bearing fruit and growing, just as it has been doing
among you since the day you heard it and understood God's
grace in all its truth. You learned it from Epaphras, our dear
fellow servant, who is a faithful minister of Christ on our behalf,
and who also told us of your love in the Spirit.
For this reason, since the day we heard about you, we have
not stopped praying for you and asking God to fill you with the
knowledge of his will through all spiritual wisdom and
understanding. And we pray this in order that you may live a life
worthy of the Lord and may please him in every way: bearing
fruit in every good work, growing in the knowledge of God,
being strengthened with all power according to his glorious
might so that you may have great endurance and patience, and
joyfully giving thanks to the Father, who has qualified you to
share in the inheritance of the saints in the kingdom of light.
For he has rescued us from the dominion of darkness and
brought us into the kingdom of the Son he loves, in whom we
have redemption, the forgiveness of sins. [Col. 1:3–14]

Devote yourselves to prayer, being watchful and thankful.
And pray for us, too, that God may open a door for our message,
so that we may proclaim the mystery of Christ, for which I am in

Praying for Others

72

chains. Pray that I may proclaim it clearly, as I should. [Col. 4:2–4]

We always thank God for all of you, mentioning you in our prayers. We continually remember before our God and Father your work produced by faith, your labor prompted by love, and your endurance inspired by hope in our Lord Jesus Christ. [1 Thess. 1:2–3]

And we also thank God continually because, when you received the word of God, which you heard from us, you accepted it not as the word of men, but as it actually is, the word of God, which is at work in you who believe. For you, brothers, became imitators of God's churches in Judea, which are in Christ Jesus: You suffered from your own countrymen the same things those churches suffered from the Jews, who killed the Lord Jesus and the prophets and also drove us out. They displease God and are hostile to all men in their effort to keep us from speaking to the Gentiles so that they may be saved. In this way they always heap up their sins to the limit. The wrath of God has come upon them at last. [1 Thess. 2:13–16]

How can we thank God enough for you in return for all the joy we have in the presence of our God because of you? Night and day we pray most earnestly that we may see you again and supply what is lacking in your faith.
Now may our God and Father himself and our Lord Jesus clear the way for us to come to you. May the Lord make your love increase and overflow for each other and for everyone else, just as ours does for you. May he strengthen your hearts so that you will be blameless and holy in the presence of our God and Father when our Lord Jesus comes with all his holy ones. [1 Thess. 3:9–13]

May God himself, the God of peace, sanctify you through and through. May your whole spirit, soul and body be kept blameless at the coming of our Lord Jesus Christ. The one who calls you is faithful and he will do it. [1 Thess. 5:23–24]

The grace of our Lord Jesus Christ be with you. [1 Thess. 5:28]

A CALL TO SPIRITUAL REFORMATION

We ought always to thank God for you, brothers, and rightly so, because your faith is growing more and more, and the love every one of you has for each other is increasing. Therefore, among God's churches we boast about your perseverance and faith in all the persecutions and trials you are enduring. . . . [2 Thess. 1:3ff.]

With this in mind, we constantly pray for you, that our God may count you worthy of his calling, and that by his power he may fulfill every good purpose of yours and every act prompted by your faith. We pray this so that the name of our Lord Jesus may be glorified in you, and you in him, according to the grace of our God and the Lord Jesus Christ. [2 Thess. 1:11–12]

May our Lord Jesus Christ himself and God our Father, who loved us and by his grace gave us eternal encouragement and good hope, encourage your hearts and strengthen you in every good deed and word. [2 Thess. 2:16–17]

And pray that we may be delivered from wicked and evil men, for not everyone has faith. But the Lord is faithful, and he will strengthen and protect you from the evil one. We have confidence in the Lord that you are doing and will continue to do the things we command. May the Lord direct your hearts into God's love and Christ's perseverance. [2 Thess. 3:2–5]

Now may the Lord of peace himself give you peace at all times and in every way. The Lord be with all of you. [2 Thess. 3:16]

I thank Christ Jesus our Lord, who has given me strength, that he considered me faithful, appointing me to his service. [1 Tim. 1:12]

I urge, then, first of all, that requests, prayers, intercession and thanksgiving be made for everyone—for kings and all those in authority, that we may live peaceful and quiet lives in all godliness and holiness. This is good, and pleases God our Savior, who wants all men to be saved and to come to a knowledge of the truth. For there is one God and one mediator between God and men, the man Christ Jesus, who gave himself as a ransom for all men—the testimony given in its proper time. . . . [1 Tim. 2:1ff.]

I thank God, whom I serve, as my forefathers did, with a clear conscience, as night and day I constantly remember you in my prayers. Recalling your tears, I long to see you, so that I may be filled with joy. I have been reminded of your sincere faith, which first lived in your grandmother Lois and in your mother Eunice and, I am persuaded, now lives in you also. For this reason I remind you to fan into flame the gift of God which is in you through the laying on of my hands. For God did not give us a spirit of timidity, but a spirit of power, of love and of self-discipline. [2 Tim. 1:3–7]

May the Lord show mercy to the household of Onesiphorus, because he often refreshed me and was not ashamed of my chains. On the contrary, when he was in Rome, he searched hard for me until he found me. May the Lord grant that he will find mercy from the Lord on that day! You know very well in how many ways he helped me in Ephesus. [2 Tim. 1:16–18]

The Lord be with your spirit. Grace be with you. [2 Tim. 4:22]

Grace be with you all. [Titus 3:15b]

I always thank my God as I remember you in my prayers, because I hear about your faith in the Lord Jesus and your love for all the saints. I pray that you may be active in sharing your faith, so that you will have a full understanding of every good thing we have in Christ. Your love has given me great joy and encouragement, because you, brother, have refreshed the hearts of the saints. [Philem. 4–7]

The grace of the Lord Jesus Christ be with your spirit. [Philem. 25]

If we follow Paul's example, then, we will never overlook the monumental importance of praying *for others*. Prayer will never descend to the level where it is nothing more than a retreat house in which we find strength for ourselves, whether through the celebration of praise or through a mystic communion with God or through the relief of casting our cares upon the Almighty. Prayer may embrace all of these elements, and more; but if we learn to pray with Paul, we will learn to pray for others. We will see it is part of our job to approach God with thanksgiving for others and with intercessions for others. In short, our praying will be shaped by our profound desire to seek what is best for the people of God.

There are two corollaries. First, we must always submit to God's definition of what is best. That means it is vitally important for us to listen to the prayers of Scripture, for how else shall we know what God judges to be best for us? Just as Scripture must reform our beliefs about God, our dealings with others, our fundamental values, so too must it shape our praying. Here is one of the places where it may do so in dramatic fashion. In particular, after we have worked through Paul's prayers and observed how often he prays for others, we need to work through them again to find out exactly what it is he asks God for on their behalf, and compare the results with what we normally ask for.

Second, praying for others demands that we examine our own hearts. How can we effectively pray for others if we nurse resentments against them? The hindrance is more than psychological, as if the principal problem were the sheer difficulty of bringing ourselves to intercede for those toward whom we feel bitter. That is a real barrier, of course: how often have you prayed for anyone whom you resent? But there is a deeper barrier. God himself declares that unconfessed sin will cut us off from communication with him, from his powerful answers. "Surely the arm of the LORD is not too short to save, nor his ear too dull to hear. But your iniquities have separated you from your God; your sins have hidden his face from you, so that he will not hear" (Isa. 59:1–2).

The sins that cut us off from effective praying may be the displays of evil condemned by Malachi—such things as half-hearted religion that offers God second best (Mal. 1:6–14), meaningless tears of repentance while adultery and divorce abound (Mal. 2:13–16), and abysmal absence of the fear of God, a lack that issues in the corruption and the oppression of the poor and unfortunate (Mal. 3:5), a wretched hankering after the ways of the arrogant and the evildoers of society, nurtured by a whispered suspicion that it is futile to serve God (Mal. 3:13–15). Small wonder that God is not moved by the prayers of people who behave in such ways.

But notoriously, what so often cuts us off from effective intercession is sheer bitterness, nurtured resentment, nicely preserved grudges, a desperate want of forgiveness. This is pitifully common among us, despite the fact that it is the Lord Jesus himself who teaches, "For if you forgive men when they sin against you, your heavenly Father will also forgive you. But if you do not forgive men their sins, your Father will not forgive your sins" (Matt. 6:14–15). More pointedly still (for the purpose of this study), he says, "And when you stand praying, if you hold anything against anyone, forgive him, so that your Father in heaven may forgive you your sins" (Mark 11:25). Indeed, if we have experienced anything of the Father's bountiful forgiveness his mercy must become the standard of our own: "Be kind and compassionate to one another, forgiving each other, just as in Christ God forgave you" (Eph. 4:32; cf. Col. 3:13).

If you are serious about reforming your prayer life, you must begin with your heart. Unconfessed sin, nurtured sin, will always be a barrier between God and those he has made in his image.

True, sometimes when we try to clean up relationships that have soured in the past, the other party remains intransigent. But that is between that party and God; you and I must watch *our* hearts.

This is true even when the offense has been entirely on the other side. Not long ago a pastor counseled a woman who, twenty years before, had been the victim of four years of incest, her own father the brutal culprit. Eventually her father went to jail. The scars on this woman's personality and faith were gathering to a head twenty years later. Her own husband did not know any of this history and therefore offered little support or understanding. They lived increasingly isolated lives, and the woman's faith shriveled until prayer became impossible, worship mere fakery.

As she and the pastor worked through this background, one of the critical steps she had to take was to forgive her own father. That did not mean she was assuming his guilt; it meant she had to deal with her own bitterness and rage. For this she needed the Lord's forgiveness; and in this context she needed to forgive the man who had abused her. This forgiveness had to be total and unqualified—and expressed to him, *regardless of whether he responded in repentance or in wretched self-justification and anger.* In fact, he chose the latter course, which did not make the woman's part any easier. But the Lord gave her strength to forgive, and that forgiveness was a decisive turning point that led to a restored relationship with her husband, to renewed joy in her Lord, and to revived praying.

Of course, the principle extends to every area of life, not just to the bitterness aroused by memories of incest. How can we intercede for our church, if we secretly hold some of its members in contempt? How can we meaningfully pray for revival, if what we want is some abstract blessing called revival and do not particularly care to see *people* revived? If we harbor bitterness and resentment, praying is little more than wasted time and effort.

Before we go any further, this is the time to examine your own heart, honestly and humbly. It is always the time to do so but especially when you seek to approach the God whose peerless holiness and forgiveness are the immutable standards for his people.

Questions for Review and Reflection

1. In what ways should our concern for people shape our selection of leaders? our Bible teaching and preaching? our praying?
2. As a spiritual discipline, slowly read through the prayers of Paul every day for one month. Record in what ways this discipline influences your own praying.
3. In what ways does nurtured sin in our lives hinder our praying?

5

A Passion for People

(1 Thessalonians 3:9–13)

Although many of Paul's prayers serve as models for what it means to pray for others, the one in 1 Thessalonians 3:9–13 is especially revealing in its portrayal of the apostle's deepest emotions. His profound concern for his readers manifests itself not only in the prayer itself, but in the surrounding verses as well. Let us look at these in turn.

Paul's Prayer: A Product of Passion for People (2:17–3:8)

1. Paul's prayer arises out of his intense longing to be with the Thessalonians. The report of Paul's planting of this church is found in Acts 17:1–9. Paul and Silas had been badly beaten in Philippi, where they were also imprisoned and then entreated to leave the district. After arriving in Thessalonica, Paul set himself the task of evangelism and church planting, but once again the opposition became so heated that he felt compelled to with-

Another of Paul's Prayers
for the Thessalonians

[17]But, brothers, when we were torn away from you for a short time (in person, not in thought), out of our intense longing we made every effort to see you. [18]For we wanted to come to you—certainly I, Paul, did, again and again—but Satan stopped us. [19]For what is our hope, our joy, or the crown in which we will glory in the presence of our Lord Jesus when he comes? Is it not you? [20]Indeed, you are our glory and joy.

[1]So when we could stand it no longer, we thought it best to be left by ourselves in Athens. [2]We sent Timothy, who is our brother and God's fellow worker in spreading the gospel of Christ, to strengthen and encourage you in your faith, [3]so that no one would be unsettled by these trials. You know quite well that we were destined for them. [4]In fact, when we were with you, we kept telling you that we would be persecuted. And it turned out that way, as you well know. [5]For this reason, when I could stand it no longer, I sent to find out about your faith. I was afraid that in some way the tempter might have tempted you and our efforts might have been useless.

draw after a few short weeks. After some success at Berea, he found himself facing the enormous spiritual and intellectual hurdles at Athens, immediately followed by the moral and cultural barriers of Corinth—a cosmopolitan port city famous for its moral decay.

It is in this environment that Paul looks back on the churches he has recently planted, churches where he has spent almost no time in discipleship and training. This failure he cannot view as nothing more than a frustrating aberration in his program. Rather, his deep concern for these believers is what pains him so greatly. Hence he can write, "But, brothers, when we were torn away from you for a short time (in person, not in thought), out of our intense longing we made every effort to see you" (1 Thess. 2:17); or again, "So when we could stand it no longer, we thought it best to be left by ourselves in Athens. We sent Timothy, who is our brother

⁶But Timothy has just now come to us from you and has brought good news about your faith and love. He has told us that you always have pleasant memories of us and that you long to see us, just as we also long to see you. ⁷Therefore, brothers, in all our distress and persecution we were encouraged about you because of your faith. ⁸For now we really live, since your are standing firm in the Lord. **⁹How can we thank God enough for you in return for all the joy we have in the presence of our God because of you? ¹⁰Night and day we pray most earnestly that we may see you again and supply what is lacking in your faith.**

¹¹Now may our God and Father himself and our Lord Jesus clear the way for us to come to you. ¹²May the Lord make your love increase and overflow for each other and for everyone else, just as ours does for you. ¹³May he strengthen your hearts so that you will be blameless and holy in the presence of our God and Father when our Lord Jesus comes with all his holy ones.

(1 Thess. 2:17–3:13)

and God's fellow worker. . . . For this reason, when I could stand it no longer, I sent to find out about your faith. I was afraid that in some way the tempter might have tempted you and our efforts might have been useless" (3:1–2a, 5).

Here is a Christian so committed to the well-being of other Christians, especially new Christians, that he is simply burning up inside to be with them, to help them, to nurture them, to feed them, to stabilize them, to establish an adequate foundation for them. Small wonder, then, that he devotes himself to praying for them when he finds he cannot visit them personally.

This is typical of Paul. He never descends to the level of the mere professional. Paul is a passionate man, deeply enmeshed in the lives of real people. That is why he can say elsewhere, "Besides everything else, I face daily the pressure of my concern for all the

A Passion for People

churches. Who is weak, and I do not feel weak? Who is led into sin, and I do not inwardly burn?" (2 Cor. 11:28–29). This is not someone intoxicated with ideas but unconcerned about people. Nor is it someone who is content to minister at a distance— through the books he has written, perhaps, or through younger emissaries. No, this man's ministry is not designed first and foremost to produce ideas, books, or junior colleagues, but to serve the people of God; and to this he is passionately committed. And that passion shapes the prayers he utters on their behalf.

2. **Paul's prayer arises out of passionate affection that seeks the good of others—not their praise, gratitude, acceptance, and still less some sense of professional self-fulfillment.** This is extraordinarily important. Often when someone expatiates on how wonderful it would be to be back home with loved ones, we are listening not only to protestations of love but also to confessions of loneliness or dislocation. We like to be with those we love because in most instances they are the ones who love us. They make us feel stable, cherished; when they are around, we belong.

Such a sense of home is entirely normal, and not to be despised. Unfortunately there is an ugly variation of it in the ministry. There are preachers who so loudly declare their love of preaching that it is unclear whether it is their own performance and their love of power that has captured them or their desire to minister to the men and women who listen to them. A church organist may buck every suggestion that a young, new musician be permitted to serve in this way, and pretty soon the reason becomes clear: the organist's self-identity is so bound up with the public performance of music that any thought of serving people has been suppressed, to the point that the thought of being replaced is intolerable.

As someone who has taught seminary students for more than fifteen years, I worry about the rising number of seminarians who, when asked where and how they think they might best serve, respond with something like this: "Well, I think I would like to teach somewhere. Every time I have taught, people have told me I have done a pretty good job. I get a tremendous sense of fulfillment out of teaching the Bible. I think I could be satisfied teaching Scripture."

How pathetic. I know pagans who find satisfaction and fulfillment by teaching nuclear physics. In any Christian view of life, self-fulfillment must never be permitted to become the controlling issue. The issue is service, the service of real people. The question is, How can I be most useful?, not, How can I feel most useful? The goal is, How can I best glorify God by serving his people?, not, How can I feel most comfortable and appreciated while engaging in some acceptable form of Christian ministry? The assumption is, How shall the Christian service to which God calls me be enhanced by my daily death, by my principled commitment to take up my cross daily and die?, not, How shall the form of service I am considering enhance my career? This is not to deny that Christians may derive joy from work honestly offered to God, whether that work is vocational ministry or research into the properties of quarks. But it is one thing to find joy in the work to which we have been called, and another to make joy the goal of life, the fundamental criterion that controls our choices. It is one thing to weigh a Christian leader's evaluation of our gifts, and another so to focus on our perception of our gifts that self-worship has crept in through the back door. It is one thing to think of people as a live audience that will appreciate our displays of homiletical prowess, and another that passionately shapes each sermon to convey the truth to God's people for their good.

Listen again to Paul: "So when we could stand it no longer, . . . [we] sent Timothy . . . to strengthen and encourage you in your faith, so that no one would be unsettled by these trials. You know quite well that we were destined for them. In fact, when we were with you, we kept telling you that we would be persecuted. And it turned out that way, as you well know. For this reason, when I could stand it no longer, I sent to find out about your faith. I was afraid that in some way the tempter might have tempted you and our efforts might have been useless" (1 Thess. 3:1–5).

Here is a man whose deep affection for these believers, these recent converts, ensures that they will not serve to feed his ego or give him a sense of importance or satisfy his longing for fulfillment. Paul is in agony out of his concern for their good. He wants to be assured that they are standing up under the persecution they

A Passion for People

84

are facing. He wants to strengthen them and encourage them in their faith, so that they will not be unsettled by trials. Paul has a pastor's heart.

In short, Paul not only wants to be with them, he wants to be with them for their good. And that is a demonstration of elementary Christianity. Christ Jesus came to us, choosing to be with us—and this for our good. He chose the path of self-denial, dying in excruciating shame and degradation so that others might live. He calls us to serve the same way, not by lording it over others but by open-eyed death to self-interest, for the good of others. This stance is not a mask to be donned as a disguise at religious conventions, but the hallmark of Christian living. Paul understood the point and lived it out. His prayers for believers are nothing more than an extension of the same love that he bore them.

3. Paul's prayer springs from unaffected delight at reports of the Thessalonians' faith, love, perseverance, and strength. Already in the first chapter, Paul wrote: "We always thank God for all of you, mentioning you in our prayers. We continually remember before our God and Father your work produced by faith, your labor prompted by love, and your endurance inspired by hope in our Lord Jesus Christ" (1 Thess. 1:2–3). Paul was referring to his memory of them during the brief period of time when he was with them. The interval since his departure awakened all sorts of worries about how the Thessalonian believers would fare on the long haul. That was why he had commissioned Timothy to go and find out.

Now he is able to add, "But Timothy has just now come to us from you and has brought good news about your faith and love. He has told us that you always have pleasant memories of us and that you long to see us, just as we also long to see you. Therefore, brothers, in all our distress and persecution we were encouraged about you because of your faith. For now we really live, since you are standing firm in the Lord" (3:6–8).

There are some people for whom the only interesting news is bad news. If they hear of Christians who are in trouble, a pastor who has fallen into sexual sin, a theological institution with internal difficulty, an evangelistic endeavor that is floundering, then they are full of concern. Their piety demands that they denounce these evil times; their rectitude ensures that they will intone their solemn analysis of the sins that have brought forth such a tragedy. But if there is really good news, if they hear of Christians who are joyful, growing in holiness and effective witness, if they learn of a pastor who is very fruitful or an institution that is proving remarkably strategic, then their interest wanes. They find nothing to denounce, no foil for their own rectitude.

How different is Paul! Every report of growth in real fundamentals—in faith and in love (v. 6)—becomes an occasion for great rejoicing. In this respect Paul and John are very close, for the latter can write, "It has given me great joy to find some of your children walking in the truth, just as the Father commanded us" (2 John 4); indeed, "[it] gave me great joy to have some brothers come and tell about your faithfulness to the truth and how you continue to walk in the truth. I have no greater joy than to hear that my children are walking in the truth" (3 John 3–4).

So once again we find ample evidence that Paul's prayers spring in part from unaffected delight at reports that Christians are pressing on in the Christian way. To put the matter at its most basic, Paul's prayer is the product of his passion for people. His unaffected fervency in prayer is not whipped-up emotionalism but the overflow of his love for brothers and sisters in Christ Jesus.

That means that if we are to improve our praying, we must strengthen our loving. As we grow in disciplined, self-sacrificing love, so we will grow in intercessory prayer. Superficially fervent prayers devoid of such love are finally phony, hollow, shallow.

Paul's Prayer: A Continuing Passion for People (3:9–13)

There are several ways that this prayer could be usefully broken up so that we might understand it better. In keeping with the theme of this chapter, however, it is worth thinking it through from one particular perspective: Exactly how do the people of God—in this case, those at Thessalonica—feature in this prayer? There are four themes that reveal Paul's continuing passion for his brothers and sisters in Christ.

1. Paul prays with rich thankfulness for the people of God (3:9). One might have thought that after reporting his thankfulness to God for the Thessalonians in the first chapter (1:2–3), and frankly disclosing his unabashed delight in the good report brought by Timothy (3:6–8), Paul could now dispense with further thanksgiving. But that is not how Paul sees things. He presses on with the same note of gratitude, if possible with still greater exuberance: "How can we thank God enough for you in return for all the joy we have in the presence of our God because of you?" (3:9).

Both in the opening chapter of this book on prayer, and in the first part of this chapter, we have had ample occasion to notice how important thanksgiving is in Paul's prayer life. Without retracing the same terrain, it remains important to underline two distinctive features of this instance of lush thankfulness.

Although the thanksgiving is not addressed to the Thessalonians, but rather to God for the Thessalonians, nevertheless it is cast in such a way as to encourage them. We may best understand this if we contrast Paul's approach with two alternatives. First, the back-slapping flatterer constantly compliments everyone. Regardless of the quality of the work, this extrovert comes alongside and bellows, "Terrific job! Wonderful piece of work. Never seen flowers better arranged." "Brilliant exposition. Absolutely brilliant!" "I don't know how the ushers would get by if it were not for your contribution." The strokes and compliments are so thickly distributed that you wonder if this person is trying to win a popularity contest. Perhaps this stream of compliments is deployed to elicit compliments in return: if you praise people long enough, they start praising you back. They feel they have very little choice. For all the jovial encouragement, doubt soon rises about the level of this flatterer's discernment. What starts off as the gift of encouragement becomes a kind of loud habit, a superficial froth regurgitated in all directions without discretion or sincerity. It may make some people feel good; it embarrasses others. It fosters holiness in no one.

Second, the sober theologically precise types are deeply committed to the truth that all praise finally belongs to God alone,

A CALL TO SPIRITUAL REFORMATION

and so they rarely thank you for anything—and then only very begrudgingly. They recognize, rightly, that anything good that we are or have or do ultimately springs from our heavenly Father's gracious hand. They conclude, wrongly, that no encouragement should be administered to those who are merely the secondary mediators of such divine grace. You can put in countless hours on the mission program and never receive a word of thanks, let alone praise. These people apparently believe that such praise might go to your head and puff you up with self-importance that might be dangerous for your spiritual well-being. Perhaps they think you should be satisfied with God's "Well done!" on the last day.

Paul's approach in many of his epistles, and not least here, is radically different from both of these extremes. He encourages Christians by thanking God for his grace in their lives. More precisely, he encourages Christians *by telling them* that he thanks God for his grace in their lives. Thus he has simultaneously drawn attention to the Thessalonians' spiritual growth, thereby encouraging them, and insisted that God is the one to be thanked for it, thereby humbling them. There is simply no way that these believers can thoughtfully listen to what Paul says and then smugly pat themselves on the back: God, and God alone, is to be praised for the signs of grace in their lives. Yet nonetheless they cannot help but feel encouraged to learn that the apostle himself has observed God's work in their lives and rejoices because of it.

This approach is standard with Paul. It might be worth again scanning his prayers, cited in chapter 4, and noting all the expressions of thanksgiving (Rom. 1:8–10; 1 Cor. 1:4–9; 2 Cor. 1:3–7; 9:12–15; Eph. 1:3ff., 15–23; Phil. 1:3–6; Col. 1:3–14; 1 Thess. 1:2–3; 2:13–16; 3:9; 2 Thess. 1:3ff.; 2 Tim. 1:3–7; Philem. 4–7).

How much would our churches be transformed if each of us made it a practice to thank God for others and then to tell these others what it is about them that we thank God for? "Bob, I thank God for the faithfulness you display in your task as usher. I can't help noticing how you greet everyone by name, even the smallest child, and that you arrive early and go out of your way to make everyone welcome. I thank God for your ministry." "Pat, I constantly thank God for your influence not only in the nursery, but

A Passion for People

88

on the parents who bring their children there. Only heaven will disclose what good God has accomplished through you." Work on your own examples! Of course, it would be hypocritical to say such things if you do not thank God along these lines. To tell others you thank God for them when in reality you don't would be cheap religious cant, mere jingoism. Worse, it would smack of manipulation.

So what we need, then, is a prayer life that thanks God for the people of God, and then tells the people of God what we thank God for.

This obvious lesson may have a bearing on the rising incidence of applause in many Western churches. Applause used to be unknown. Then it came to be deployed after special music. Now it is sometimes heard punctuating sermons. This is, I think, a regressive step. True, some might consider this to be a kind of cultural equivalent to a voiced "Amen!" I take the point, and would not want to introduce new legalism by banning applause outright. But the fundamental difference between "Amen!" and applause must be noted: the "Amen!" is directed to God, even if it serves to encourage the person who is ministering, while applause in our culture signals approval of the performer. God is left out, and the "performer" may the more easily be seduced into pride. This is one of several ways by which the rules of the entertainment world have subtly slipped into corporate worship and are in danger of destroying it from within.

Paul's thanks to God for the Thessalonian Christians is in some measure Paul's thanks to God for his own greatest sources of joy. Paul's wording is remarkable: "How can we thank God enough for you in return for all the joy we have in the presence of our God because of you?" (3:9). Read superficially, of course, this could mean that Paul is simply thanking God for his own joy, thereby betraying a rather self-centered assessment: the Thessalonians are important to him only because they make him happy. If they are doing well, Paul's ministry is vindicated; he therefore feels joyful, and so he thanks God for the joy. Paul then begins to take on the shadings of a narcissistic preacher who evaluates everything by the idolatrous criterion of the joy it affords him.

In fact, that would be a wretched misreading of the apostle. Paul's wording is important: he speaks of the joy he has "in the presence of our God" because of the Thessalonians. The apostle does not use such language lightly. The joy that he experiences, far from making himself the center of the universe, is akin to the joy in heaven among the angelic hosts when a sinner on earth turns to the Lord. This is joy "in the presence of our God"—the kind of joy shared with God, based on the kind of event that makes God himself joyful. Paul's values are so aligned with God's that the things that bring joy to God bring joy to Paul.

In fact, Paul's exuberant testimony discloses another aspect of his prayer. Paul does not observe the growth among the Thessalonian believers with analytic objectivity, still less with Olympian detachment. This is not the comment of the professional sociologist evaluating the depth of this startling "people movement." Nor is it the condescending approval of a self-declared "great man," coolly and haughtily acknowledging that his protégés are on the right track. Rather, this is the joy of a man who says, in effect, "I love you so much that when I see God's grace in your life I am utterly elated. Indeed, your spiritual growth affords me so much joy in the presence of God that I am profoundly indebted to you— and I am impelled all the more to thank God for you." It is in this spirit that Paul tells his readers, "Indeed, you are our glory and joy" (2:20). Paul is never a mere professional; he is passionately involved with these people.

There is another hint in the text that assures us Paul's joy is not narcissistic. A true narcissist would never move to the second point in Paul's prayer that proves his passionate attachment to the people of God.

2. Paul prays that he might be able to strengthen these believers (3:10–11). "Night and day," he writes, "we pray most earnestly that we may see you again and supply what is lacking in your faith" (v. 10). Then he changes the form of his prayer, referring to God in the third person, but continuing the same theme: "Now may our God and Father himself and our Lord Jesus clear the way for us to come to you" (v. 11). This is the prayer, not of a narcissist, but of a servant.

A Passion for People

90

There are three details that demand attention. First, Paul claims he utters this petition "night and day." Whenever Paul avows that he "always" thanks God (e.g., 1 Cor. 1:4; Phil. 1:4) or "continually" thanks God (e.g., 1 Thess. 1:2; 2:13) or, as here, petitions God "night and day," we are not to think Paul is resorting to hyperbolic language, which if taken literally would mean that the apostle never had time for eating and sleeping. Still less are we to think of him floating in a constant (if ill-defined) "spirit of prayer," with very little concrete praying. He means that, in his regular times for prayer, day and night, he remembers the Thessalonians before the Lord.[1] There are two lessons to learn: the importance of frequent, regular prayer times, and the importance of remembering the right things when we set out to pray. But more of this in the next chapter. For the moment it is enough to note that Paul is constantly praying for other Christians. When we contrast this with the penchant many of us have for praying almost exclusively for ourselves, we are ashamed.

Second, the burden of Paul's constant prayer, as he remembers them at his prayer times night and day, is that he might see them again so as to supply what is lacking in their faith. Their deficiency stems not from rebellion but from ignorance. Paul was with them such a short time that he did not have the opportunity on that first visit to establish them in the Scriptures. Now he longs to see them again, for no other purpose than to strengthen their faith.

What is remarkable in this petition is not only the light it sheds on what Paul thinks is important and on his commitment to brothers and sisters in Christ, but also the way it mingles intercessory prayer and his own service. He does not simply pray that the faith of the Thessalonians might be strengthened, leaving the means unstated (would it be strengthened by some other apostle or teacher? by God himself?); rather, he prays that he himself might do it. He is like Isaiah after his vision of the Almighty: "Here am I. Send me!" (Isa. 6:8).

For Paul, prayer is not a substitute for Christian service; it is part of it. And apparently he cannot long pray for believers without longing to serve them himself. This was true even with respect

A CALL TO SPIRITUAL REFORMATION

to believers Paul had not yet met but for whom he nevertheless prayed (Rom. 1:11).

This mindset ought to be in all of us. Relatively few of us are called to cross-cultural ministry; few of us will be able to minister personally to all the believers for whom we ought to be praying. But the mindset of service should belong to all of us, especially when we pray. Certainly all of us can be doing something. As we pray for believers we know, we may be able to write an encouraging letter, befriend a teenager who is beginning to go adrift, take a fatherless child fishing, start an inductive Bible study for young Christians in the subdivision, quietly administer a humble word of admonition to someone who is doing damage with unguarded speech, send some free books to a pastor in the so-called Third World. These things ought not to be done without prayer; conversely, praying with Paul will impel us to do some of these things, and more. Both in our praying and in our immediate, personal service, we will strive to make up what is lacking in someone's faith.

Third, it is remarkable that Paul is aware of factors that prevent him from serving as he would like. Earlier he testified, "For we wanted to come to you—certainly I, Paul, did, again and again— but Satan stopped us" (2:18). What form this satanic opposition took we have no idea, but Paul's prayer now is that "our God and Father himself and our Lord Jesus clear the way for us to come to you" (3:11). These hindrances do not curtail his praying but incite him to greater fervency. They are not grounds for discouragement but for renewed intercession.

All three of these details strengthen the connections between Paul's prayer life and his passion for the people of God.

3. Paul prays that there might be an overflow of love among these believers (3:12). "May the Lord make your love increase and overflow for each other and for everyone else, just as ours does for you" (3:12). "The Lord" here refers to the Lord Jesus, just mentioned in the previous verse. A more literal translation might read: "May the Lord [Jesus] enlarge you and make you abound in love for one another. . . ." The enlargement Paul here envisages is not in numbers, but in spirit, strength, perspective, heart (as in

2 Cor. 6:11, 13, though the verb there is a little different; hence the New International Version's periphrastic but accurate rendering).

Considering how little Christian instruction the Thessalonians received before Paul was forced to leave them, is it not remarkable that this is one of the burdens of Paul's prayer? He does not restrict his prayer to doctrinal considerations, praying only that the understanding of the believers in Thessalonica might increase. He prays that their love might increase and overflow.

It is important to recognize how much such conduct would fly in the face of the conventions of the ancient world. In most layers of Greco-Roman society, a kind of social contract existed between those perceived to be "benefactors" and everyone else. Entire sets of relationships turned on these customs. A fairly well-to-do person might dispense food, preferment, employment, honor, money; in return that person demanded loyalty, various forms of service, or privileged information. If you had any hope of climbing up within the system, it was essential to meet these obligations. An ordinary worker would not be inclined to show particular affection or loyalty to his coworkers; he would want to show loyalty and affection to someone who was his "benefactor," someone a little higher up the pecking order.

Paul will not have it, not in the church or even in the way Christians treat outsiders. True, he elsewhere insists that Christians honor those to whom honor is due. Nevertheless he here prays that the Christians' love will increase and overflow "for each other" (that is, for fellow believers in the church) "and for everyone else" (that is,for those outside the fellowship). Similarly he writes a little later in the letter, "Make sure that nobody pays back wrong for wrong, but always try to be kind to each other and to everyone else" (5:15).

This is a hard, brutal world. There are many protestations of affection, many forms of pseudo-love, whether in ancient Greco-Roman civilization or in our own. But Christian love, mature, deep, and unqualified, is a rare commodity. When it is displayed, it speaks volumes to a society that gorges itself in self-interest, lust, mutual-admiration pacts, even while it knows very little of love.

Show me a church where the choir is known as the War Department, where people divide over evangelistic strategies or over the color of the carpet, and I'll show you a church that has not been praying along these lines for some time. Conversely, we will see profound spiritual renovation if by God's grace we make it our commitment not to put anyone down—except on our prayer list.

That is why Paul turns to this petition again and again. It will surface in one form or another in the next two prayers we examine. For the moment it is enough to compare our own praying with that of Paul and to ask ourselves to what extent we have made this petition a passionate interest in our own prayers.

4. Paul prays that these believers will be so strengthened in heart that they will be blameless and holy when the end comes (3:13). "May he strengthen your hearts so that you will be blameless and holy in the presence of our God and Father when our Lord Jesus comes with all his holy ones" (3:13). In biblical thought, the heart is not only the center of personality, the seat of will and understanding, but also the place where hidden motives are shaped (cf. 2:4: "We are not trying to please men but God, who tests our hearts."). If our hearts are strengthened, if our resolve and guileless allegiance to Jesus Christ are enlarged, then we will not need to fear the day of the Lord. We serve one of whom it is said that he "will bring to light what is hidden in darkness and will expose the motives of men's hearts. At that time each will receive his praise from God" (2 Cor. 4:5).

Paul prays that Christians will be so strengthened that they will become "blameless and holy in the presence of our God and Father"—not according to temporal, worldly standards, but blameless and holy in the presence of a holy God. Paul wants us to "become blameless and pure, children of God without fault in a crooked and depraved generation, in which [we] shine like stars in the universe" (Phil. 2:15). That is what he prays for.

Paul prays for these things in the light of the end, "when our Lord Jesus comes with all his holy ones" (v. 13). Now the connection with the first chapter of this book becomes clear. There we saw how Paul prays with eternity's values in view; here we discover that he prays with burning passion for people. But in fact,

A Passion for People

94

these are not two distinct poles; they are facets of the same vision. When we pray for people, we must do so knowing that these people, and we ourselves, are inevitably moving toward the last day. When we pray with eternity's values in view, we are driven to pray for people, because people like you and me are the ones who must give account to God on the last day.

From that perspective, there is no prayer we can pray for others more fundamental than this: that God might strengthen their hearts so that they will be blameless and holy in the presence of our God and Father on the last day.

When was the last time you offered up these petitions for the people of God?

Questions for Review and Reflection

1. In what ways does Paul's prayer in 1 Thessalonians 3:9–13 show his passion for people?
2. Set yourself the task of faithfully praying for a Christian (or Christians) for whom you do not now pray. After you have been at it a few months, tell the person you are doing so—and then keep on doing so.
3. According to this passage, what is Paul's source of joy? What is yours? How is our source of joy likely to be related to what we pray for?

The Content of a Challenging Prayer

(Colossians 1:9–14)

y far the most important and the most authoritative of the sources that continue to shape my prayer life is the Bible itself. The study of the Scriptures with a view to strengthening one's prayer life has two foci. The first is general and comprehensive: the more we learn about God and his ways and his perspectives, the more we improve our grasp not only of elemental theology but of prayer as well. All praying presupposes an underlying theology; conversely, our theology will have a decisive influence on our praying. Of course, the direction of influence is not just one way: it is also true to say that our praying (or lack of praying) will also influence our theology. Even so, deepening grasp of Scripture is bound to have a reforming influence on our praying.[1]

The second focus is narrow and powerful: the study of the prayers of Scripture. Learn to argue in prayer with Moses, to sing with David, to be farsighted and expansive with Solomon at the

Paul's Prayer for the Colossians

³We always thank God, the Father of our Lord Jesus Christ, when we pray for you, ⁴because we have heard of your faith in Christ Jesus and of the love you have for all the saints—⁵the faith and love that spring from the hope that is stored up for you in heaven and that you have already heard about in the word of truth, the gospel ⁶that has come to you. All over the world this gospel is bearing fruit and growing, just as it has been doing among you since the day you heard it and understood God's grace in all its truth. ⁷You learned it from Epaphras, our dear fellow servant, who is a faithful minister of Christ on our behalf, ⁸and who also told us of your love in the Spirit.

⁹**For this reason, since the day we heard about you, we have not stopped praying for you and asking God to fill you with the knowledge of his will through all spiritual wisdom and understanding. ¹⁰And we pray this in order that you may live a life worthy of the Lord and may please him in every way: bearing fruit in every good work, growing in the knowledge of God, ¹¹being strengthened with all power according to his glorious might so that you may have great endurance and patience, and joyfully**

dedication of the temple. Think through what it means to pray the prayer taught us by the Lord Jesus himself. Learn to pray with Paul. Such study will help us identify what to pray for, how to approach God, the proper grounds for our petitions. To restrict ourselves for a moment to the petitions in the prayers of Paul, we must ask ourselves how far the petitions we commonly present to God are in line with what Paul prays for. Suppose, for example, that 80 or 90 percent of our petitions ask God for good health, recovery from illness, safety on the road, a good job, success in exams, the emotional needs of our children, success in our mortgage application, and much more of the same. How much of Paul's praying revolves around equivalent items? If the center of our praying is far removed from the center of Paul's praying, then even our very praying may serve as a wretched testimony to the remark-

> [12]giving thanks to the Father, who has qualified you to share in the inheritance of the saints in the kingdom of light. [13]For he has rescued us from the dominion of darkness and brought us into the kingdom of the Son he loves, [14]in whom we have redemption, the forgiveness of sins.
>
> [15]He is the image of the invisible God, the firstborn over all creation. [16]For by him all things were created: things in heaven and on earth, visible and invisible, whether thrones or powers or rulers or authorities; all things were created by him and for him. [17]He is before all things, and in him all things hold together. [18]And he is the head of the body, the church; he is the beginning and the firstborn from among the dead, so that in everything he might have the supremacy. [19]For God was pleased to have all his fullness dwell in him, [20]and through him to reconcile to himself all things, whether things on earth or things in heaven, by making peace through his blood, shed on the cross.
>
> (Col. 1:3–20)

able success of the processes of paganization in our life and thought.

That is why we need to study the prayers of Paul. The one before us provides us with lessons in two areas.

Lessons from the Setting of the Prayer

1. Paul prays for Christians he has never met personally. Paul writes that "since the day *we heard about you*, we have not stopped praying for you" (1:9, emphasis added). In the first three prayers we examined, Paul was praying for Christians whom he personally knew. Indeed, they were Christians in a church he himself had founded. But here Paul is writing to a church he has never visited, a church apparently founded by Epaphras, himself a Coloss-

98

ian who was probably led to the Lord through Paul's ministry in Ephesus (Col. 1:7; 4:12–13; Acts 19:1, 8–10).

Though he has never visited them, Paul assures the Colossian Christians he is praying for them—for his spiritual grandchildren, as it were. Apparently Paul has added the Colossian believers to his prayer list, ensuring that he never stops praying for them, and as each new report comes in of God's work in that place it becomes grist for Paul's constant intercession to God for them.

We must ask ourselves how extensive our own praying is. Do all our petitions revolve around our own families and churches, our own cherished but rather small circle of friends? Of course, we are primarily responsible for praying for our own circle. If we do not pray for our own circle, who will? But if that is the farthest reach of our prayers, we become parochial, introverted. Our prayers may be an index of how small and self-centered our world is.

Of course, we cannot pray for all believers everywhere, except in the most general ways. But it will do us good to fasten on reports of Christians in several parts of the world we have never visited, find out what we can about them, and learn to intercede with God on their behalf. Not only is this an important expression of the fellowship of the church, it is a critical discipline that will enlarge our horizons, increase our ministry, and help us to become world Christians.

2. Paul prays unceasingly. We have come across this element of Paul's prayer life before. Here we find it again: "since the day we heard about you, *we have not stopped praying* for you" (1:9, emphasis added). We have already observed that this does not mean that Paul's praying was an incessant mystical experience, or that his claim is a rather exaggerated and extravagant use of language. Rather, however much Paul maintained a spirit of prayer as he pursued his normal rounds of activities, he maintained set times for prayer (as Rom. 1:9–10 suggests). In short, Paul is telling the Colossians that since hearing about them he has made it a point to intercede with God on their behalf in his disciplined, regular prayer times; he has "not stopped praying" for them.

The point to be emphasized here is that there are some things for which we should not stop praying. Some books on prayer so

urgently advocate making specific requests that this broader perspective is overlooked. When Paul tells the Colossians that he
has "not stopped praying for them," he implies that there are some
things for which we must pray again and again. Prayer is God's
appointed means for appropriating the blessings that are ours in
Christ Jesus. Many of the best of those blessings we need again
and again, and so we must constantly ask—like the child brought
up in a home stamped with courtesy, where the means of obtain-
ing things, even necessary things, is a respectful request. For
instance, Christians learn to thank God, at each meal, for their
food; the prayer that our Lord taught us to pray assumes we should
ask for food on a daily basis. Likewise, it will not do to set aside
time today to ask God to sanctify us, if we do not return to the
request for six months or so. We need some of God's blessings
constantly, and as we ask God for them constantly, so he constantly meets our need.

That is the sort of thing Paul has in mind when he tells the
Colossians that he has "not stopped praying" for them. There are
certain things that Christians need again and again, constantly,
if they are to live and serve as Christians. For these things Paul
intercedes with his heavenly Father on the Colossians' behalf.
This unceasing nature of his praying serves, of course, as a model
to encourage us to learn persistence in prayer. But perhaps more
importantly, it piques our curiosity: what does Paul think he should
pray for constantly, whether on behalf of the Colossians or on
behalf of anyone else? Is this what we pray for constantly?

3. Paul links prayers of thanksgiving to prayers of petition.
"*For this reason,*" Paul writes, "since the day we heard about you,
we have not stopped praying for you" (1:9, emphasis added). Once
again we observe that Paul's petitions are in some ways linked to
his thanksgiving (vv. 3–7). The kinds of things for which Paul
thanks God are the kinds of things for which Paul asks. But
because we have observed this link in two of Paul's prayers already,
I do not want to dwell on the same point. Rather, I want to
observe that these links between Paul's thanks to God and his
intercession before God drive us to an extremely important conclusion: although we are inclined to pray for people and situa-

tions when they have fallen into desperate need, Paul's common practice is to pray for going concerns.

Consider, first, our own practice. We may of course pray when things are going well. But is it not true that we are inclined to pray with a great deal more urgency when things are going badly? When there is illness, financial pressure, moral failure, dissension in the church, a difficult decision, tensions in the family—those are the times when we are driven to prayer. In itself, that is not bad. It is always encouraging to find Christians instantly taking their needs and fears to God.

But if we pray only at those times, we are overlooking a great lesson from the apostle's prayer life. The frequency with which he links his thanksgiving for signs of grace in the lives of this or that group of believers, with his petitions for more signs of grace in the lives of the same believers, cannot be accidental. When Paul learns of the work of God in some church, he gives thanks; then he prays for still more of the same, shaped, perhaps, by his knowledge of the special needs and propensities of this particular body of believers. The good news he hears of them does not inspire thanks alone. Paul does not give thanks for a particular church in such a way as to suggest that his petitions can now move on to other groups of believers, perhaps those in more difficult circumstances.

Doubtless Paul intercedes when there are barriers to be hurdled; the point here is that he also intercedes when there are signs of life and power and grace, for his concern is that such signs should be protected and increased.

What we must ask ourselves is whether our instinct is in the same direction. Do we feel most constrained to pray when our church is about to split, or when there have been several conversions? Are we as eager to intercede for our children when they seem to be making great progress in the faith as when they are succumbing to the influences of ill-chosen friends? Do we petition God for evidence of perseverance and generous love among Christians we know when we witness some of those virtues in them already?

Do we seriously pray for going concerns?

A CALL TO SPIRITUAL REFORMATION

Lessons from the Content of the Prayer (1:9–14)

What is it, then, that Paul again and again prays for on behalf of the Colossian believers, as if the supply must be constantly renewed? In this prayer, there is but one petition, followed by a statement of its purpose and a description of the way God's answer to the petition works out in daily life.

1. Paul asks God to fill believers with the knowledge of his will. "For this reason," he writes, "since the day we heard about you, we have not stopped praying for you and asking God to fill you with the knowledge of his will through all spiritual wisdom and understanding" (1:9).

We must think through what Paul means by "the knowledge of his [i.e., God's] will" with which he wants believers to be filled. Very frequently we are inclined to use the expression *the will of God* to refer to God's will for my vocation or for some aspect of my future that is determined by an impending choice. We "seek the Lord's will" over whom we should marry, over major purchases, over what church to attend when we move to a new city.

None of this is intrinsically bad. There are many ways in which the Lord does lead us, and we should not despise them. Nevertheless this focus is often quite misleading, perhaps even dangerous, for it encourages me to think of "the Lord's will" primarily in terms of my future, my vocation, my needs—and that is often another form of self-centeredness, no matter how piously put. Worse, it expunges from my consciousness the dominant ways in which the Bible speaks of the will of the Lord.

Consider such passages as the following: "Teach me to do your will, for you are my God; may your good Spirit lead me on level ground" (Ps. 143:10). To do the will of God in this passage is virtually synonymous with obeying what God has mandated. What God has mandated is his will; our responsibility is to do it. The psalmist does not here encourage us to find God's will, for he assumes it is already known. Rather, he is concerned with performance of that will. When he says "Teach me," he does not say, "Teach me your will," but "Teach me *to do* your will."

Paul exhorts the Roman Christians, "Do not conform any longer to the pattern of this world, but be transformed by the

The Content of a Challenging Prayer

renewing of your mind. Then you will be able to test and approve what God's will is—his good, pleasing and perfect will" (Rom. 12:2). Here the assumption is that the transformation of character and conduct brought about by the renewal of the Christian's mind is precisely what equips such a Christian to test and approve God's will—that is, to discover personally and experientially that his ways are best.

Elsewhere we are told, "Be very careful, then, how you live—not as unwise but as wise, making the most of every opportunity, because the days are evil. Therefore do not be foolish, but understand what the Lord's will is" (Eph. 5:15–17). In such a context, to "understand what the Lord's will is" cannot be reduced to a merely intellectual pursuit. Over against the evil and folly of the surrounding society, where, because of laziness and hedonism, people squander opportunities that the Lord graciously gives, Christians are to make the most of every opportunity, to avoid foolishness, and thus to show they understand what the Lord's will is. The next verses contrast the debauchery of inebriation with the joy of being filled with the Spirit, a filling which issues in right relationship at every level of society (Eph. 5:18–6:9). That is the way understanding "what the Lord's will is" will be worked out in believers' lives.

Elsewhere, Paul writes, "It is God's will that you should be sanctified" (1 Thess. 4:3); and again, "Be joyful always; pray continually; give thanks in all circumstances, for this is God's will for you in Christ Jesus" (1 Thess. 5:16–18). When some perpetually morose and whining Christians come to me, I tell them I know what God's will is for their lives: "Give thanks in all circumstances, for this is God's will for you in Christ Jesus." It is folly to pretend to seek God's will for your life, in terms of a marriage partner or some form of Christian vocation, when there is no deep desire to pursue God's will as he has already kindly revealed it.

The second part of this verse that needs explanation is the phrase *through all spiritual wisdom and understanding*. This rendering assumes that spiritual wisdom and understanding constitute the means by which God fills us with the knowledge of his will. It is perhaps better to take the Greek preposition to mean "which consists of":[2] the knowledge or perception of God's will consists of all spiritual wisdom and understanding. Knowledge of God's will is more than knowledge of a certain corpus of doctrine (though it cannot easily be less). Knowledge of God's will consists of wisdom (so often tied in the Scripture to knowing *how* to live) and understanding of all kinds, at the spiritual level.

That is what Paul prays for the Colossians. His prayer is motivated in part by his concern over their flirtation with the syncretism and pluralism of their own day. These dangerous tendencies end up reducing Christ to merely relative importance, and Paul will not have it. In the next chapter he writes, "See to it that no one takes you captive through hollow and deceptive philosophy, which depends on human tradition and the basic principles of this world rather than on Christ. For in Christ all the fullness of the Deity lives in bodily form, and you have been given fullness in Christ, who is the head over every power and authority" (2:8–10). So also here: Paul prays that they may be filled with the knowledge of the will of God, a knowledge that consists of wisdom and understanding of all kinds, at the spiritual level. How else will they withstand the pressures of their surrounding pagan culture, pressures that are as subtle as they are endemic? How else will they think Christianly, and genuinely bring their minds and hearts and conduct into conformity with God's will?

Is there anything that our own generation more urgently needs than this? Some of us have chased every fad, scrambled aboard every bandwagon, adopted every gimmick, pursued every encounter with the media. Others of us have rigidly cherished every tradition, determined to change as little as possible, worshiped what is aged simply because it is aged. But where are the men and women whose knowledge of God is as fresh as it is profound, whose delight in thinking God's thoughts after him ensures that their study of Scripture is never merely intellectual and self-distancing, whose desire to please God easily outstrips residual and corrupting desires to shine in public?

People cannot live by bread and Jacuzzis alone. We desperately need meditative and reflective dependence on every word that proceeds from the mouth of God (Deut. 8:3; Matt. 4:4). The need

The Content of a Challenging Prayer

takes on painful urgency when we discover that even within our churches, let alone the nation at large, there are rapidly declining standards of the most basic Bible knowledge. True, basic Bible knowledge does not ensure the kind of knowledge of God's will that Paul has in mind. But ignorance of the Bible, the focal place where God has so generously disclosed his will, pretty well ensures that we will not be filled with this knowledge of God's will, this knowledge that consists in all spiritual wisdom and understanding.

Small wonder, then, that this is something for which we must constantly pray. It is to our great shame if we have not constantly been praying along these lines. Few needs more urgently demand our intercession before our merciful heavenly Father than this one. The rapid growth of many churches in, say, sub-Saharan Africa and in Latin America, as humbling and as thrilling as it may be, will be jeopardized unless it is accompanied by a deepening knowledge of God's will. And in the Western world, where much of the church continues to squander its remarkable heritage in the grace of God, the knowledge of God declines while our fascination with techniques and fads increases. Are these not reasons to join Paul in his prayer that God might fill believers with the knowledge of his will?

2. The purpose of Paul's petition is that believers might be utterly pleasing to the Lord Jesus. After articulating his petition, Paul discloses the reason for his prayer: "And we pray this in order that you may live a life worthy of the Lord and may please him in every way" (1:10). We have come across this thought before. In 2 Thessalonians 1:5, for instance, Paul assures the Christians in Thessalonica that they "will be counted worthy of the kingdom of God" for which they are suffering (see chap. 1 of this book). But here the language is stronger yet, because it is more personal. The purpose of Paul's praying as he does is that believers might live a life "worthy of the Lord"—an astonishingly high standard, and somehow more embarrassingly demanding than "worthy of the kingdom of God."

In case his readers are slow to discover just what "worthy of the Lord" means in practical terms, Paul spells it out: he wants them to "please him [i.e., the Lord Jesus] in every way." That is what it means to live a life worthy of the Lord.

We might have a clearer vision of what this means if we lived in a shame culture. In a shame culture, one of the worst things you can do is bring shame on your family, clan, or tribe. Usually a host of known and accepted taboos exists, and the people who belong to that culture will go to extraordinary lengths to avoid transgressing those taboos, since to do so would incur terrible shame.

Not long ago a Korean student pursuing a research degree at a well-known British university approached me to ask if I could give him some advice. His problem was both simple and complex. At the simple level, he was failing rather badly in all his work, and it was clear the university was going to squeeze him out of the program. He needed to come to terms with this hard reality. Yet at a deeper level, he had to deal with his family back home in Seoul. His mother and father had sacrificed to send him to the United Kingdom, and they could not conceive of the possibility that their son would not make the grade. The student was utterly distraught. His parents and siblings were pressuring him to succeed in some way—to transfer to another university, perhaps, or to another program, or to another degree. If he were to return home without a degree, he would bring devastating shame upon the entire family.

In the Western world, we do not, by and large, think in such terms. Of course, some families operate that way, and no one with any sensitivity at all wants to disappoint loved ones who have sacrificed to enable us to forge ahead. Still, we do not live in a shame culture. Rugged individualism pervades much Western ideology, and whatever shame we feel is rather slight compared with the shame brought on by corporate pressures imposed on people in many cultures of the world. But in a shame culture, people are taught they must be worthy of their family's name, worthy of their country, worthy of their heritage. By contrast, many Westerners are applauded when they act in stubborn independence of their peers.

Most cultures in the first century were close to the pattern of a shame culture. But instead of insisting that Christians live up to the church's expectations—our tribe, if you will—Paul

The Content of a Challenging Prayer

tells them they must live up to the expectations of the church's Lord. They are not to live a life worthy of the church, but worthy of the Lord.

That would be an immensely powerful plea in a shame culture. In the Western world, it is far too often taken as nothing more than one option. But in Paul's world, to be a Christian, to confess Jesus as Lord, meant to adopt a world view in which you are bound to please him in every way. Not to do so would be to bring shame on him whom you have confessed as Lord.

Of course, a shame culture can manipulate individuals with terrible cruelty. The price of social cohesion can be destruction of individual integrity. In the same way, the church can thunder the truth that Jesus' name is to be lifted up, yet do so in such a way that people are manipulated, driven by guilt without pardon, power without mercy, conformity without grace. But most of our churches in the West are plagued with a different sort of problem. Many of us think we can sin with impunity. We have been debilitated by the virus of indifferentism.

If we are to join Paul in his petition, we will have to align ourselves with his motives: "And we pray this in order that you may live a life worthy of the Lord and may please him in every way." In thought, word, and deed, in action and in reaction, I must be asking myself, "What would Jesus have me do? What is speech or conduct worthy of him? What sort of speech or conduct in this context should I avoid, simply because it would shame him? What would please him the most?"

Rightly pursued, these simple questions would transform how we work, what we do with leisure time, how we talk with our spouses and children, what responsibilities we take on in our churches, what we read, what we watch on television, how we treat our neighbors, what we do with our money.

Transparently, we cannot begin to be utterly pleasing to Jesus unless God fills us with the knowledge of his will. Conversely, the knowledge of his will is not an end in itself but has as its goal such Christian maturity that our deepest desire is to please the Lord Christ.

Even here, Paul will not permit these concerns to remain at a theoretical or abstract level. He goes on to describe what it means to be utterly pleasing to the Lord.

3. Paul sketches, in terms of four characteristics, what a life pleasing to the Lord looks like (1:10b–14). These four characteristics are not the only marks of the believer. Rather, they are typical traits, and they flesh out what living "a life worthy of the Lord" really means. They are borne along by four participles in the Greek text.

Christians bear fruit in every good work. That is Paul's language in verse 10b. True, Christians are saved "by grace" and "through faith," "and this . . . not by works, so that no one can boast" (Eph. 2:8–9). But God's free grace in our lives has an irreducible purpose: "For we are God's workmanship, created in Christ Jesus to do good works, which God prepared in advance for us to do" (Eph. 2:10).

The kinds of good works demonstrated and the degree of fruitfulness will vary a great deal from believer to believer. Even in the parable of the soils, the percentage increase among the productive soils varied considerably (Mark 4:8). But Paul cannot imagine anyone being pleasing to Christ without fruitfulness in good works. Or again, Paul's thought can be put the other way around: he prays that believers might be filled with the knowledge of God's will, so that they may live a life worthy of the Lord Jesus and utterly pleasing to him—and this means abounding in good works. It is not a question of ascetic temperament or self-flagellation: it is a question of bearing fruit (see John 15:1–8).

Christians grow in the knowledge of God. Paul is never satisfied with the mere status quo: Christians are organisms that grow, not machines that simply perform a designated function for which they were designed.

At the same time, when Paul describes these believers as "growing in the knowledge of God" (1:10b), he has come full circle. The petition in Paul's prayer is that these believers might be filled with the knowledge of God, to the end that they might live a life worthy of Jesus Christ. When he describes a little of what such a life looks like, however, he says it is characterized by growth in the knowledge of God. This is not a vicious circle. What Paul means is that knowledge of God's will, knowledge that consists of all spiritual wisdom and understanding, turns in part on obedience, on conformity to the will of God. We must learn something of that will in order to obey it; discovery of more of that will is contingent on obeying what we know of it.

To put the matter another way, there is a moral basis to the knowledge of God. Did not Jesus say, along somewhat similar lines, "If any one chooses to do God's will, he will find out whether my teaching comes from God or whether I speak on my own" (John 7:17)? To learn something of God's will and to use such knowledge to live a life worthy of the Master and utterly pleasing to him, is to engage in the business of obedience. But as you get busy in the business of obedience, you get to know God better. That in turn impels you to more obedience, which in turn opens up new vistas in the knowledge of God and his will. Of course, as your knowledge of God and his will improves, you are driven to greater obedience. Such obedience is one point of access to greater knowledge of God; and on, and on, and on. . . .

Christians grow in the knowledge of God.

Christians are strengthened so as to display great endurance and patience. That is how Paul thinks of believers: they are "being strengthened with all power according to [God's] glorious might, so that [they] may have great endurance and patience" (1:11). What is remarkable is that the power for which Paul prays is frequently tied to the power of the resurrection (Eph. 1:19–20; Col. 2:12), but its demonstration among believers, at least in the first instance, is found not in miracles or in their own resurrection, but in great endurance and patience.

"Great endurance and patience": the expression suggests both the kind of stamina that gets under a burden and carries it with enduring fortitude, and the kind of stamina that knows how to possess its soul in patience. Those are not virtues that are popular in our age. We extol champagne: lots of fizz and a pretty good high, but having no nutritional value for the long haul. In an age when tempers are hot, quick solutions are ardently courted, success is revered, victory is cherished, independence is lauded, and easy

A CALL TO SPIRITUAL REFORMATION

triumphs are promised, "great endurance and patience" at first glance seem like less than stellar qualities. But the truth is, they are so far beyond human capacity that they require the power of the Spirit of God. Not to be confused with mere Stoicism (which loses its moral center and therefore its capacity for righteous outrage), still less with mere physical stamina, these virtues enable the believer to survive with joy when persecuted, to triumph in self-composure and contentment when insulted, to trust God's all-wise and all-gracious providence when one is suffering like Job. When Jesus sees these virtues in us, he is well pleased.

Christians joyfully give thanks to the Father. Thanksgiving, too, pleases Jesus Christ. Not to give thanks would be mute testimony to a catastrophic loss of perspective; to give thanks, to give thanks with joy, is to remember that the Father has "qualified [us] to share in the inheritance of the saints in the kingdom of light. For he has rescued us from the dominion of darkness and brought us into the kingdom of the Son he loves, in whom we have redemption, the forgiveness of sins" (1:12–14).

If God had perceived that our greatest need was economic, he would have sent an economist. If he had perceived that our greatest need was entertainment, he would have sent us a comedian or an artist. If God had perceived that our greatest need was political stability, he would have sent us a politician. If he had perceived that our greatest need was health, he would have sent us a doctor. But he perceived that our greatest need involved our sin, our alienation from him, our profound rebellion, our death; and he sent us a Savior.

What Paul is saying is that to live a life worthy of Jesus Christ is to overflow with joyful thanksgiving in the light of the salvation we have received at his hand. If we have been transferred out of the dominion of darkness and into the kingdom of the Son beloved by God, our only appropriate response is joyful gratitude.

Indeed, as Paul thinks along such lines, his mind is so compellingly drawn to Jesus that he breaks out in a paean to Christ (1:15–20). Of course, it is important for Paul to remind his Colossian readers that Christ is the Lord of the universe, since he was God's agent in creation, and to tell them that Jesus is not only

The Content of a Challenging Prayer

110

creation's agent but its goal: "all things were created by him and for him" (1:16). Because of the syncretism all around them, the Colossians needed to be reminded that Christ alone is the head of the church. Yet Paul reminds them in such a way that he displays the joyful exuberance that he has just been describing. It is the inevitable heritage of those who dwell on the countless blessings they have received from God through the merits of Christ Jesus.

The line of thought in this prayer of the apostle is straightforward. He prays constantly that these Christians will be filled with the knowledge of God's will. Then he tells them the purpose of his prayer: he wants them to live a life worthy of the Lord, utterly pleasing to him, and Paul assumes that such a life is utterly impossible unless there is a growing and spiritual grasp of what God's will is. Finally, unwilling to leave undefined such expressions as "worthy of the Lord" and "please him in every way," he fleshes them out with some concrete characteristics of Christians who live this way. His list is not meant to be exhaustive, merely typical, but it is no less revolutionary for that. Christians, he says, bear fruit in every good work. They grow in the knowledge of God, they are strengthened by God's power so as to display great endurance and patience, and they joyfully give thanks to the Father for the astonishing salvation he has granted them through the Son he loves, Jesus Christ. That sublime thought elicits a burst of praise for Jesus himself.

When was the last time you prayed like that? Does not the example of the apostle suggest we should be constantly praying along these lines?

Questions for Review and Reflection

1. Granted that one aim in praying is that you might be utterly pleasing to the Lord Jesus, what concrete things in your own life should you be praying about?
2. What praying do you do for believers you have never met? How can you improve in this area?
3. What connections do joyful thanksgiving and faithful endurance have with prayer?

7

Excuses for Not Praying

*L*et's pause now to reflect on the most common excuses we advance to justify our relative prayerlessness, and what Scripture says about those excuses.

I Am Too Busy to Pray

This is surely one of our most overworked excuses. We live in a frenetic age. Both in our work and in our play, we rush, we perform, we accomplish, we strive, we do. We are not living in a contemplative age. When we stop rushing and performing and doing, many of us park ourselves in front of a television, possibly a television attached to a video recorder, and simply absorb what is dished out. The result is that we seldom take time to think, to meditate, to wonder, to analyze; we seldom take time to pray.

Lillian Guild[1] tells an amusing story of an occasion when she and her husband were driving along and happened to notice a late-model Cadillac with its hood up, parked at the side of the road. Its driver appeared somewhat perplexed and agitated. Mrs. Guild and her husband pulled over to see if they could offer assistance. The stranded driver hastily and somewhat sheepishly explained that he had known when he left home that he was rather low on fuel, but he had been in a great hurry to get to an important business meeting so he had not taken time to fill up his tank. The Cadillac needed nothing more than refueling. The Guilds happened to have a spare gallon of fuel with them, so they emptied it into the thirsty Cadillac, and told the other driver of a service station a few miles down the road. Thanking them profusely, he sped off.

Twelve miles or so later, they saw the same car, hood up, stranded at the side of the road. The same driver, no less bemused than the first time, and even more agitated, was pathetically grateful when they pulled over again. You guessed it: he was in such a hurry for his business meeting that he had decided to skip the service station and press on in the dim hope that the gallon he had received would take him to his destination.

It is hard to believe anyone would be so stupid, until we remember that that is exactly how many of us go about the business of Christian living. We are so busy pressing on to the next item on the agenda that we choose not to pause for fuel. Sadly, Christian leaders may be among the worst offenders. Faced with constant and urgent demands, they find it easy to neglect their calling to the ministry of the Word and prayer because they are so busy. Indeed, they are tempted to invest all of their activity with transcendental significance, so that although their relative prayer-lessness quietly gnaws away at the back of their awareness, the noise and pain can be swamped by the sheer importance of all the things they are busily doing.

Of course, they tell themselves, in their heart of hearts praying is of utmost importance. It's just that the overburdened calendar ensures that this month prayer cannot be given the attention it deserves.

What is God's response? The well-known story of Mary and Martha (Luke 10:38–42) must surely tell us something of Jesus' perception of our busyness. Martha was so sure her choices and her activism were right that she was rather indignant over Mary's quiet pietism. Moreover, it was not as if Martha was engaged in trivial things: she was, after all, looking after this large party, feeding people, "distracted by all the preparations that had to be made" (10:40). Eventually her exasperation with her sister spills over into resentment against Jesus himself: "Lord, don't you care that my sister has left me to do the work by myself? Tell her to help me!" (10:40).

But Jesus' quiet answer still confounds us today: "Martha, Martha . . . you are worried and upset about many things, but only one thing is needed. Mary has chosen what is better, and it will not be taken away from her" (10:41–42).

Another startling insight as to where the Bible ranks prayer is found in a chapter dealing with marriage and sexual relations. There Paul tells married couples they ought to meet each other's sexual needs: "The wife's body does not belong to her alone but also to her husband. In the same way, the husband's body does not belong to him alone but also to his wife" (1 Cor. 7:4). Someone might ask whether there is any possible ground for suspending this principle. Of all the exceptions Paul might have thought of, what he actually says betrays what he thinks of prayer: "Do not deprive each other except by mutual consent and for a time, so that you may devote yourselves to prayer. Then come together again so that Satan will not tempt you because of your lack of self-control" (7:5). In other words, Paul will allow a married couple to turn aside from their obligation to meet each other's sexual needs, but only on three conditions: (1) there must be mutual consent; (2) the purpose must be that they wish to devote themselves to prayer; (3) the suspension must be temporary, for an agreed time, after which the marital obligations must be reaffirmed.

A superficial glance at the passage may leave the reader wondering why sexual intimacy in the context of marriage should be set aside, even temporarily, for the purpose of prayer. Such a glance really is superficial: it knows little of real life. Busy couples can be so active and therefore so tired that they scarcely have time to make love to each other. Doubtless in some instances the problem was even worse in the first century, where husband/wife slaves might have to be the first in the household to get up in the morning and the last to go to bed at night. When will this couple pray

114

together? As highly as Paul values marital obligations, he can envisage a couple self-consciously choosing not to have sex together for a while, so that the time they would have spent pleasing each other sexually will be devoted to prayer. That says something about Paul's valuation of prayer.

It matters little whether you are the mother of active children who drain away your energy, an important executive in a major multinational corporation, a graduate student cramming for impending comprehensives, a plumber working overtime to put your children through college, or a pastor of a large church putting in ninety-hour weeks: at the end of the day, if you are too busy to pray, you are too busy. Cut something out.

I Feel Too Dry Spiritually to Pray

Some of us may set aside a time to pray, only to find that when the time comes we feel too discouraged, or too unbelieving, or too empty—in short, too dry—to pray. We may then be tempted to put off praying until we feel like it a little more.

Whether or not we have given in to our feelings, all of us have sometimes felt that way. What triggers our discouragement or spiritual dryness may be one of a hundred things. We may be short of sleep, and therefore we start seeing the world through spectacles tinted with pessimism. Someone may have hurt our feelings and made our spirits sag by venting unrestrained or injudicious criticism. Stress may be taking its emotional toll, and in such cases this second excuse is also tied to the first. Whatever the cause, the challenge to pray seems too mountainous to surmount in our state of spiritual depletion.

Hidden behind this excuse are two presuppositions that are really quite monstrous. The first is that the acceptability of my approach to God in prayer ought to be tied to how I feel. But is God especially impressed with us when we feel joyful or carefree or well rested or pious? Is not the basis of any Christian's approach to the heavenly Father the sufficiency of Christ's mediating work on our behalf? Is not this a part of what we mean when we pray "in Jesus' name"? Are we not casting a terrible slur on the cross when we act as if the usefulness or acceptability of our prayers turns on

A CALL TO SPIRITUAL REFORMATION

whether we feel full or dry? True, when we feel empty and dispirited we may have to remind ourselves a little more forcefully that the sole reason why God accepts us is the grace that he has bestowed upon us in the person and work of his Son. But that is surely better than giving the impression that we are somehow more fit to pray when we feel good.

The second unacceptable presupposition behind this attitude is that my obligation to pray is somehow diminished when I do not feel like praying. This is to assign to my mood or my feelings the right to determine what I ought to do. And that, of course, is unbearably self-centered. It means that I, and I alone, determine what is my duty, my obligation. In short, it means that I am my own god. It is to act as if the Bible never says, "Be joyful in hope, patient in affliction, *faithful in prayer*" (Rom. 12:12, emphasis added).

What is God's response? Two of Jesus' parables are especially relevant. In Luke 18, Jesus tells of a persistent widow who took her case to a corrupt judge who "neither feared God nor cared about men" (18:2). Although he began by ignoring her, eventually her persistence paid off: "Even though I don't fear God or care about men, yet because this widow keeps bothering me, I will see that she gets justice, so that she won't eventually wear me out with her coming!" (18:4–5). Jesus draws the conclusion: "And will not God bring about justice for his chosen ones, who cry out to him day and night? Will he keep putting them off? I tell you, he will see that they get justice, and quickly" (18:7–8). The point is not that God is rather like a corrupt judge who responds only to constant badgering. Rather, the argument is *a fortiori*: if even a corrupt judge responds to persistence, how much more will the righteous God respond to persistence? After all, the opening verse of the chapter reminds us that "Jesus told his disciples a parable to show them that they should always pray and not give up" (18:1). Indeed, as far as Jesus is concerned the real question is not whether or not God answers prayer but whether or not we have the faith to persevere; for the passage ends with Jesus' asking the probing question, "However, when the Son of Man comes, will he find faith on the earth?" (18:8). To fall back on the excuse that we feel too

116

dry or the like is merely to admit that we do not exercise the kind of faith that perseveres.

Another parable with a similar point is the story of the person who goes at midnight to the home of his friend. He wakes him up and says, "Friend, lend me three loaves of bread, because a friend of mine on a journey has come to me, and I have nothing to set before him" (Luke 11:5–6). Initially the man inside the house begs off. He and his family are already in bed, and they do not want to be disturbed. But Jesus, knowing the community commitment to hospitality that characterized first-century Palestine, comments, "I tell you, though he will not get up and give him the bread because he is his friend, yet because of his *desire to be without shame*[2] he will get up and give him as much as he needs" (11:8). Not to do so, in that culture, would bring shame upon himself and his family. He may not want to help the man at the door, and he may resent the prospect of getting out of bed, but it is simply unthinkable, in that shame culture, that he would finally refuse.

Jesus draws the moral: "So I say to you: Ask and it will be given to you; seek and you will find; knock and the door will be opened to you. For everyone who asks receives; he who seeks finds; and to him who knocks, the door will be opened" (11:9–10). The point is not that God has to be shamed into answering prayer. Once again, the argument is implicitly *a fortiori*: if even a lazy and inconsiderate neighbor finally does the right thing for no other reason than that he does not want to bring shame on his name and house, how much more will God answer the prayers of his people? After all, he has his own name to keep up! He has pledged himself in covenant grace to meet the needs of his people, to prove utterly reliable and trustworthy. He cannot be less than trustworthy, or he would bring shame on his own name. Therefore ask, knock, seek.

Implicit in both of these parables is the assumption that God may not answer immediately, that it is part of his wisdom to wait, even to resist us, so that we may exercise our faith and pursue him with sincerity. A moment's reflection shows that this is a good thing. If God were to answer all prayers the instant they were

A CALL TO SPIRITUAL REFORMATION

uttered, he would become an automaton, the power link in a clever bit of magic. He would not be the God who wisely responds to his people, and who disposes of all things according to his sovereign goodness, but a powerful genie constrained by a magic bottle called prayer.

God insists that we learn not to hide behind our feelings of dryness, behind our chronic unbelief, behind our lapses into discouragement. He wants us to learn to trust him, to learn to persevere in prayer. In short, in prayer as in other areas of life, God wants us to trust and obey.

I Feel No Need to Pray

This excuse is a trifle trickier than the first two. Few of us are so crass that we self-consciously reason, "I am too important to pray. I am too self-confident to pray. I am too independent to pray." Instead, what happens is this: Although abstractly I may affirm the importance of prayer, in reality I may treat prayer as important only in the lives of other people, especially those whom I judge to be weaker in character, more needy, less competent, less productive. Thus, while affirming the importance of prayer, I may not feel deep need for prayer in my own life. I may be getting along so well without much praying that my self-confidence is constantly being reinforced. That breeds yet another round of prayerlessness.

What is God's response? If Christians who shelter beneath such self-assurance do not learn better ways by listening to the Scriptures, God may address them in the terrible language of tragedy. We serve a God who delights to disclose himself to the contrite, to the lowly of heart, to the meek. When God finds us so puffed up that we do not feel our need for him, it is an act of kindness on his part to take us down a peg or two; it would be an act of judgment to leave us in our vaulting self-esteem.

This lesson is taught in countless passages of Scripture. One thinks, for instance, of the Gibeonite deception, reported in Joshua 9. At this point the people of God have witnessed God's power in the crossing of the Jordan and in the destruction of Jericho. After a setback occasioned by Achan's sin, they have by God's power and wisdom overpowered Ai (Josh. 7–8). At that point in Israel's history, the people of Gibeon approach, wearing old clothes and dilapidated sandals, and carrying moldy bread to generate the illusion they have come from a great distance. They pretend they are not part of the corrupt tribes of the land whom the Israelites have been ordered to drive out, but foreigners who simply want to secure a peace treaty with Israel because Israel is perceived to be a rising power (Josh. 9:9–13).

What was Israel's response? "The men of Israel sampled their provisions but did not inquire of the LORD. Then Joshua made a treaty of peace with them to let them live, and the leaders of the assembly ratified it by oath" (9:14–15).

What a damning indictment! Yet could not the text be paraphrased somewhat and applied to many of us? "John Smith weighed the alternative employment opportunities before him, but did not inquire of the Lord." "Jane Brown sought a lot of advice before she made her decision, but did not inquire of the Lord." "The Evangelical Community Church formed a committee to explore possible approaches to evangelizing their community, but did not inquire of the Lord."

It is painfully easy for us to come to all kinds of critical points in ministry, service, family development, changes in vocation, and, precisely because we have enjoyed spiritual victories in the past, approach these matters with sophisticated criteria but without prayer. We love our independence. As a result we may repeatedly stumble and fall, because although we have exercised all our intellectual ingenuity we have not sought God's face, we have not begged him for his wisdom.

Consider Hezekiah. He begged God for fifteen more years of life, and they were granted to him. Most of these years were filled with productive service. In one matter, however, Hezekiah failed miserably. When envoys from the mighty Babylonian Empire showed up, Hezekiah, flattered by their attention, gave them a guided tour of the wealth of his kingdom. Doubtless the written reports of the envoys remained on file. This small incident became a crucial factor in the decision of Babylon to pillage the kingdom decades later (2 Kings 20:12–21). But perhaps the most startling assessment comes from the Chronicler. He acknowledges that Hezekiah did many good things, and then adds, "But when envoys were sent by the rulers of Babylon to ask him about the miraculous sign that had occurred in the land, God left him to test him and to know everything that was in his heart" (2 Chron. 32:31). Because it was not in Hezekiah's heart to seek the Lord's face, because his heart was self-confident and self-assured, he badly stumbled at this critical point.

We need not think that the only sins that will keep us from prayer are large and gross. We so often fall at the subtle points.

I Am Too Bitter to Pray

We cannot live long in this world without coming across injustice, chronic lack of fairness. Many of us accept such sin with reasonable equanimity, reasoning that it is, after all, a fallen world. But when the injustice or unfairness is directed against us, our reaction may be much less philosophical. Then we may nurture a spirit of revenge, or at least of bitterness, malice, and gossip. Such sins in turn assure that our prayers are never more than formulaic; eventually such sin may lead to chronic prayerlessness. "How can I be expected to pray when I have suffered so much?" "Don't talk to me about praying for my enemies: I know who has kept me from being promoted."

Life itself is consumed by the petty assessment of how well you are perceived by those around you. In this morass of self-pity and resentment, real prayer is squeezed out. In other words, many of us do not want to pray because we know that disciplined, biblical prayer would force us to eliminate sin that we rather cherish. It is very hard to pray with compassion and zeal for someone we much prefer to resent.

What is God's response? At the end of Matthew's version of the Lord's Prayer, Jesus adds, "For if you forgive men when they sin against you, your heavenly Father will also forgive you. But if you do not forgive men their sins, your Father will not forgive your sins" (Matt. 6:14–15). Elsewhere Jesus says, "And when you stand praying, if you hold anything against anyone, forgive him, so that your Father in heaven may forgive you your sins" (Mark 11:25).

Excuses for Not Praying

The idea is not that by our act of forgiving others we somehow earn the Father's forgiveness, but that by our forgiving others we demonstrate we really want the Father's forgiveness. By such an approach to God we signal that our repentance is genuine and our contrition real. Christians must never approach God as if they enjoy an inside track with the Almighty that allows them to experience his blessings but not his discipline. Precisely because we know ourselves to be sinners in need of forgiveness, we recognize that to ask for forgiveness while we withhold it from others is nothing more than cheap religious cant.

In fact, we can look at this matter of bitterness not only from the vantage of those who need forgiveness, but from the vantage of those who have received it. The Bible tells us, "Get rid of all bitterness, rage and anger, brawling and slander, along with every form of malice. Be kind and compassionate to one another, forgiving each other, just as in Christ God forgave you" (Eph. 4:31–32). In the light of the matchless forgiveness we have received because Christ bore our guilt, what conceivable right do we have to withhold forgiveness?

I Am Too Ashamed to Pray

We remember the response of Adam and his wife after their willful disobedience of God's one prohibition. When they "heard the sound of the LORD God as he was walking in the garden in the cool of the day . . . they hid from the LORD God among the trees of the garden" (Gen. 3:8). Shame encourages us to hide from the presence of God; shame squirrels behind a masking foliage of pleasantries while refusing to be honest; shame fosters flight and escapism; shame engenders prayerlessness.

What is God's response? God sought Adam and Eve and dealt with their sin. We cannot successfully hide from God anyway, "for a man's ways are in full view of the LORD, and he examines all his paths" (Prov. 5:21). "Nothing in all creation is hidden from God's sight. Everything is uncovered and laid bare before the eyes of him to whom we must give account" (Heb. 4:13). But if it is futile to run from God, our sense of shame can scarcely be an adequate ground to excuse our prayerlessness. Rather, it ought to be a goad that drives us back to the only one who can forgive us and grant us utter absolution, back to the freedom of conscience and the boldness in prayer that follow in the wake of the joyful knowledge that we have been accepted by a holy God because of his grace.

I Am Content with Mediocrity

Some Christians want enough of Christ to be identified with him but not enough to be seriously inconvenienced; they genuinely cling to basic Christian orthodoxy but do not want to engage in serious Bible study; they value moral probity, especially of the public sort, but do not engage in war against inner corruptions; they fret over the quality of the preacher's sermon but do not worry much over the quality of their own prayer life. Such Christians are content with mediocrity.

What is God's response? Many passages could be brought to bear on the condition. One of the most intriguing is the letter written by James, the half-brother of our Lord. Writing to Christians, he nevertheless finds it necessary to say, "You quarrel and fight. You do not have, because you do not ask God" (James 4:2). Here are Christians, bickering and squabbling, profoundly frustrated because of their prayerlessness. When they do pray, they are no better off: "When you ask, you do not receive, because you ask with wrong motives, that you may spend what you get on your pleasures" (James 4:3).

From God's perspective, such Christians are "adulterous people" (4:4), because while nominally maintaining an intimate relationship with God, they are trying to foster an intimate relationship with the world. "You adulterous people, don't you know that friendship with the world is hatred toward God [in exactly the same way that a physically adulterous relationship is hatred toward the spouse]? Anyone who chooses to be a friend of the world becomes an enemy of God" (James 4:4).

God's response is utterly uncompromising: "Submit yourselves, then, to God. Resist the devil, and he will flee from you. Come near to God and he will come near to you. Wash your hands, you sinners, and purify your hearts, you double-minded. Grieve, mourn and wail. Change your laughter to mourning and your joy to gloom. Humble yourselves before the Lord, and he will lift you up" (4:7–10).

The sad truth is that at various times all of us need to apply these words to our lives.

Questions for Review and Reflection

1. What excuses, other than the ones mentioned in this chapter, are sometimes used to justify prayerlessness? Critique them from a biblical perspective.
2. Do you ever appeal to any excuses to justify your own prayerlessness? Which ones? Are they any good?
3. Does God accept us on the basis of whether or not we feel like praying? If not, on what basis does he accept us? How should this affect the priority we assign to prayer?

Overcoming the Hurdles

(Philippians 1:9–11)

All of us recognize that some believers are gifted with a peculiar ministry of prayer. While William Carey is often referred to as "the father of modern missions," it was his sister, bedridden for years, who spent hours each day interceding for the ministry of her brother and for others who were beginning to follow the trail he blazed. George Müller of Bristol was extraordinarily gifted in prayer.

Still, we have come far enough to recognize that we cannot justify our relative prayerlessness by saying that those who are peculiarly effective are more gifted than we. Wherever we stand in the spectrum of Christian maturation, we could do better than we do, and many of us could do much better. One of the most important steps we can take is to recognize where we are. We quietly confess that we are dangerously dry. Our knowledge of God is slight, and we long to pray with a greater sense of reality and a greater degree of fruitfulness. We want to learn how to pray.

124

> ## Paul's Prayer for the Philippians
>
> [1]Paul and Timothy, servants of Christ Jesus,
> To all the saints in Christ Jesus at Philippi, together with the overseers and deacons:
> [2]Grace and peace to you from God our Father and the Lord Jesus Christ.
> [3]I thank my God every time I remember you. [4]In all my prayers for all of you, I always pray with joy [5]because of your partnership in the gospel from the first day until now, [6]being confident of this, that he who began a good work in you will carry it on to completion until the day of Christ Jesus.
> [7]It is right for me to feel this way about all of you, since I have

Few of Paul's prayers have greater potential to help us surmount the hurdles of spiritual dryness and lack of faith than the one in Philippians 1:9–11. It can help us overcome our excuses for prayerlessness. Formally this is a short and simple prayer. For our purposes it may be helpful to think through what Paul prays for by breaking the prayer into three steps.

Paul Prays for What Is Excellent

At one level, one could say that what Paul is asking God for is constantly increasing love: "And this is my prayer," he writes, "that your love may abound more and more in knowledge and depth of insight" (1:9). But as one reads on, it becomes clear that, at least in this prayer, the love for which Paul prays is not an end in itself but a means to an end. Paul tells the Philippians that he prays that their love may increase "so that [they] may be able to discern what is best" (v. 10).

So although Paul is here praying that the Philippians' love may increase, that petition is so tightly cast with a different end, namely, that they may discern and approve what is best, that it is no less fair to say that Paul is praying for what is best, for what is

A CALL TO SPIRITUAL REFORMATION

you in my heart; for whether I am in chains or defending and con-
firming the gospel, all of you share in God's grace with me. [8]God
can testify how I long for all of you with the affection of Christ
Jesus.
   [9]And this is my prayer: that your love may abound more and
more in knowledge and depth of insight, [10]so that you may be
able to discern what is best and may be pure and blameless until
the day of Christ, [11]filled with the fruit of righteousness that comes
through Jesus Christ—to the glory and praise of God.

(Phil. 1:1–11)

excellent. We have not yet unpacked exactly what these excellent things are; nor have we explored how an increase in love
moves the church toward the goal of approving these excellent
things, the best things. What is immediately clear, however, is
that Paul's prayer spells the death of entrenched mediocrity, of
smug self-satisfaction, of contentment with our own excuses. Paul
prays for what is excellent.
   Paul does not expect excellence to be dropped on the church in
a package. He prays that believers may discern and approve what
is best, that is, that they may experientially test and thereby
approve[1] what is best. But what are these distinguishing things,
these excellent things for which Paul prays?
   Three clues in the text help us answer that question. First, Paul
assumes that if the Philippians are going to discern and approve
what is best, their love will have to "abound more and more in
knowledge and depth of insight." That is why he prays for such
love. The excellence he wants the Philippian believers to pursue
is not easily discerned. To discern and approve what is excellent
Christians must be characterized by this abounding love.
   Why does Paul describe Christian love in exactly this way?
Love that "abounds more and more" is plain enough, but what

about love that "abounds more and more in knowledge and depth of insight"? Perhaps we will get at Paul's point rather quickly if we replace the phrase with the opposite qualities. Paul does not pray that their love might "abound more and more in ignorance and insensitivity" or in "stupidity and ham-fistedness" or in "cheap sentimentality and myopic nostalgia." He prays, rather, that their love might "abound more and more in knowledge and depth of insight." The ever-increasing love for which Paul prays is to be discriminating. It is to be constrained by "knowledge" and "depth of insight." Without the constraints of knowledge and insight, love very easily degenerates into mawkish sentimentality or into the kind of mushy pluralism the world often confuses with love. Christian love will be accompanied by "knowledge"—that is, in Paul's use, that mature grasp of the meaning of the gospel that is the fruit of sound instruction and full experience. Christian love is also accompanied by (literally) "all insight": the "all" does not here signal total insight or "depth of insight" (NIV), but breadth of insight—that is, moral perception across the entire gamut of life's experiences.

Clearly, knowledge and discernment without love could easily become supercilious, overbearing, casuistical. But love without knowledge and discernment is soon a parody of itself. The Christian love for which Paul prays is regulated by knowledge of the gospel and comprehensive moral insight. These constraints do not stifle love. Far from it: they ensure its purity and value. Such love, Paul insists, must abound more and more.

The point is that Christians must abound more and more in this quality of love if they are to test and approve what is best. So "what is best" must be delicate or subtle or difficult to spot to those whose love is not abounding in this way. Paul simply assumes that unless your love is abounding more and more in knowledge and depth of insight, you will not be able to discern and approve what is best. In other words, if the discernment of "what is best" is utterly dependent on such multiplying love, a little light is shed on the content of "what is best," on the excellent things Paul wants Christians to pursue.

The second clue is in the expression rendered in the New International Version by "what is best." Scholars have debated whether the expression[2] means something like "things that differ" or "superior things." The first option means Paul wants believers to grow in their love "in order that they may put to the proof things that differ"; the second means Paul wants believers to grow in their love "in order to discern and approve [i.e., to test] superior things, the things that really matter." But perhaps the two notions are not as far apart as some think. Paul's thought is that there are countless decisions in life where it is not a question of making a straightforward decision between right and wrong. What you need is the extraordinary discernment that helps you perceive how things differ, and then make the best possible choice. That is what Paul means by choosing "what is best." His point thus far, then, is that love shaped and honed by knowledge and moral insight is the absolute requirement for testing and approving "what is best," for developing "a sense of what is vital" (*Moffatt*).

There is a third clue that will help us understand the content of "what is best," the content of the excellent things for which Paul prays. This clue is nothing other than one of the dominant themes in this entire epistle. Already in verse 6 of this chapter, Paul tells the Philippians that he always prays for them with joy, because he is confident "that he who began a good work in you will carry it on to completion until the day of Christ Jesus." In other words, Paul does not envisage mere maintenance of the Philippians' faith, but positive improvement in their discipleship, until it is capped by the perfection effected by the last day, the day of Jesus Christ.

If we may judge from his own example, Paul's confidence that the Lord will bring about such growth does not in the least diminish the need for personal resolution to grow. Thus, two chapters later the apostle testifies to his own aim: "I want to know Christ and the power of his resurrection and the fellowship of sharing in his sufferings, becoming like him in his death, and so, somehow, to attain to the resurrection from the dead" (3:10–11). Then he explains just where he sees himself in this process: "Not that I have already obtained all this, or have already been made perfect, but I press on to take hold of that for which Christ Jesus took

128

hold of me. Brothers, I do not consider myself yet to have taken hold of it. But one thing I do: Forgetting what is behind and straining toward what is ahead, I press on toward the goal to win the prize for which God has called me heavenward in Christ Jesus" (3:11–14).

When we bring these three clues together, the nature of the excellent things Paul wants believers to pursue, of "what is best," comes into focus. These excellent things are nothing less than all the elements characteristic of maturing Christian discipleship, and we cannot discern and approve them unless our love abounds more and more in knowledge and depth of insight. "What is best" includes increasing experience of the power of the resurrection and increasing participation in Christ's sufferings. Above all, these excellent things result in a growing knowledge of Jesus Christ (Phil. 3:10), in anticipation of the day of Christ when all of God's good work in us is brought to culmination.

The pursuit of such excellence does not turn on transparent distinctions between right and wrong. It turns, rather, on delicate choices that reflect one's entire value system, one's entire set of priorities, one's heart and mind. That is why Paul prays that the love of the Philippians might abound more and more in knowledge and depth of insight: he wants their hearts and minds to become profoundly Christian, for otherwise they will not discern and approve what is best.

Perhaps some practical examples will help clarify Paul's prayer.

What do you do with your time? How many hours a week do you spend with your children? Have you spent any time in the past two months witnessing to someone about the gospel? How much time have you spent watching television or in other forms of personal relaxation? Are you committed, in your use of time, to what is best?

What have you read in the past six months? If you have found time for newspapers or news magazines, a couple of whodunits, a novel or two or perhaps a trade journal, have you also found time for reading a commentary or some other Christian literature that will help you better understand the Bible or improve your spiritual discipline or broaden your horizons? Are you committed, in your reading habits, to what is best?

How are your relationships within your family? Do you pause now and then and reflectively think through what you can do to strengthen ties with your spouse and with your children?

Do you make time for personal prayer? For prayer meetings? Have you taken steps to improve in this regard?

How do you decide what to do with your money? Do you give a set percentage, say, 10 percent, of your income to the Lord's work, however begrudgingly, and then regard the rest of your income as your own? Or do you regard yourself as the Lord's steward, so that all the money you earn is ultimately his? Are you delighted when you find yourself able to put much more of your money into strategic ministry, simply because you love to invest in eternity?

Has your compassion deepened over the years, so that, far from becoming more cynical, you try to take concrete steps to serve those who have less than you do?

Is your reading and study of the Bible so improving your knowledge of God that your wholehearted worship of the Almighty grows in spontaneity, devotion, and joy?

At what points in your life do you cheerfully decide, for no other reason than that you are a Christian, to step outside your "comfort zone," living and serving in painful or difficult self-denial?

Behind your answers to all of these questions are choices. The last thing I want to do is generate a load of guilt because of the choices constantly before us, choices we frequently fail to exploit for the glory of God. In fact, I hesitated over including these paragraphs for just that reason. Feelings of guilt will not by themselves help us to make the right choices; they may simply increase our stress and resentments.

But if our love abounds more and more, shaped all the while by knowledge and moral insight, then these are the kinds of choices we will be wanting to make—and we will be wanting to make them well. They are the kinds of choices that cannot be made on the basis of mere law. They spring from a heart transformed by God's grace.

Overcoming the Hurdles

130

"Ah," you reply, "since God demands that we love him with heart, soul, mind, and strength, since he demands that we be holy as he is holy, is not the goal of such perfection demanded by God? Don't the choices you are talking about come our way because God demands our total allegiance? So isn't it simply a question of obeying his demands, his law?"

If by God's law you mean his demands that we submit without reservation to his lordship and aim for perfect obedience, then of course you are right. But my point is that mere statutes, mere case law, cannot possibly cover all the cases. Consider, for example, our use of time. Each of us has twenty-four hours a day to spend. But each of us needs different amounts of sleep. We vary in our ability to concentrate—and each one varies in that particular balance of time, rest, and experience. To "redeem the time because the days are evil" may signal quite different things to different Christians, both in the number of hours they invest and in the ways they invest them. The call to use time wisely may suggest to activist Christians that they slow down and learn to intercede with God; to reflective, meditative Christians, it may become a challenge to active evangelism or work among the poor. How should the time reserved for relaxation be used? The mature Christian may relax by memorizing some Scripture, reading a Puritan classic, or perusing a fresh commentary on Isaiah. But would a Christian necessarily be less mature if he or she picked a whodunit to read? Would one want to say that less mature Christians have actually fallen into sin just because they do not use leisure time quite so profitably?

Paul's prayer cuts through this tangle. What he wants Christians to pray for, at every stage of their spiritual pilgrimage, is excellence, "what is best." Of course, the pursuit of what is best can never be carried on without constant appeal to the standard of God's gracious self-disclosure in the Scriptures. Even so, Paul refuses to set up an arbitrary set of checkpoints against which Christians are to measure themselves; he refuses to erect hoops through which believers must jump. Rather, he simply prays to his heavenly Father and asks him that these believers may pursue what is best. Knowing full well that they cannot pursue excellence without transformed hearts and minds, he further specifies, in his prayer, that God will make their love abound more and more in knowledge and depth of insight, so that they will be able to discern what is best.

Paul cannot be satisfied with the status quo. Knowing that we are destined for the perfection to be achieved when Christ returns, already Paul wants us to press toward it. He cannot be lackadaisical in his praying, because the more fruitful and the more holy he becomes, the more he perceives how much farther he has to go; and he wants the Philippian believers to share the same vision. In short, Paul is passionate about pursuing spiritual excellence, and as he pursues it himself (3:10–14) so he prays for it for others (1:9–11).

Now I would like to address rather directly the clergy who read these pages.

Do you desire, with all your heart, what is best for the congregation you serve? Then you must ask yourself how much time you devote to praying this sort of prayer.

Part of the problem we ministers in the West face when we butt up against this challenge is that, while we know we have been called to the ministry of the Word and prayer, several notable pressures impose themselves, pressures so persistent they end up shaping our values and therefore our schedules.

The pastor's job has been diversified. We no longer give ourselves to the ministry of the Word and prayer, because we have become professional counselors, fund-raisers, administrators, committee members, referees, politicians, and media personalities.

Many pastors are confused about their own identity and may suffer from low estimates of the value of their work. Up until thirty years or so ago, clergy were generally respected in the Western world. Three decades of rising secularism, of the media's persistent presentation of clergy as wimps or charlatans or both, of public perceptions that we are obsolete (like dinosaurs) and arrogant, and we may feel a little insecure. Many of us work with professionals and even teach professionals, but we quickly discover that we are not treated like professionals ourselves. It can be argued that such pressures should not bother those who follow in the way of the

132

cross. In practice, however, many clergy overcompensate, acting far too much like professionals and far too little like those given to the ministry of the Word and prayer.

Not a few clergy feel discouraged and unfruitful. Many pastors work for months and years without seeing a single convert. Some have bright ideas but feel they cannot pull the weight of ecclesiastical tradition with them; others value the traditions from which they spring and feel threatened by the endless succession of faddish innovation. The years trickle past, and dispirited resignation sets in.

Some clergy bury themselves in endless activism. Through no one's fault but their own, they give themselves to endless work, always keeping busy but never carving out time to study, think, meditate, and pray.

These and similar pressures corrode our values, deflect our aims, and finally corrupt our schedules. If we regain biblical priorities, all of these pressures will appear in a different light. Has the job been diversified? Once our priorities are straight, we will learn to relegate tasks to their appropriate rank according to the values of Scripture. Delegate some things; cancel others. You do not have to have a bulletin; you have to pray. You do not have to chair every committee or attend every meeting; you have to pray. Are we confused about our roles? If we remember what we have been called to and devote ourselves to praying for what is best, we may care a little less about the opinions of a secular world and devote ourselves more scrupulously to serving the only Master whose opinion matters. Do we feel unfruitful and discouraged? Not only must we remind ourselves that our Master is more interested in faithfulness than in statistics, we shall also be bold enough to ask if some of our unfruitfulness is the result of being diverted from the ministry of the Word and prayer. How much have we prayed for what is best—for a spiritual harvest, for conversions, for demonstrations of the fruit of the Spirit? Could it be that we have experienced little because we have asked for little? Is our unfruitfulness proportionate to our prayerlessness? Paul's prayer knifes through so many of our excuses. Finally, do we bury ourselves in activism? When, then, do we devote ourselves to that to which we have been called, to the ministry of the Word and prayer? When do we pray for what is best?

Of course, Paul's determination to pray along these lines for the believers in Philippi must not be restricted in its application to clergy. Each believer must ask: To what extent do I pray for excellent things, things judged excellent in God's eyes, both for myself and for those around me? Do I pray that my love may abound more and more in knowledge and depth of insight, so that I can distinguish between what is passable and what is excellent, between what is acceptable and what is best, testing out and approving what is best in my own life? Do I pray this for my church?

Or, quite frankly, do I prefer sullen mediocrity?

Paul prays for what is excellent, and it is quite certain that this sort of excellence cannot be attained without prayer.

Paul's Prayer Is Tied to the Long View

The New International Version gives the impression that two things depend upon love's increase: "[1] so that you may be able to discern what is best and [2] may be pure and blameless until the day of Christ, filled with the fruit of righteousness that comes through Jesus Christ" (1:10b–11a). In fact, the Greek begins a new construction, without any "and," where I have inserted [2]. This suggests that everything before "may be pure and blameless" prepares us for this fresh purpose. In other words, Paul prays that believers will test and approve what is excellent "in order [he tells them] that you may be pure and blameless until the day of Christ, filled with the fruit of righteousness that comes through Jesus Christ."

One might want to understand the testing and approving of what is excellent to be a merely intellectual exercise. That path is cut off not only by Paul's insistence that discerning love is a precondition of the exercise but also by his insistence that the goal of the exercise is transparent purity (that is what the word suggests), utter blamelessness, and a life full of righteousness. So although this pursuit of the excellent is certain to challenge one's mental powers, it is not restricted to them. In fact, it will chal-

134

lenge all of our powers, our whole being, and it issues in a transformed life.

Two expressions in this part of Paul's prayer need explanation.
The first is "filled with the fruit of righteousness" (v. 11). The
Greek word for "righteousness"[3] is often rendered "justification,"
and some have argued that that is what Paul means here. In this
view, "the fruit of righteousness" is the life that results from justification, that is, from that decisive act of God whereby my sins
are credited to Christ and his righteousness credited to me. There
is nothing intrinsically objectionable in this interpretation, but
it is probably wrong. The expression *the fruit of righteousness* or *the
fruit of the righteous* is a sufficiently stereotyped expression that it is
doubtful that Paul could have profitably used it outside its regular
meaning (see Prov. 11:30; Amos 6:12). Moreover the entire
expression, "filled with the fruit of righteousness," is here paral-
lel to "pure" and "blameless." It seems best therefore to take all
three as ethical qualities. To be filled with "the fruit of righteousness" is to be characterized by the conduct—the actions, words,
and thoughts—that God himself judges to be right.

Even so, this basket of righteous qualities is the fruit of righteousness; indeed, it is the fruit of righteousness that comes through
Jesus Christ. The picture is of an organism that produces fruit,
and the one who makes the growth and fruitfulness possible is
Jesus Christ. We are to pour our energy into the task, but we must
understand that where this fruit appears it is the product of spiritual growth made possible by Jesus Christ. Just as in Galatians
love, joy, peace, patience, kindness, goodness, faithfulness, gen-
tleness, and self-control constitute the "fruit of the Spirit" (Gal.
5:22–23), so here every righteous thing the Philippians say or do or
think is the "fruit of righteousness that comes through Jesus
Christ." Paul never exhorts us merely to try harder apart from trying harder to be Christians worthy of Christ Jesus; and he is the
first to acknowledge that the righteous living that ensues is, finally,
the product of the grace of God.

The second expression, and the one that is more crucial to our
purposes, is the phrase *until the day of Christ* (v. 10). In English,
the preposition *until* has purely temporal force. The expression in

the original suggests rather "with a view to the day of Christ." Putting the line of thought together, Paul prays that the love of these Christians might abound more and more in knowledge and depth of insight, so that they will be able to discern and approve what is truly excellent—and all of this so that they may be pure and blameless and filled with the fruit of righteousness, with a view to the day of Christ. We have returned to the forward-looking dimension so characteristic of other prayers of Paul (see chaps. 1 and 2 of this book). At the same time, we have returned to the theme of perseverance: we have already noted that just a few verses earlier Paul expresses his confidence that the One who has begun a good work in the Philippian believers will carry it on to completion until the day of Christ Jesus. That is the theme Paul is picking up again here.

Paul does not appeal to the "day of Christ," the day of his return, in order to introduce a veiled threat. He is not saying, "You really must start showing more signs of this righteous conduct I have been talking about, or you may be caught out at the end, and face horrible judgment, or at the very least have a great deal of explaining to do." Rather, he is saying something that most Christians will find even more compelling. Paul is telling them that they must live with a view to the day of Christ—that is, they must live in such a way that they show they remember they are moving toward that day and are utterly constrained by it. On that day, in "a new heaven and a new earth, the home of righteousness" (2 Pet. 3:13), the fruit of our lives will be entirely righteous. Even now, Paul says, Christians will live with that day in view and will produce much righteous fruit in anticipation of that day. That is part of the call toward excellence.

The church is to see itself as an outpost of heaven. It is a microcosm of the new heaven and the new earth, brought back, as it were, into our temporal sphere. We are still contaminated by failures, sin, relapses, rebellion, self-centeredness; we are not yet what we ought to be. But by the grace of God, we are not what we were. For as long as we are left here, we are to struggle against sin, and anticipate, so far as we are able, what it will be like to live in the

Overcoming the Hurdles

136

untarnished bliss of perfect righteousness. We are to live with a view to the day of Christ.

That means, of course, that Christians constitute a kind of intrinsic missionary community. Our proper citizenship is in heaven; positionally, we have already been seated with Christ in the heavenlies (Eph. 2:6). But until the consummation, we live out our lives down here, a heavenly, missionary outpost in a lost, dying, and decaying world. We are to see ourselves as an outpost of a new heaven and a new earth in an old world that stands under the judgment of God.

This means that when Paul prays this prayer, he is praying for nothing less than revival. He is praying that Christians might be, right now, what we ought to be, what we certainly one day will be. The text teaches us to pray that we will test out and approve for ourselves the highest and best and holiest things—all with a view to the day of Jesus Christ. Even now, Paul's prayer insists, Christians are to be as holy as pardoned sinners can be this side of eternity. And we are to pray toward that end. It is in this way that Paul's prayer for what is excellent is tied to the long view, to the day of Jesus Christ.

It does not take much reading in the history of revivals[4] to discover that when true revival dawns, resentments are dissolved. When revival comes, self-promotion is seen to be ugly, and withers away. When revival comes, men and women are concerned to be holy, they are serious about integrity, they embrace genuine self-denial and learn to love. When revival comes, our worrying sense of unreality disappears, and heaven seems more real, and certainly more important, than this transient world order. When revival comes, worship is no longer an exercise but one of the chief characteristics of our lives. Buffoonery, gimmicks, and entertainment fade away; the day of Jesus Christ seems to draw near. Out of this fresh experience of the grace of God powerfully working in our lives, evangelism becomes not only a passion but immeasurably more fruitful.

Inevitably, some soon imitate the revival by applying techniques and tests, trying, as it were, to codify grace and domesticate the power of God. Abuses occur, and sometimes multiply so quickly that the revival is quenched or diverted to a pale imitation of itself. Still, those who have witnessed even a little of the powerful work of the Holy Spirit in times of blessing are often stamped with peculiar unction. As one revival convert put it, "I was born again in the fires of revival, and I do not intend to die in the ashes of its memory."

The point to stress in this context is that although Paul's prayer for what is excellent is equivalent to praying for revival, what he is doing is praying. He is not simply exhorting people to be better, nor is he trying to organize revival, still less is he berating fellow believers for lack of revival. What he is doing is praying for revival. For if true revival is a work of God, if transforming and discerning love that enables believers to approve what is best is at bottom the fruit of God's work in our lives, if true righteousness is fruit that comes through Jesus Christ, then however much God may use means, the means themselves do not guarantee anything. Only God can produce transformation; only God can grant a revival. Judging by Paul's example, however much we must work out our own salvation with fear and trembling, we must also acknowledge that our best efforts in this regard are nothing other than God's working in us both to will and to act according to his good purpose (2:12–13). So it is urgent that we ask God to work in us; it is vital that we learn to pray this prayer with Paul.

The Western church needs nothing more urgently than groups of believers, unknown, unsought, privately, faithfully, without promotion or fanfare, covenanting together to seek God's face, praying urgently for what is best as we contemplate the day of Jesus Christ—praying, in short, for revival. What would the end of these things be? God is sovereign and full of compassion: who knows what he might do?

Paul's Prayer Is Not Idolatrous, but Praises God

Sadly, the pursuit of the excellent can be wretchedly idolatrous. The point can be observed in a thousand contexts. You marry someone you know to be something of a perfectionist, and the first night you discover just what that means when you are berated for squeezing the tube of toothpaste instead of rolling it. People can be perfectionists in some areas and not in others. In our family both my wife and I are born organizers. Inevitably, problems arise when, without consulting each other, we organize the same thing quite differently and fully expect the other person to fall in with our own "perfect" plans.

Perfectionist parents can be desperately hard on their children. Not only in the area of basic conduct, but in skills, sports, schoolwork, recreational activities, we can end up belittling their efforts and angrily chiding them for not meeting standards that are frankly unrealistic.

Perfectionism in its unhappier guises also invades the church. A couple of years ago I sat down for coffee, after prayer meeting, with one of the most able preachers I have ever heard. This man is extraordinary. I have never heard him preach without finding my mind informed and my heart challenged. On the relatively rare occasions when I can listen to him, his ministry invariably reshapes my thinking by the Word of God. Though only in his late forties, he serves in a strategic church. But that night, over coffee, he quietly began to speak words along these lines: "Don," he said, "if the truth be told, I am getting tired. For the first time I understand why some able preachers end up in administration or teaching at the age of fifty. I cannot maintain this level of ministry, Sunday after Sunday, week after week, without burning out. I am tired. And I confess I am enough of a perfectionist that I do not want to go into the pulpit unless I am thoroughly prepared. Unless I feel the message is ready, I am not content to preach it."

I responded with a few platitudes, and we prayed together. Some months later, I was preaching and lecturing in Australia, when someone passed on to me one of the sayings of Broughton Knox, formerly the principal of Moore Theological College. According to this report, Knox told his students, "God is not interested in one hundred percentism."

There is a sense, of course, in which that is the only thing God is interested in. He wants us to trust and obey him wholly; he wants us to serve him with 100 percent loyalty. But then the focus is on him. What Broughton Knox meant is that very often what we call "one hundred percentism" is not unrestrained allegiance to

God and his gospel but merely a reflection of a perfectionist personality. For some people, unless they tackle whatever they are
doing with 100 percent of their energy and competence, the task
is not worth doing at all. They cannot live with themselves unless
they work that way. Frequently they are the high achievers. But
from a Christian perspective, this attitude may turn out to be
nothing more than another form of self-worship—in short, a form
of idolatry.

So I wrote to my fellow preacher and cited Broughton Knox:
"God is not interested in one hundred percentism." The fact is,
I told him, I would much rather listen to him preach for thirty or
forty more years at 80 percent of his capacity, than for three or
four more years at 100 percent of his capacity. If the choice is to be
made on the basis of what is for the good of the church, of the
number of people who would hear the gospel powerfully and intel-
ligently presented, and therefore on the basis of what would bring
most glory to Christ, the same decision would be called for. In all
our pursuit of excellence, we must never worship excellence. That
would simply be idolatrous.

The same problem arises at many levels. The perfectionist
housewife who constantly insists the house be perfect can be so
"perfect" she is almost impossible to live with. The perfectionist
corporate executive can make success in business an idol to be
worshiped at all cost. The Christian student who cannot face himself or herself with anything less than an A+ may be far more
interested in preserving a personal reputation than in serving the
risen Christ.

None of this should be taken as an excuse for laziness, carelessness, lack of discipline. From a biblical perspective, the deep
question we must ask is what our motives are. There are different
kinds of personalities, each with its own strengths. But the question is this: Are we concerned to utilize the gifts and graces God
has given us, to utilize them for his glory and for his people's good?
Or are we simply interested in doing our own thing?

It is at this point that Paul is so careful. He prays for "what is
best," and understands that this best must issue in "the fruit of

140

righteousness that comes through Jesus Christ," and then carefully adds that all of this is to the glory and praise of God (1:11b).

That is the ultimate test: it is the test of our motives. Some of us pursue what is excellent, even in the spiritual arena, simply because we find it hard to do anything else. Our perfectionist natures are upset when there is inferior discipline, inferior preaching, inferior witness, inferior praying, inferior teaching. If we are concerned over these things because we sense in them a church that has sunk into contentment with lukewarmness and spiritual mediocrity, if we try to change these things because in our heart of hearts we are zealous for the glory of Christ and the good of his people, that is one thing; if on the other hand our concern over these matters is driven primarily by our own high, perfectionist standards, we will be less inclined to help, and more inclined to belittle. Our own service will become a source of secret pride, precisely because it is more competent than much of what we see around us. And sadly, much of this ostensible concern for quality may be nothing more than self-worship, the ugliest idolatry of them all.

Paul has in fact already tried to quash pursuit of this kind of excellence. By praying that the love of the Philippian believers might abound more and more, as a precondition and a means to discerning and approving what is best, he establishes the nature of the excellence that interests him. Love is essentially self-denying; it seeks God's interests, our fellow-believer's good. Now Paul gives his prayer the sharpest focus: the apostle intercedes with God along these lines to the end that God himself might be glorified and praised.

By the same token, if our pursuit of what is excellent, both in prayer and in our Christian lives more generally, is bound up with our own egos and with unarticulated notions of self-fulfillment, it is worthless. To the degree that our pursuit of what is excellent is increasingly impelled by discerning love, and directed "to the glory and praise of God," so far are we joining the apostle in his prayers, and learning to live with eternity's values in view.

These lessons may be especially important for those who are more senior. Retirement can betray where our hearts really are;

so can medical incapacity. Bishop Stanway was used by God to multiply churches and strengthen the outreach of the gospel throughout East Africa. In Tanzania alone he was responsible for creating more than twenty dioceses; some referred to him as the apostle to Tanzania. In retirement he helped to found a seminary in North America. But when I met him, he had returned to his native Australia, and Parkinson's disease had so debilitated him that he could no longer talk. He communicated by writing on a pad of paper; more precisely, he could no longer write, but printed his answers in scarcely legible block letters. By the time I got to know him a little, I felt emboldened to ask him how he was coping with his crippling disease. He had been so active and productive throughout his life; how was he handling being shunted aside? He had to print his answer on that pad of paper three times before I could read it: "There is no future in frustration."

In short, Bishop Stanway would not allow himself the luxury of frustration. He lived with eternity's perspective before him, and frustration plays no part there. He simply had not tied his ego to his service, so that when the active, fruitful forms of service he had enjoyed for decades were withdrawn, he himself was not threatened. He could still trust his Master, and pursue what was best within the constraints imposed on him.

Martyn Lloyd-Jones was one of the most influential preachers of the century. A few weeks before he died, someone asked him how, after decades of fruitful ministry and extraordinary activity, he was coping now he was suffering such serious weakess it took much of his energy to move from his bed to his armchair and back. He replied in the words of Luke 10:20: "Do not rejoice that the spirits submit to you, but rejoice that your names are written in heaven." In other words, do not tie your joy, your sense of wellbeing, to power in ministry. Your ministry can be taken from you. Tie your joy to the fact you are known and loved by God; tie it to your salvation; tie it to the sublime truth that your name is written in heaven. That can never be taken from you. Lloyd-Jones added: "I am perfectly content."

Here then is a practical test as to whether the excellence I pursue is really for the glory and praise of God or for my own self-

Overcoming the Hurdles

image. If the things I value are taken away, is my joy in the Lord undiminished? Or am I so tied to my dreams that the destruction of my dreams means I am destroyed as well?

Paul's pursuit in prayer of what is excellent is not idolatrous; rather, it is bound up with praising God. He would have understood the ancient Irish hymn:

> Be Thou my vision, O Lord of my heart,
> All else but naught to me, save that Thou art;
> Thou my best thought in the day and the night,
> Waking and sleeping, Thy presence my light.
>
> Be Thou my wisdom, Thou my true word;
> Thou ever with me, and I with Thee, Lord;
> Thou my great Father, and I Thy true son;
> Thou in me dwelling, and I with Thee one.
>
> Be Thou my breastplate, my sword for the fight;
> Thou my whole armour and Thou my true might;
> Thou my soul's shelter, and Thou my strong tower,
> Raise Thou me heavenward, great power of my power.
>
> Riches I heed not, nor man's empty praise,
> Thou mine inheritance now and always;
> Thou and Thou only the first in my heart,
> Sovereign of heaven, my treasure Thou art.
>
> High King of heaven, Thou heaven's bright sun,
> Grant me its joys after victory is won;
> Heart of my own heart, whatever befall,
> Still be my vision, O Ruler of all.
>
> Translated by Mary E. Byrne

Hear then this prayer that God has placed in his Word that we might learn what we should ask him for: "And this is my prayer: that your love may abound more and more in knowledge and depth of insight, so that you may be able to discern what is best [in order that you] may be pure and blameless until the day of

Christ, filled with the fruit of righteousness that comes through Jesus Christ—to the glory and praise of God" (1:9–11).

Questions for Review and Reflection

1. Enlarge on the connection between growing in love shaped by knowledge and moral insight . . . and approving what is best.
2. Enlarge further upon the nature of the best things for which we should be praying.
3. What percentage of your praying is for things of eternal value? Do you think your prayers should change? Why or why not?
4. How does Paul avoid making the pursuit of what is excellent an idolatrous exercise? How should his example apply to you?

A Sovereign and Personal God

rayer changes things. You find plaques promulgating this notion everywhere. You may have one in your home. Countless sermons have been preached, countless prayers prayed, under this assumption: "Prayer changes things."

Or does it?

If prayer changes things, how can we believe that God is sovereign and all-knowing? How can we hold that he has his plans all worked out and that these plans cannot fail? If not a bird falls from the heavens without his decree, if we live and move and have our being under his sovereignty, if he works out everything in conformity with the purpose of his will (Eph. 1:11), then in what meaningful sense can we say that prayer changes things?

Indeed, that is precisely why some people argue that God must be severely limited in certain ways. They reason something like this: "Frankly, it seems to us that although God is extraordinarily powerful, it is unreasonable to think he is all-powerful, absolutely sovereign. Surely that would reduce the entire universe to a toy, God's toy. We would lose our freedom; we would become mere puppets, chunks of matter moved around by a despotic Deity. If in that sort of universe we pray, well, we pray only if God has ordained

145

that we pray; if we do not pray, God has ordained that, too. In either case it is hard to see how our prayers actually change anything. Certainly there is little point in encouraging people to be fervent or passionate in prayer: your encouragement has been ordained, and if they listen to you and offer fervent prayer that, too, has been ordained. The entire business becomes pretty phony. Surely there is no other reasonable option: we simply have to conclude that God cannot be utterly sovereign, absolutely omnipotent."

If God is not absolutely sovereign, goes this line of reasoning, maybe the reason he does not answer your prayers as you would like is that he can't. Suppose you are praying for the conversion of your sister. If God has already done everything he can to bring her to himself, but somehow she won't give in, why bother asking him to save her? Isn't it a little indecent to pressure God to do more when he has already done the best he can?

Or, one might reason that God is powerful, but somewhat aloof, unwilling to do very much until we ask him. Then, of course, he grants some requests but turns down others simply because he can't do any better.

So prayer does change things, after all—even if the price of these sorts of reasoning is that God is not as powerful, and therefore not as trustworthy, as we might have thought. In fact, if God is not really all-powerful, one might wonder, in darker moments, how we can be certain that he will make the universe turn out all right in the end.

Others argue that the only change prayer effects is within the person praying. Because I pray for certain things (they hold), I focus on them and strive for them, and I myself am changed. I may pray to do a good job at work, and because I am praying along such lines my determination is reinforced, I am slightly changed for the better, and the result may be that my work really improves. But the only immediate change effected by the prayer is in me. Put crudely, this means it does not really matter if God is out there at all. Prayer is nothing but a psychological crutch. Prayer is all right, but only for weak and insecure people.

Christians will never think along any of these lines, for such thoughts are basically atheistic. Ironically, some of us adopt a Christian version of the same approach. We, too, sometimes say that what prayer changes is primarily the person who prays, but we attribute this change not to psychology but to obedience. The only meaningful prayer, we may think, is, "Not my will, but yours be done." If that is answered, then we have become better attuned with the will and purpose of God, and that is a good thing.

Yet despite the importance of praying that God's will be done, it is certainly not the only prayer in the Bible. In the Scriptures, believers not only pray for themselves, they ask for things. They ask God to change circumstances, to give them things, even to change his mind. In many passages, as we shall see, we are told that God, on hearing such prayers, "relented"—which is not much different from saying that he "changed his mind."

But if God changes his mind, why do other passages of Scripture picture him as steadfast, reliable, immutable?

Sad to tell, we are sufficiently perverse that we can find reasons for not praying no matter what perspective we adopt. Consider missions. If you believe that God "elects" or chooses some people for eternal life, and does not choose others, you might be tempted to conclude that there is no point praying for the lost. The elect will infallibly be saved: why bother praying for them? So you have a good reason not to pray. If on the other hand you think that God has done all he can to save the lost, and now it all depends on their free will, why ask God to save them? He has already done his bit; there's very little else for him to do. Just get out there and preach the gospel. Either way you have another reason not to pray.

You can really hurt your head thinking about this sort of thing.

The Bible insists that we pray, urges us to pray, gives us examples of prayer. Something has gone wrong in our reasoning if our reasoning leads us away from prayer; something is amiss in our theology if our theology becomes a disincentive to pray. Yet sometimes that is what happens. The slightly ingenuous but enthusiastic believer may have more experience at prayer than the theologian who thinks a lot about prayer. Or again, sometimes when a Christian develops an increasing appreciation of "the doctrines of

A Sovereign and Personal God

grace"—truths that underline God's sovereignty, freedom, and grace—one of the first results is a tragic decrease in the discipline of prayer. That was part of my own pilgrimage at one point. The fault was not in the doctrines themselves, but in me and in my inability to mesh them properly with other biblical teachings.

God's Sovereignty and Human Responsibility

In this chapter I want to take some steps that have helped me to think about prayer a little more biblically than I used to. Although I am far from the kind of maturity in prayer I would like to achieve, these biblical reflections have helped me not only to think about prayer but to pray. I shall begin by articulating two truths, both of which are demonstrably taught or exemplified again and again in the Bible:[1]

1. God is absolutely sovereign, but his sovereignty never functions in Scripture to reduce human responsibility.
2. Human beings are responsible creatures—that is, they choose, they believe, they disobey, they respond, and there is moral significance in their choices; but human responsibility never functions in Scripture to diminish God's sovereignty or to make God absolutely contingent.

My argument is that both propositions are taught and exemplified in the Bible. Part of our problem is believing that both are true. We tend to use one to diminish the other; we tend to emphasize one at the expense of the other. But responsible reading of the Scripture prohibits such reductionism.

We might begin by glancing at the large picture. Proverbs 16 pictures God as so utterly sovereign that when you or I throw a die, which side comes up is determined by God (16:33). "The LORD works out everything for his own ends—even the wicked for a day of disaster" (16:4). "In his heart a man plans his course, but the LORD determines his steps" (16:9). "Why do the nations say, 'Where is their God?' Our God is in heaven; he does whatever pleases him" (Ps. 115:2–3).

According to Jesus, if the birds are fed it is because the Father feeds them (Matt. 6:26); if wild flowers grow, it is because God clothes the grass (6:30). Thus God stands behind the so-called natural processes. That is why biblical writers prefer to speak of the Lord sending the rain, rather than to say, simply, "It's raining"—and this despite the fact that they were perfectly aware of the water cycle. The prophets understood the sweep of God's sway: "I know, O LORD, that a man's life is not his own; it is not for man to direct his steps" (Jer. 10:23). "The LORD does whatever pleases him, in the heavens and on the earth, in the seas and all their depths" (Ps. 135:6). The passage (Eph. 1:3–14) is as strong as any: God "works out everything in conformity with the purpose of his will" (Eph. 1:11). In some mysterious way, and without being tainted with evil himself, God stands behind unintentional manslaughter (Exod. 21:13), family misfortune (Ruth 1:13), national disaster (Isa. 45:6–7), personal grief (Lam. 3:32–33, 37–38), even sin (2 Sam. 24:1; 1 Kings 22:21ff.). In none of these cases, however, is human responsibility ever diminished. Thus although it is God in his wrath who incites David to take the prohibited census (2 Sam. 24:1), David is nevertheless held accountable for his actions.

The second of my two statements is no less strongly supported in Scripture. There are countless passages where human beings are commanded to obey, choose, believe, and are held accountable if they fail to do so. God himself offers moving pleas to incite us to repentance, because he finds no pleasure in the death of the wicked (Isa. 30:18; 65:2; Lam. 3:31–36; Ezek. 18:30–32; 33:11). In his day, Joshua can challenge Israel in these words: "Now fear the LORD and serve him with all faithfulness. . . . But if serving the LORD seems undesirable to you, then choose for yourselves this day whom you will serve. . . . But as for me and my household, we will serve the LORD" (Josh. 24:14–15). The commanding invitation of the gospel itself assumes profound responsibility: "That if you confess with your mouth, 'Jesus is Lord,' and believe in your heart that God raised him from the dead, you will be saved. . . . As the Scripture says, 'Anyone who trusts in him will never be put to shame'" (Rom. 10:9, 11). Of course, none of this jeopardizes God's sovereignty: only a few verses earlier we find the apostle quoting Scripture (Exod. 33:19) to prove that "God has mercy on whom he wants to have mercy, and he hardens whom he wants to harden" (Rom. 9:18).

Hundreds of passages could be explored to demonstrate that the Bible assumes both that God is sovereign and that people are responsible for their actions. As hard as it is for many people in the Western world to come to terms with both truths at the same time, it takes a great deal of interpretative ingenuity to argue that the Bible does not support them.

In fact, not only does the Bible support both these truths in a large number of disparate passages, both truths come together in many passages. We have space to mention only seven.

Genesis 50:19–20

After the death of their father, Jacob's sons approach Joseph and beg him not to take revenge on them for having sold him into slavery. Joseph's response is instructive: "Don't be afraid. Am I in the place of God? You intended to harm me, but God intended it for good to accomplish what is now being done, the saving of many lives."

We shall best understand what Joseph says if we carefully observe what he does not say. Joseph does not say, "Look, miserable sinners, you hatched and executed this wicked plot, and if it hadn't been for God coming in at the last moment, it would have gone far worse for me than it did." Nor does he say, "God's intention was to send me down to Egypt with first-class treatment, but you wretched reprobates threw a wrench into his plans and caused me a lot of suffering."

What Joseph says is that in one and the same event the brothers intended evil and God intended good. God's sovereignty in the event, issuing in the plan to save millions of people from starvation during the famine years, does not reduce the brothers' evil; their evil plot does not make God contingent. Both God's sovereignty and human responsibility are assumed to be true.

2 Samuel 24

We have already mentioned that God in his anger incites David to number the people, and then when David performs this prohibited action David is conscience-stricken and must ultimately choose one of three severe judgments that God metes out. The result is that seventy thousand people die.

It is important to remember that the Bible insists that God is good, perfectly good. "He is the Rock, his works are perfect, and all his ways are just. A faithful God who does no wrong, upright and just is he" (Deut. 32:4). "God is light; in him there is no darkness at all" (1 John 1:5). Heaven echoes with the praise, "Great and marvelous are your deeds, Lord God Almighty. Just and true are your ways, King of the ages. Who will not fear you, O Lord, and bring glory to your name? For you alone are holy" (Rev. 15:3–4).

Yet on the other hand, there are numerous passages, like this one in 2 Samuel 24, where God is presented as in some way behind the evil. The evil does not just happen, leaving God to splutter, "Whoops! I missed that one; it sort of slipped by. Sorry about that." Thus God sends certain people a "strong delusion" so that they will believe the great lie (2 Thess. 2:11); he seduces Ahab's prophets, so that their prophecies are rubbish (1 Kings 22:21ff.); ultimately he stands behind Job's sufferings. The story of Job is important when we reflect on 2 Samuel 24 and God's incitement of David to sin by taking a census. The reason is that in 1 Chronicles 21, where the story is retold in a slightly different way, it is Satan and not God who incites David to number the people. Some readers think this is an intolerable contradiction. Certainly the emphasis is different, but it is not a contradiction. Similarly in Job, one could either say that Satan afflicts Job, or that God afflicts Job: the two are not necessarily mutually exclusive.

Of course, this introduces all sorts of difficult questions about secondary causality and the like. My sole point at the moment, however, is that God is presented as sovereign over David's life, including this particular sin in his life, while David himself is not thereby excused: David is still responsible for his actions. Both propositions are assumed to be true.

Isaiah 10:5–19

This passage is typical of many in the Prophets. God addresses the cruelest superpower of Isaiah's day: "Woe to the Assyrian, the rod of my anger, in whose hand is the club of my wrath! I send him against a godless nation, I dispatch him against a people who

A Sovereign and Personal God

anger me, to seize loot and snatch plunder, and to trample them down like mud in the streets" (10:5–6). The context makes clear that the people against whom God is sending the Assyrians is none other than his own covenant community. God is angry with his people for their sin, and so he is sending the Assyrians against them. Even so, God here pronounces a woe on the Assyrians in connection with this mission. Why? Because they think they are doing this all by themselves. They think Samaria and Jerusalem are just like the capital cities of the pagan nations they have already overthrown. Therefore when the Lord has finished his work against Mount Zion and Jerusalem (that is, when he has finished punishing them by using the Assyrians), he will say, "I will punish the king of Assyria for the willful pride of his heart and the haughty look in his eyes" (10:12). "Does the ax raise itself above him who swings it, or the saw boast against him who uses it? . . . Therefore, the Lord, the LORD Almighty, will send a wasting disease upon his sturdy warriors; under his pomp a fire will be kindled like a blazing flame" (10:15–16).

Here we find God using a military superpower as if it were nothing more than a tool—an ax or a saw—to accomplish his purposes of bitter judgment. But that does not mean the Assyrians are not responsible for their actions. Their "willful pride" and their "haughty look" and above all their arrogance in thinking they have made themselves strong are all deeply offensive to the Almighty, and he holds them to account. They may be tools in his hands, but that does not absolve them of responsibility.

John 6:37–40

In the context of the "Bread of Life" discourse, Jesus declares, "All that the Father gives me will come to me, and whoever comes to me I will never drive away" (6:37). This means, on the one hand, that all of the elect, all of God's chosen people, are viewed as a gift the Father presents to the Son, and, on the other, that once they have been given to Jesus, Jesus for his part will certainly keep them in: he will never drive them away. That this is the meaning of the last part of verse 37 becomes especially clear when we follow the argument into the next few verses. "I will never drive [them] away," Jesus says, "for I have come down from heaven not to do my will but to do the will of him who sent me. And this is the will of him who sent me, that I shall lose none of all that he has given me, but raise them up at the last day" (6:37–39).

Thus God is seen as so sovereign in the process of salvation that the people of God are said to be given as a gift by the Father to the Son, while the Son preserves them to the last day when (he promises) he will raise them up. Nevertheless, this does not make these privileged people automata. The next verse can describe these same people in terms of what they do: "For my Father's will is that everyone who looks to the Son and believes in him shall have eternal life, and I will raise him up at the last day" (6:40).

Both of our propositions are assumed to be true, and neither is allowed to diminish the other.

Philippians 2:12–13

After powerfully presenting the unique example of Jesus Christ (2:6–11), Paul writes, "Therefore, my dear friends, as you have always obeyed—not only in my presence, but now much more in my absence—continue to work out your salvation with fear and trembling, for it is God who works in you to will and to act according to his good purpose" (2:12–13). The meaning of these verses has been disputed, and this is not the place to engage the disputants. On the face of it, however, Paul's meaning may become a little clearer if we recognize what he does not say.

Paul does not tell his readers to work out their own salvation, since God has done his bit and now it is all up to them. Still less does he tell them that God does everything, so that all they need is to become supremely passive: "Let go and let God" or some equivalent slogan. Rather, he tells them to work out their own salvation precisely because it is God working in them, both at the level of their will and at the level of their actions ("to will and to act according to his good purpose").

Not only is the truth of our two propositions assumed, but God's sovereignty, extending so far that it includes our will and our action, functions as an incentive to our own industry in the spiritual arena.

A Sovereign and Personal God

154

Acts 18:9–10

A similar argument is displayed in Acts 18, where God's election becomes an incentive to evangelism. Paul arrives in Corinth, doubtless a little discouraged from the rough treatment he has suffered as he has made his way south through Macedonia into Achaia. Now, in a night vision, the Lord speaks to him: "Do not be afraid; keep on speaking, do not be silent. For I am with you, and no one is going to attack and harm you, because I have many people in this city" (18:9–10). The prospect of the conversion of many people, a prospect ensured by God's purposes in election, is what gives Paul stamina and perseverance as he settles down in Corinth for extended ministry.

I first understood something of that argument when I was growing up and beginning to ask difficult questions. My father was a church-planter in Québec. At the time, there was very little fruit. An exceedingly prosperous French-speaking evangelical church in Québec during that period might have had twenty or thirty core people. Many is the time my father preached to a crowd of twenty. At one point, several Americans who had proved remarkably effective in ministry in French West Africa came to Québec to look the situation over. One or two managed to convey the subtle message (without, of course, being so crass as to articulate it), "Shove over, you guys, and we'll show you how it's done."

Not one of those missionaries stayed. All left within months. I was old enough to ask my father why none of them remained to help. He quietly explained that they had served in areas where they had known great blessing, and it was hard for them to envisage working in an area where there seemed to be such dearth. I pressed my father further: why then did he stay? Why shouldn't he go some place where the power of the Lord was abundant? Why commit yourself to working where there is so much to discourage, and so little fruit? He gently rounded on me: "I stay," he said, "because I believe with all my heart that God has many people in this place."[2]

Of course Dad could have gone to his grave without seeing any of this fruit. But in the Lord's mercy, the harvest began in 1972. From a base of fewer than fifty evangelical churches, many hundreds sprang up. Where a major evangelistic effort in a metropolitan area might have drawn a few hundred people to hear the gospel, thousands began to attend. But the point is that this is merely another illustration of what Paul understood in Acts 18:9–10: God's sovereignty in election, far from discouraging evangelism, becomes an incentive to get on with the task. Once again, both of our propositions are assumed to be true.

Acts 4:23–30

This passage in Acts is the most revealing of the seven I have briefly discussed.

As it opens, Peter and John, freshly released from arrest—an arrest that is an omen of worse persecution to come—report on their experiences to "their own people" (4:23), that is, to Christians living in Jerusalem. Their response is to pray. They begin their prayers with an affirmation of God's sovereignty: "Sovereign Lord . . . you made the heaven and the earth and the sea, and everything in them" (4:24). Not only do they confess God as the Creator of the universe, they quote a psalm that affirms God's continuing sovereignty over the nations, even when those nations rebel against him: "The kings of the earth take their stand and the rulers gather together against the Lord and against his Anointed One" (4:26, citing Ps. 2:2). In this psalm, God is not flummoxed by such opposition: "The One enthroned in heaven laughs; the Lord scoffs at them" (Ps. 2:4).

The Christians praying in Jerusalem doubtless remember that context. Even so, they do not quote the entire psalm. Having mentioned the kings of the earth and the rulers gathering together to oppose the Lord and his Anointed One, they think of the most shocking instance of this rebellion against the God who created them: "Indeed Herod and Pontius Pilate met together with the Gentiles and the people of Israel in this city to conspire against your holy servant Jesus, whom you anointed" (Acts 4:27). The early Christians understood that the most wretched fulfillment of Psalm 2 lies in the events leading up to the cross. An ugly conspiracy to pervert justice and gain political advantage was nothing other than a conspiracy against God himself, and against his "anointed one," his Messiah.

A Sovereign and Personal God

156

But the prayer of these Christians does not stop there. They realistically outline the blame to be laid at the feet of Herod, Pontius Pilate, and various Gentile and Jewish authorities, and then they add, "They did what your power and will had decided beforehand should happen" (4:28).

Even brief reflection demonstrates that any other alternative destroys the fabric of the Christian faith. Suppose God had not been sovereign over the conspiracy that brought Jesus to Calvary. Would we not have to conclude that the cross was a kind of afterthought in the mind of God? Are we to think that God's intention was to do something quite different, but then, because these rebels fouled up his plan, he did the best he could, and the result was Jesus' atoning death on the cross? All of Scripture cries against the suggestion. Then should we conclude, with some modern theologians, that if God is as sovereign as the early Christians manifestly believed him to be—so sovereign in fact that the conspirators merely did what God's "power and will had decided beforehand should happen"—then the conspirators cannot reasonably be blamed? But that too destroys Christianity. The reason Jesus goes to the cross is to pay the penalty due to sinners; the assumption is that these sinners bear real moral accountability, real moral guilt for which a penalty has been pronounced. If human beings are not held responsible for this act, why should they be held responsible for any act? And if they are not held responsible, then why should God have sent his Anointed One to die in their place?

God is absolutely sovereign, yet his sovereignty does not diminish human responsibility and accountability; human beings are morally responsible creatures, yet this fact in no way jeopardizes the sovereignty of God. At Calvary, all Christians have to concede the truth of these two statements, or they give up their claim to be Christians.

Mystery and the Nature of God

If we agree, then, that the Bible frequently affirms or exemplifies the truth of these two statements, where do we go from there?

First, we refuse to think of these two statements as embracing a deep contradiction. Granted there is mystery in them, and we

A CALL TO SPIRITUAL REFORMATION

shall have to explore just where that mystery lies. But if we are careful about semantics, we can avoid setting up these two statements as if they were mutually exclusive. Christianity is not interested in tempting you to believe contradictory nonsense. It invokes mystery now and then; it does not invoke nonsense.

That means, for instance, that we must be careful with the notion of freedom. Many Christians today think that if human beings are to be thought of as morally responsible creatures, they must be free to choose, to believe, to disobey, and so forth. But what does "freedom" mean? Sometimes without thinking about it, we assume that such freedom must entail the power to work outside God's sovereignty. Freedom, we think, involves absolute power to be contrary—that is, the power to break any constraint, so that there is no necessity in the choice we make. If we are constrained to choose a certain option, if what we decide is in fact utterly inevitable, then how could it be ours? And if not truly ours, how can we be held morally accountable?

Yet the passages we have just surveyed cry out in protest. To go no further than the last example: Herod and Pontius Pilate and the rest conspired together; they did what they wanted to do, even though they did what God's power and will had determined beforehand should be done. That is why many theologians have refused to tie "freedom" to absolute power to act contrary to God's will. They tie it, rather, to desire, to what human beings voluntarily choose. Joseph's brothers did what they wanted to do; Herod and Pilate and the rulers of the Jews did what they wanted to do; the Assyrians did what they wanted to do. In each case, God's sovereignty was operating behind the scenes: the human participants, to use the language of the early Christians, did what God's power and will had decided beforehand should happen. But that did not excuse them. They did what they wanted to do.

The only reason for bringing this up is to insist that our two propositions, as difficult and mysterious as they are, can be made to look silly, even flatly contradictory, if we begin with questionable assumptions and definitions that are not borne out by the Scriptures.

A Sovereign and Personal God

Second, it is vital to see that God does not stand behind good and evil in exactly the same way. There are two positions to avoid: (1) Some suppose that God does not stand in any sense behind evil and (2) others think that God stands behind good and evil in exactly the same way.

In the first case, the thinking is that certain things take place in the universe, namely, every evil event, that are entirely outside God's control. That would mean there is another power, apart from God and outside the domain of God's sovereignty, that challenges him. In philosophy, such a viewpoint is called dualism. In such a universe, it is hard to be sure which side, good or evil, will ultimately win. We have already taken notice of enough texts to be certain that the Bible does not sanction this view of God.

The second view maintains that what God ordains takes place; what he does not ordain does not take place. If both good and evil take place, it can only be because God ordains them both. But if he stands behind good and evil in exactly the same way, that is, if he stands behind them *symmetrically*, he is entirely amoral. He may be powerful, but he is not good.

The Bible's witness will not let us accept either of these positions. The Bible insists God is sovereign, so sovereign that nothing that takes place in the universe can escape the outermost boundary of his control; yet the Bible insists God is good, unreservedly good, the very standard of goodness. We are driven to conclude that God does not stand behind good and evil in exactly the same way. In other words, he stands behind good and evil *asymmetrically*. He stands behind good in such a way that the good can ultimately be credited to him; he stands behind evil in such a way that what is evil is inevitably credited to secondary agents and all their malignant effects. They cannot escape his sway, in exactly the same way that Satan has no power over Job without God's sanction; yet God remains mysteriously distant from the evil itself.

I say "mysteriously" because how he does this is mysterious, for reasons still to be explored. In fact, it is the very mysteriousness of his control that prompts not a few biblical writers to wrestle in agony over the problem of evil—not only the writer of Job, but Habakkuk, some of the psalmists, and others.

Third, and most importantly, our two propositions concerning God's sovereignty and human responsibility are directly tied to the nature of God. If God were sovereign and nothing more, we might all become Christian fatalists, but it would be hard to carve out a place for human interaction with Deity, a place for human responsibility. If God were personal and no more—talking with us, responding to us, asking and answering questions—it would be easy to understand how human beings are responsible to him, but it would be harder to grasp just how this sort of God could be transcendent, sovereign, omnipotent.

The wonderful truth is that God is both transcendent and personal. He is transcendent: he exists above or beyond time and space, since he existed before the universe was created. From this exalted and scarcely imaginable reach he sovereignly rules over the works of his hands. Yet he is personal: he presents himself to us not as raw power or irresistible force, but as Father, as Lord. When he speaks and issues a command, if I obey I am obeying him; if I disobey, I am disobeying him. All of my most meaningful relationships with God are bound up with the fact that God has disclosed himself to be a person.

Part of our problem is that virtually all that we understand by "personal" is shaped by our experience within time and space. We find it hard to imagine how God can be both transcendent and personal, even though we clearly see that the Bible presents him in just such categories.

So whatever mystery is locked up in our initial pair of statements, it is no more and no less than the mystery of God himself. Christians are prepared to accept certain mysteries. We confess that the Father is God, the Son is God, and the Holy Spirit is God—yet there is but one God. Christian thinkers across the ages have taken pains to show how there is no necessary contradiction in such an understanding of the trinitarian character of God, even if there are huge swaths of mystery involved. So also here: God is sovereign and transcendent, and he is personal.

Perhaps it is the way God apparently stands outside time and space that enables him to handle secondary causes the way he does. I do not know. What does time look like to a transcendent God? I

A Sovereign and Personal God

160

do not know. I only know that the Bible speaks of his *predestinat-ing* power and his *fore*ordination of events, even though these are categories of time. I suppose that if he is to communicate effec-tively with us, he must graciously stoop to use categories that we can understand. But despite all the mysteries bound up with the nature of God, I perceive, on the basis of Scripture, that he is simul-taneously personal and transcendent. He is utterly sovereign over his created order, yet he is nothing less than personal as he deals with me. Sometimes it is more important to worship such a God than to understand him.

Conclusion

What bearing does all this have on prayer?

Before answering that question directly, it is essential to draw one crucial lesson out of the previous discussion. Let us grant that the Bible insists that God is utterly sovereign, and human beings are morally responsible creatures; let us grant that God himself is both transcendent and personal. Let us frankly admit that this involves a significant degree of mystery. The question we must then ask ourselves is this: How can we assure that these comple-mentary pairs of truths operate the right way in our lives? If there is so much mystery about them, will we not always be in danger of using these truths in a way that denies the mystery or contradicts something else we should know?

The answer is simple, but has profound effects. We must do our best to ensure that these complementary truths function in our lives in the same ways they function in the lives of believers described in Scripture.

For example, how does election function in Scripture? How should election function in our lives? It never functions in Scripture to foster fatalism; it never functions to douse evangelistic zeal. Repeatedly it functions to emphasize the wonder of grace (John 6:68–70; Rom. 9). It also functions, among other things, to ensure the certainty of spiritual fruitfulness among God's people (John 15:16) and to encourage perseverance in evangelism (Acts 18:9–10).

How do the constant exhortations to believe and obey function in Scripture? They never function to picture God as fundamentally at the end of his own resources and utterly dependent on us; they never reduce God to the absolutely contingent. Rather, they function to increase our responsibility, to emphasize the urgency of the steps we must take, to show us what the only proper response is to this kind of God.

How does the repeated truth of God's sovereign providence function in Scripture? It never serves to authorize uncaring fatalism; it never allows me to be morally indifferent on the ground that I can't really help it anyway. Rather, the biblical emphasis on God's sovereignty functions in quite different ways. For example, it give me ground for believing that everything is in God's gracious control, so that all things will work out for good in the lives of God's people (Rom. 8:28).

We must deploy exactly the same approach when we come to prayer.

How does God's sovereignty function in passages of Scripture where prayer is introduced? Certainly it never functions as a disincentive to pray! It can forbid certain kinds of preposterous praying: for instance, Jesus forbids his followers from babbling on like pagans who think they will be heard because of their many words. "Do not be like them, for your Father knows what you need before you ask him" (Matt. 6:8). On the other hand, this prohibition cannot be taken as a blanket condemnation of all perseverance in prayer, since the same Jesus elsewhere urges that such perseverance is important (Luke 11, 18).

God's sovereignty can also function as an incentive to pray in line with God's will. Thus Jesus prays, "Father, the time [lit., hour] has come. Glorify your Son, that your Son may glorify you" (John 17:1). This is important. The hour in John's Gospel is the time appointed by the Father at which Jesus will in fact be glorified by means of the cross, and thus returned to the glory that he enjoyed with the Father before the world began (John 12:23–24; 17:5). By saying that the hour has come, Jesus is acknowledging that his Father's appointed time has arrived. This does not prompt Jesus to say only "Your will be done." Still less does it breed silence: the

A Sovereign and Personal God

hour has arrived and there is not much anyone can do about it, since everything has been ordained by my heavenly Father. Rather, Jesus' logic runs like this: My Father's appointed hour for the "glorification" of his Son has arrived; so then, Father, glorify your Son.

This sort of logic is not in any way unusual. Those who pray in the Scriptures regularly pray in line with what God has already disclosed he is going to do. A wonderful example is found in Daniel 9. Here we are told that Daniel understands from the Scriptures, "according to the word of the LORD given to Jeremiah the prophet" (Dan. 9:2), that the period of seventy years of exile was drawing to an end. A fatalist would simply have wiped his or her brow and looked forward to the promised release as soon as the seventy years were up. Not Daniel! Daniel is perfectly aware that God is not an automaton, still less a magic genie that pops out of a bottle at our command. God is not only sovereign, he is personal, and because he is personal he is free.[3] So Daniel addresses this personal God, confessing his own sins and the sins of his people: "So I turned to the Lord God and pleaded with him in prayer and petition, in fasting, and in sackcloth and ashes" (9:3). In other words, precisely because Daniel is aware of the promise of this personal, sovereign God, he feels it his obligation to pray in accord with what he has learned in the Scriptures regarding the will of that God. Most of the rest of the chapter records Daniel's prayer. Daniel reminds God that while Daniel and the children of Israel have sinned, God is the one "who keeps his covenant of love" (9:4), that God is "merciful and forgiving, even though we have rebelled against him" (9:9). "For your sake, O Lord," he prays, "look with favor on your desolate sanctuary. . . . O Lord, listen! O Lord, forgive! O Lord, hear and act! For your sake, O my God, do not delay, because your city and your people bear your Name" (9:17, 19). In other words, he appeals to God to preserve the integrity of his own name, the sanctity of his own covenant, his reputation for mercy and forgiveness.

And the exile ends.

Perhaps the most startling passages that mingle God's sovereignty and God's personhood are those that speak of God relenting. While Moses is on Mount Sinai receiving the tables of the law, the children of Israel succumb to the terrible idolatry of the golden calf. God is furious: "I have seen these people . . . and they are a stiff-necked people. Now leave me alone so that my anger may burn against them and that I may destroy them. Then I will make you into a great nation" (Exod. 32:9–10).

But Moses simply will not "leave God alone." The arguments in his intercession are remarkable, appealing to God both as the Sovereign and as the supreme personal Deity. Moses argues that if God carries through with this plan of destruction, the Egyptians will sneer that the Israelite God is malicious and that he led his people into the desert to destroy them. At the same time, Moses reminds God of his own sovereign promises: "Remember your servants Abraham, Isaac and Israel, to whom you swore by your own self [for there is none higher by whom to swear]: 'I will make your descendants as numerous as the stars in the sky and I will give your descendants all this land I promised them, and it will be their inheritance forever'" (32:12). In other words, if God destroys his people, will he not be breaking his own promises? How can a faithful God do that? In Moses' eyes, this is not an argument for pietistic fatalism—simply trust the promises of God and everything will work out—but for intercession. So Moses comes to the point: "Turn from your fierce anger; relent and do not bring disaster on your people" (32:12).

"Then the LORD relented and did not bring on his people the disaster he had threatened" (32:14).

A casual reader might be tempted to say, "See? God does change his mind. His purposes are not sovereign and steadfast. Prayer does change things because it changes the mind of God."

But such a conclusion would be both one-sided and premature. If God had not relented in his declared purpose to destroy the children of Israel, then, paradoxically, he would have proved fickle with respect to the firm promises he gave to Abraham, Isaac, and Jacob. On the other hand, if God is to remain faithful to the promises made to the patriarchs, then, as Moses realizes, God cannot destroy the Israelites, and he must therefore turn from the judgment he has pronounced against Israel. It is that very point Moses is banking on as he prays.

A Sovereign and Personal God

164

We gain additional insight into God's relenting when we compare the prayers of Amos, a true prophet of God, with the prayerlessness of false prophets. Amos learns of God's threatening judgments against the people, and he passionately intercedes on their
behalf: "I cried out, 'Sovereign LORD, forgive! How can Jacob survive? He is so small!'" (Amos 7:2). Amos's prayer proves effective.
Twice we are told, "So the LORD relented" (7:3, 6). By contrast,
God berates the false prophets of Israel precisely because they do
not intercede for the people. "You have not gone up to the breaks
in the wall to repair it for the house of Israel [an idiom that means
they have not interceded with God on behalf of the people] so
that it will stand firm in the battle on the day of the LORD" (Ezek.
13:5). No one was seriously interceding with God: "I looked for a
man among them who would build up the wall and stand before me
in the gap on behalf of the land so I would not have to destroy it,
but I found none. So I will pour out my wrath on them and con-
sume them with my fiery anger, bringing down on their own heads
all they have done, declares the Sovereign LORD" (Ezek. 2:30–31).

The extraordinary importance of these passages must not be
missed. God expects to be pleaded with; he expects godly believers
to intercede with him. Their intercession is his own appointed
means for bringing about his relenting, and if they fail in this
respect, then he does not relent and his wrath is poured out. If we
understand something similar to have happened in the life of
Moses, we must conclude that Moses is effective in prayer not in
the sense that God would have broken his covenant promises to
the patriarchs, nor in the sense that God temporarily lost his self-
control until Moses managed to bring God back to his senses.
Rather, in God's mercy Moses proved to be God's own appointed
means, through intercessory prayer, for bringing about the relenting
that was nothing other than a gracious confirmation of the
covenant with Abraham, Isaac, and Jacob.

The really wonderful truth is that human beings like Moses and
you and me can participate in bringing about God's purposes
through God's own appointed means. In that limited sense, prayer
certainly changes things; it cannot be thought to change things
in some absolute way that catches God out.

Of course, we are circling around the fundamental mystery, the mystery of the nature of God. This God presents himself to us as personal, and so we can pray to him, argue with him, present reasons to him, intercede with him. But he is also sovereign, the kind of God who works in us—not least in our prayers!—"both to will and to act according to his good purpose" (Phil. 2:13). His sovereignty does not diminish his personhood; that he is a person does not diminish his sovereignty. He is always not less than sovereign and personal.

The perverse and the unbeliever will appeal to God's sovereignty to urge the futility of prayer in a determined universe; they will appeal to passages depicting God as a person (including those that speak of his relenting) to infer that he is weak, fickle, and impotent, once again concluding that it is useless to pray. But the faithful will insist that, properly handled, both God's sovereignty and his personhood become reasons for more prayer, not reasons for abandoning prayer. It is worth praying to a sovereign God because he is free and can take action as he wills; it is worth praying to a personal God because he hears, responds, and acts on behalf of his people, not according to the blind rigidities of inexorable fate.

It is also helpful to remember that the prayer we offer cannot be exempted from God's sovereignty. If I pray aright, God is graciously working out his purposes in me and through me, and the praying, though mine, is simultaneously the fruit of God's powerful work in me through his Spirit. By this God-appointed means I become an instrument to bring about a God-appointed end. If I do not pray, it is not as if the God-appointed end fails, leaving God somewhat frustrated. Instead, the entire situation has now changed, and my prayerlessness, for which I am entirely responsible, cannot itself escape the reaches of God's sovereignty, forcing me to conclude that in that case there are other God-appointed ends in view, possibly including judgment on me and on those for whom I should have been interceding![4]

In short, despite the fact that God's nature is in many respects profoundly mysterious to us, we shall not go far wrong if we allow the complementary aspects of God's character to function in our lives the way they function in the lives of his servants in the Scrip-

A Sovereign and Personal God

ture. Then we will learn the better how to pray, and why we should pray, and what we should pray for, and how we should ask. We shall discover that the biblical emphasis on God's sovereignty and on God's personhood, if they function in our lives properly, will serve both as powerful incentives to prayer and as direction for the way in which we approach God.

Questions for Review and Reflection

1. What are the two truths that must be held together if we are to think biblically about prayer? How are these truths tied to the very nature of God?
2. If we grant that there is some mystery in the way these two truths hang together, how can they function in our lives without constant distortion? Give some examples. Include some comment on Daniel's reasoning in the prayer recorded in Daniel 9.
3. Select one of the following passages and explain it to someone: Genesis 50:19–20; Isaiah 10:5–16; Acts 4:23–30; Philippians 2:12–13.
4. Does prayer change things?

10

Praying to the Sovereign God

(Ephesians 1:15–23)

As he frequently does elsewhere, Paul links the content of his prayer (1:15–23) with the praise he offers to God (1:3–14). His opening words to the Ephesians forge this link: "For this reason . . . I have not stopped giving thanks for you, remembering you in my prayers" (1:15–16). The words *this reason* refer to the line of thought in the earlier verses. There God is praised because he "has blessed us in the heavenly realms with every spiritual blessing in Christ" (1:3). The crowning evidence for this blessing is stunning: "For he chose us in him before the creation of the world to be holy and blameless in his sight" (1:4). This was not an act of sovereign whimsy, but of sovereign love: "In love he predestined us to be adopted as his sons through Jesus Christ, in accordance with his pleasure and will" (1:4b–5).

None of these blessings was bestowed on us because of our intrinsic goodness or worth. They are all "to the praise of his glorious grace, which he has freely given us in the One he loves" (1:6). This

167

One of Paul's Prayers for the Ephesians

³Praise be to the God and Father of our Lord Jesus Christ, who has blessed us in the heavenly realms with every spiritual blessing in Christ. ⁴For he chose us in him before the creation of the world to be holy and blameless in his sight. In love ⁵he predestined us to be adopted as his sons through Jesus Christ, in accordance with his pleasure and will—⁶to the praise of his glorious grace, which he has freely given us in the One he loves. ⁷In him we have redemption through his blood, the forgiveness of sins, in accordance with the riches of God's grace ⁸that he lavished on us with all wisdom and understanding. ⁹And he made known to us the mystery of his will according of his good pleasure, which he purposed in Christ, ¹⁰to be put into effect when the times will have reached their fulfillment—to bring all things in heaven and on earth together under one head, even Christ.

¹¹In him we were also chosen, having been predestined according to the plan of him who works out everything in conformity with the purpose of his will, ¹²in order that we, who were the first to hope in Christ, might be for the praise of his glory. ¹³And you also were included in Christ when you heard the word of truth, the gospel of your salvation. Having believed, you were marked in him with a seal, the promised Holy Spirit, ¹⁴who is a deposit guaranteeing our inheri-

reference to Jesus spurs Paul to enlarge a little on what Jesus has accomplished at his Father's behest (1:7–10). Then the apostle returns to his central theme: "In him we were also chosen, having been predestined according to the plan of him who works out everything in conformity with the purpose of his will" (1:11), so that we, too, "might be for the praise of his glory" (1:12). Paul wants his readers to rest assured that the "we" of whom he has been speaking includes them: "And you also were included in Christ when you heard the word of truth, the gospel of your salvation" (1:13). The blessings of God, including the wonderful gift of "the promised Holy Spirit" (1:13), belong to "those who are God's possession"—and all of this is "to the praise of his glory" (1:14).

tance until the redemption of those who are God's possession—
to the praise of his glory.
¹⁵For this reason, ever since I heard about your faith in the Lord Jesus and your love for all the saints, ¹⁶I have not stopped giving thanks for you, remembering you in my prayers. ¹⁷I keep asking that the God of our Lord Jesus Christ, the glorious Father, may give you the Spirit of wisdom and revelation, so that you may know him better. ¹⁸I pray also that the eyes of your heart may be enlightened in order that you may know the hope to which he has called you, the riches of his glorious inheritance in the saints, ¹⁹and his incomparably great power for us who believe. That power is like the working of his mighty strength, ²⁰which he exerted in Christ when he raised him from the dead and seated him at his right hand in the heavenly realms, ²¹far above all rule and authority, power and dominion, and every title that can be given, not only in the present age but also in the one to come. ²²And God placed all things under his feet and appointed him to be head over everything for the church, ²³which is his body, the fullness of him who fills everything in every way.

(Eph. 1:3–23)

For this reason, Paul says, he sets himself to pray. For what reason? Some think that Paul is saying no more than that since he heard of the faith of his readers he decided to pray for them. But that is surely to focus too narrowly on one tiny part of verses 3–14. Moreover, verse 15 mentions Paul's hearing about the faith of his readers, yet treats that report as something different from this reason that accounts for the content of Paul's prayer. It is far more likely that the words *for this reason* refer to all of verses 3–14, or, more specifically, to its central and repeated themes. In a spirit of profound worship, Paul has been outlining God's sovereignty, especially in redemption, as the anchor for his grace and as the source of the blessings enjoyed by his people. As he thinks about these

Praying to the Sovereign God

things, Paul finds specific things to pray for. What God has already sovereignly accomplished constitutes a specific reason for him to pray as he does—in line with God's purposes.

In short, Paul's prayer in this chapter is a model of how to pray under the sovereignty of God. In particular, Paul's prayer report emphasizes three aspects of God's sovereignty.

1. Because God is sovereign, Paul offers thanksgiving for God's intervening, sovereign grace in the lives of his readers (1:15–16). Paul, having heard about his readers' "faith in the Lord Jesus" and their "love for all the saints" (1:15),[1] sees in their conversion and transformation a wonderful example of God's sovereign and gracious intervention in the lives of men and women. Their "faith" (which probably here includes both trust and fidelity) reposes securely in the Lord Jesus; their characters have been transformed—not in some mystical, mawkish, or merely sentimental and privatized fashion, but in the public arena where they richly display "love for all the saints." Paul has heard of their faith and love, and he gives thanks for them and prays for them.

Nevertheless, by the words *for this reason*, Paul ties his prayer more dramatically to what God has sovereignly done in them, doubtless as exemplified in their faith and love, than to the reports of faith and love themselves. Because it is God who has worked in them, Paul has not stopped thanking God; because it is God alone who sovereignly and graciously continues to effect such transformation, he is the one who must be petitioned to continue his good work. So Paul commits himself (he tells his readers) to "remembering you in my prayers." In short, because God is sovereign, Paul offers thanksgiving for God's intervening, sovereign grace in the lives of his readers.

The assumption, of course, is that apart from God's powerful, transforming work, these people would never have been converted. Without God, they would never have begun to display the trust, faithfulness, and love now richly displayed in their lives. Therefore whatever Christian virtues characterize them become the occasion for heartfelt praise to God.

We Christians know this; sometimes we sing it better than we articulate it in other ways. One of my favorites is the anonymous hymn:

> I sought the Lord, and afterward I knew
> He moved my heart to seek him, seeking me;
> It was not I that found, O Savior true;
> No, I was found by Thee.
>
> Thou didst reach forth Thy hand and mine enfold;
> I walked and sank not on the storm-vexed sea;
> 'Twas not so much that I on Thee took hold
> As Thou, dear Lord, on me.
>
> I find, I walk, I love, but O the whole
> Of love is but my answer, Lord, to Thee!
> For Thou wert long beforehand with my soul;
> Always Thou lovedst me.

In the same way that we give thanks to God when we recognize his quiet and effective work in our lives, so also we thank God when we hear of his work in others. If we hear of substantial numbers of people in another city or country who have been genuinely transformed by the gospel, we would not think of going to them to thank them for becoming Christians. Instead, we thank God for so working in them that they have become Christians. That is what Paul is doing.

So if we intend to imitate the prayers of Paul, we will be attentive to reports of the progress of the gospel, not only in circles immediately around us, but also from places we have never visited. We may subscribe to a missionary organization's newsletter; we may receive the prayer letters of some who are working abroad; we may glance at the news reports found in some Christian magazines. When we find reliable reports of people who have by God's grace become Christians, we will learn to respond as Paul does: we immediately turn to the God whose grace has sovereignly intervened in their lives, with such happy result, and offer him praise and thanksgiving.

Praying to the Sovereign God

172

If even the angels of heaven rejoice over a single sinner who repents, it does not seem too much to ask the people of God to offer thanksgiving at the same news.

When was the last time you offered such thanksgiving to God? Is it conceivable that we could hear news of people coming to Christ without expressing our gratitude to God?

2. Because God is sovereign, Paul offers intercession that God's sovereign, holy purposes in the salvation of his people may be accomplished (1:17–19a). Just as Daniel prayed for the end of the exile because God had promised that the exile would end, so Paul prays that Christians may grow in their knowledge of God because God has declared his intention to expose his people to the glories of his grace, both now and for eternity. Just as Christians cry "Even so come, Lord Jesus!" precisely because they know Jesus has promised to do just that, so also they pray that God will continue to work out his sovereign, gracious purposes in those in whom he has begun to do the same. It is because God has chosen us in Christ (1:4), it is because he has in love predestined us to be adopted as his sons through Jesus Christ (1:4–5), it is because God has lavished on us the riches of his grace (1:7–8)—it is, in short, for this reason that we must pray as Paul does. God's sovereign grace in our lives must not serve as a disincentive to prayer, but as an incentive, just as it is for Paul: "For this reason . . . I keep asking . . . the God of our Lord Jesus Christ, the glorious Father . . ." (1:15, 17).

What is it, precisely, that Paul asks for?

Paul's prayer is that the Ephesians might know God better. That is what the text says. Of all the things Paul might have asked for, that is what he puts at the top of his list: "I keep asking that the God of our Lord Jesus Christ, the glorious Father, may give you the Spirit of wisdom and revelation, so that you may know him better" (1:17).

Do you feel you know God well enough? Surely no thoughtful Christian would want to answer such a question in the affirmative. Indeed, the more we get to know God, the more we want to know him better.

How shall this growing knowledge of God come about? It comes about by approaching God in prayer, by asking him to give us the

Spirit of wisdom and revelation, to the end that we may know him better.

There are two details in this verse which, properly understood, go a long way toward clarifying what Paul is after. First, when he asks God for something, very frequently Paul addresses God or describes God in terms that are related to the request. For example, in Romans 15:4 Paul says that what was written in the earlier Scriptures was written to teach us, so that through "endurance and the encouragement of the Scriptures" we might have hope. Then he prays that "the God who gives endurance and encouragement" might "give you a spirit of unity among yourselves as you follow Christ" (Rom. 15:5). It is clear that Paul thinks a spirit of unity among Christians depends on the endurance and encouragement of the Scriptures, and so he describes God as he does when he offers his prayer.

Similarly here. The one Paul addresses in prayer is "the God of our Lord Jesus Christ" and "the glorious Father" (lit., the Father of glory). The first expression reminds us that the one to whom we pray has supremely disclosed himself to us in his Son Jesus the Christ, Jesus our Lord. All of God's blessings are mediated through his Son; more, all of God's new covenant blessings have already been secured for us by his Son, so that to pray in Jesus' name, or to address God as the Father of Jesus Christ, is to recognize the ground on which God answers such requests: Jesus himself.

The second expression, "the Father of glory," does not imply that the Father has somehow sired glory. The New International Version's "the glorious Father" is pretty close to the mark. But glory is often associated both with God's domain and with his gracious self-disclosure. Thus it is the God of glory who appears to Abraham when he is still in Mesopotamia (Acts 7:2). When Moses wants to know more of God, he begs the Almighty to show him his glory—and this God does, even if it is only the trailing edge of his glory (Exod. 33:18–23). Jesus wants to return to the domain of his Father, to the glory he shared with the Father before the world began (John 17:5). Even so, what he has been doing on earth, what he does supremely on the cross, is to manifest God's glory (John 1:14; 2:11; 12:27–28). Glory is the Christian's ultimate destination, and already we "are being transformed into [the Lord's] likeness with ever-increasing glory" (2 Cor. 3:18). Thus for Paul to pray to the Father of glory is to confess his awareness of God's proper domain, to articulate his gratitude for God's gracious self-disclosure, and to hold up the Father's domain as the Christian's ultimate hope.

Now recall the petition, and it is clear how these two descriptions of God are tied to it. Paul prays that God might give his readers the Spirit of wisdom and revelation, so that they might know him better. What kind of God will answer such a prayer? It is the God and Father of our Lord Jesus Christ, for all of God's blessings have been won for us through Christ's work. More: we are related to God through Christ. In him we were chosen (1:11); God "made known to us the mystery of his will according to his good pleasure, which he purposed in Christ" (1:9). Moreover, unless God whose domain is glory graciously reveals to us more of his glory, how shall we press on to know him better and thus prepare for the day when we too enter his glory?

Second, Paul does not simply pray that we might know God better, but that God might give us the Spirit of wisdom and revelation to the end that we might know God better. There is a set means to the desired end. What is required is wisdom and revelation mediated by the Spirit. This is not simply a corpus of truth to be picked up by reading a book on systematic theology (though such reading may do us a great deal of good!). It is growth in wisdom—probably here referring to how to live in God's universe so as to please him—and in revelation.

Today some people are nervous when they find Paul praying that God might give us the Spirit of revelation. Did not revelation reach its climax in Jesus Christ? Is not this sort of talk today likely to lead us to reach for revelation outside the canon? In fact many Christians today make a distinction between revelation and illumination, reserving the latter term for nonnormative experience, the enlightenment of an individual's mind so that God's truth and claims, values and norms, are absorbed and embraced. But Paul can use "revelation" for both concepts. His context always makes his particular point clear enough. "Revelation" can refer to

God's unique self-disclosure issuing in the normative Scriptures; it can also refer to what we mean by "illumination." Thus, writing to the Philippians, Paul says, "All of us who are mature should take such a view of things. And if on some point you think differently, that too God will make clear [lit., will reveal] to you" (Phil. 3:15). So also here: Christians need the Spirit of God to reveal more of himself and his ways to us, if we are to know God better, for it is the Spirit's task to take things that belong to the domain of God, the domain of glory, and bring them to us so that we can receive them (2 Cor. 2:9–16).

Only such work by God's Spirit will enable us to know him better. Therefore we must pray for it. If we fail to do so, we betray our cool interest in really knowing God better, even though a moment's reflection shows us there is nothing more important in God's universe, both in time and in eternity, than knowing God better. Therefore with Paul we must earnestly pray to God that we might know him better.

In particular, Paul's prayer to God is that we might have the insight needed to grasp certain crucial truths. As he asks God to reveal himself by his Spirit, so he asks God that the eyes of his readers' hearts might be enlightened, so that his readers might learn certain things. Thus in one sense this is a continuation of the same request; or, otherwise put, it is the flip side of the same request. The Spirit reveals; we must have our spiritual faculties attuned to receive what God reveals by his Spirit. But that Paul prays for both shows that he understands that it is ultimately God, God alone, who both reveals and enables us to grasp what he reveals. That is why Paul prays; that is why we must pray. We will never grow in the knowledge of God the way we ought if we do not ask God for such things as these. They are fundamental to all of Christian experience and maturation. If they are omitted, everything else we do is little more than playing religious games.

What is it, then, that Paul particularly wants his readers to see with enlightened eyes?

First, Paul wants the Ephesians to understand the hope of their calling—that is, the goal of their salvation. As we have observed in other examples of Paul's prayers, God's calling of his people is effective. If you have been called, you have been saved. The hope of one's calling is therefore the aspect of one's calling or salvation for which one still looks forward. If you are a Christian, the hope of your calling is the component of your salvation that you look forward to in the future.

In other words, this "hope" is nothing less than life in the new heaven and the new earth, life in the presence of God. It is the "hope of the glory of God" (Rom. 5:2), the hope of sharing that glory, the hope of appearing with Christ in glory at the end (Col. 3:4). It is the anticipation of being presented to Christ "without stain or wrinkle or any other blemish, but holy and blameless" (Eph. 5:27).

In our generation, which reflects too little on the future and almost never on eternity, it is distressingly obvious that we need help, help from God, so as to be able to know the hope to which we have been called. Only then will we become more interested in living with eternity's values constantly before our eyes. What we will have to show before the great King on the last day will be infinitely more important to us than what we leave behind here.

The second blessing Paul wants his readers to be able to grasp is "the riches of his glorious inheritance in the saints"; or more literally, "the riches of the glory of [God's] inheritance in the saints," thus continuing the "glory" theme. Already in this chapter Paul has told us that God will redeem those who constitute his possession at the consummation (1:14). We are God's inheritance; to use the language of the fourth Gospel, we are those whom the Father has given to the Son, his gift to his Messiah. The thought would be incredible were it not for the fact that God sees us in Christ (1:11; see Col. 2:1–10). God's valuation of his people is established by his valuation of Christ.

We need to know who we are, as God sees us. Paul wants us to appreciate the value that God places on us, not because we are intrinsically worthy but because we have been identified with Christ. We have been chosen in Christ; his righteousness has been reckoned ours; our destiny is to be joint-heirs with him. If we maintain this vision before our eyes of who we are—nothing less than God's inheritance!—we will be concerned to live in line with this unimaginably high calling. This does not mean that we focus on ourselves, as if we were to strut around and commend ourselves for being part of God's inheritance. Rather, Paul wants us to grasp "the riches of the glory" of God's inheritance, that is, the ineffably great privileges that belong to God's inheritance, simply because we are God's inheritance. Can there be any greater and higher incentive to live in the light of the glory of God and of heaven? In view of the grace and glory to be lavished on us, for no other reason than that God has made us his inheritance in Christ, we ought to live to God's praise. That is why Paul wants us to grasp just who we are.

Third, Paul wants us to know God's "incomparably great power for us who believe" (1:19a). Just what that power does, as it operates in us, is something Paul does not enlarge upon until his next prayer, in Ephesians 3:14–21, the prayer we shall study in the next chapter. Only this much must be said at the moment: Paul cannot be satisfied with a brand of Christianity that is orthodox but dead, rich in the theory of justification but powerless when it comes to transforming people's lives. We shall see that he has very specific ideas in mind about what that power accomplishes. But whatever those descriptions and constraints, since it is God's power that Paul envisages in the lives of believers, he knows that he must pray for it, and he knows that he must pray that believers will know it, experience it in their own existence.

In summary: Because God is sovereign, Paul offers intercession that God's sovereign, holy purposes in the salvation of his people may be accomplished. In particular, his prayer to God is that we might know him better and might have the insight to grasp certain crucial truths—the hope of our calling, the riches of God's glorious inheritance in the saints, and his incomparably great power for us who believe.

When was the last time you prayed for such things?

3. Because God is sovereign, Paul offers a review of God's most dramatic displays of power (1:19b–23). Having introduced the power of God he wants Christians to experience, Paul, before explaining just what he expects that power to do in us (something he does not take up until chap. 3), outlines its standard and controlling analogy. The power for which Paul prays is "like the work-

Praying to the Sovereign God

ing of [God's] mighty strength, which he exerted in Christ" when certain things took place. What things?

What would you have chosen to describe God's power? When you think of God's sovereignty, to what does your mind turn? I confess I am inclined to think of God's power in creation. He speaks, and worlds leap into being. He designs the water molecule, with its remarkable atomic structure that ensures greater density is achieved at four degrees Centigrade than at the freezing point, so that lakes and rivers freeze not from the bottom up but from the top down, providing a blanket of ice with water underneath so that fish can survive. I think of God calculating the mathematics of quarks, with half-lives in billionths of a second. I think of God designing each star and upholding the universe by his powerful word. I think of the pleasure he takes in the woodpecker, with its specially designed tailfeathers that enable it to peck with such force. I marvel at a God who creates emus and cheetahs and the duck-billed platypus. His power extends beyond the limits of our imagination.

But that is not what Paul turns to. After all, for an omnipotent God there cannot be degrees of difficulty. There is no one act that is "most powerful." Paul does not hunt for the most powerful or the most difficult displays of God's power, since such categories are essentially meaningless. Rather, he hunts for the most glorious, the most revealing. As a result, he focuses on three events.

Paul mentions the power exerted when Christ was raised from death. The power that Christians must experience is like the power God exerted in Christ "when he raised him from the dead" (1:20). Paul thinks of the resurrection of Jesus Christ. Here is the undoing of death, the destruction of sin; Christ's resurrection is the firstfruits of the mighty resurrection that will mock the death of death and inaugurate a new heaven and a new earth. Small wonder Paul elsewhere declares that he wants to know Christ and the power of his resurrection (Phil. 3:10).

Paul describes the power displayed in the exalted Christ. The power that Christians must experience is like the power God exerted in Christ "when he . . . seated him at his right hand in the heavenly realms, far above all rule and authority, power and dominion, and

every title that can be given, not only in the present age but also in
the one to come" (1:20–21). There are levels of authority of which
we know very little, demonic powers and seraphic powers, not only
in this world but in the heavenlies (see Col. 1:16). But over all of
them is Christ Jesus, elevated to the Father's right hand in consequence of his obedience to death and his victorious resurrection
(see Phil. 2:6–11).

Indeed, this vision controls part of the line of argument in chapter 2. There Paul says that although we were dead in our trespasses
and sins and were by nature objects of wrath (2:1), nevertheless
because of his great love for us, God, "who is rich in mercy, made us
alive with Christ even when we were dead in transgressions. . . .
[and] raised us up with Christ and seated us with him in the heavenly realms in Christ Jesus" (2:4–6). Of course, in one sense I'm
still here, not there. But because God views me as "in Christ," and
Christ is seated with his Father in the heavenlies, therefore God
views me as there in principle. That is my destination; that is where
I properly belong, because of God's great love for me. That is why
my Canadian citizenship can never be more than secondary: I'm
already a citizen of the new Jerusalem, and I am seated with Christ
in the heavenlies.

*Paul declares the power exercised by Christ over everything—for the
church.* "God placed all things under his feet and appointed him
to be head over everything for the church, which is his body, the
fullness of him who fills everything in every way" (1:22–23). All of
God's sovereignty is mediated through Christ (see 1 Cor. 15:27;
Ps. 110:1), and all of this sovereign power is for the good of the
church. Christ is the head over everything: that is, he exercises
authority over everything. But this "head" metaphor takes a sudden
shift when the "body" is introduced. Although Christ is the head
over everything, he is in particular the head of the church, which
is his body.[2] He is ideally placed to ensure that all of his sovereignty is exercised for his people's good.

Not a drop of rain can fall outside the orb of Jesus' sovereignty.
All our days—our health, our illnesses, our joys, our victories, our
tears, our prayers, and the answers to our prayers—fall within the
sweep of the sovereignty of one who wears a human face, a thorn-

shadowed face. All of God's sovereignty is mediated through one who was crucified on my behalf. For Christians, that means God's sovereignty can no longer be viewed as a merely credal point, still less as the source of endless mystery. There is more than enough material for credal confession here, and not a little mystery; but these mysteries revolve around one who died in my place. The mysteries of prayer remain, but they dissolve in worship and gratitude. It is far easier to accept the mysteries of divine sovereignty when the divine love is as great as the divine sovereignty.

All of this sovereignty is exercised for the church. This is a stunning thought. God "placed all things under his feet and appointed him to be head over everything for the church" (1:22). What gratitude should this call from us! What an incentive to pray in line with God's purposes for his people!

Brothers and sisters in Christ, we will sometimes come to places where, as we try to think about God, we will conclude that these things are way beyond us, that we cannot take them in, that we cannot comprehend him. But if we focus on what God has revealed of himself, such meditation will become a ground not for complaint, not for self-interest, not for fatalism or an excuse for sin, but a ground for worship—and an incentive to approach this sovereign, loving God and intercede with him according to his own plan and purpose declared in Scripture, for his Son's glory and his people's good.

Questions for Review and Reflection

1. What are Paul's petitions in Ephesians 1? Summarize them in your own words. Do you regularly pray for such things? Why or why not? How can you improve in this respect?
2. Of what relevance to your prayer life is the stunning conclusion to Paul's prayer, where he records the best analogy to the power he wants to see operating in every believer's life?
3. What does this passage teach us about how to pray under the sovereignty of God?

11

Praying for Power

(Ephesians 3:14–21)

How did you learn to pray? If like me you were reared in a conservative Christian home and early taught the King James Version of the Bible, then you learned to pray in Elizabethan English. When I was growing up, this was not judged to be a holier or more reverent form of English; it was simply the language of the English Bible that almost all English-speaking Protestants used at the time. I do not recall what I said when I first dared to pray out loud at a public prayer meeting. But even though I was very young, it opened something like this: "We thank Thee, heavenly Father, that in Thy grace Thou hast condescended to visit us." Ironically, when our family prayed in French (I was reared in a bilingual home), our prayers were in reasonably up-to-date French. This owed a great deal to the fact that our French Bibles were more current, linguistically speaking, than our English ones.

On the other hand, if you grew up in a modern, pagan home, and did not become a Christian until you were in your third year at

---

Another of Paul's Prayers for the Ephesians

14For this reason I kneel before the Father, 15from whom his whole family in heaven and on earth derives its name. 16I pray that out of his glorious riches he may strengthen you with power through his Spirit in your inner being, 17so that Christ may dwell in your hearts through faith. And I pray that you, being rooted and established in love, 18may have power, together with all the saints, to grasp how wide and long and high and deep is the love of

---

university, your first public prayer sounded a little different. Perhaps you were led to Christ by a Campus Crusade group. You went to their studies and meetings, and eventually, when you had enough courage to pray in public, your prayer began like this: "Jesus, we just want to thank you for being here."

I am not suggesting that one of these prayers is better than the other. God, after all, looks on the heart. My only point is that Christians learn to pray by listening to those around them.

Nothing is intrinsically bad about this. If we lived in a time and place where Christians were characterized by knowledgeable, anointed praying, it would be a wonderful privilege to learn from them. Sadly, although there are a few signs of resurgence, prayer in the West has fallen on hard times, and there are few models to hold up to a new generation of believers.

Then how shall we reform our praying?

Surely the best answer is to turn again to the prayers of the Bible. If every part of our lives is to be renewed and reformed by the Word of God, how much more should that be so of our praying? If our generation does not cast up many prayer warriors whose habits in prayer accurately reflect the standards of Scripture, it is all the more urgent that we return to the primary source. Then we shall learn afresh what to pray for, what arguments to use, what themes on which to focus, what passion is seemly, how these prayers fit

A CALL TO SPIRITUAL REFORMATION

Christ, ¹⁹and to know this love that surpasses knowledge—that
you may be filled to the measure of all the fullness of God.
²⁰Now to him who is able to do immeasurably more than all
we ask or imagine, according to his power that is at work within
us, ²¹to him be glory in the church and in Christ Jesus throughout
all generations, for ever and ever! Amen.

(Eph. 3:14–21)

---

into a larger Christian vision, how to maintain the centrality of
God himself in our praying.

The prayer before us has two rich and lengthy petitions, which
we shall examine in depth. Paul roots them in two grounds or reasons, and he ends the prayer with a word of praise, a powerful doxology.

Two Central Petitions

Two petitions emerge directly from the text. Paul prays (1) that
God might strengthen us with power through his Spirit in our
inner being (3:16–17a) and (2) that we might have power to grasp
the limitless dimensions of the love of Christ (3:17b–19).

At heart, the first petition is a prayer for power. Paul regularly
prays for power. Already in this epistle (as we saw in chap. 10), Paul
has asked God for power for his readers: "I pray also that the eyes of
your heart may be enlightened in order that you may know the
hope to which he has called you, the riches of his glorious inheritance in the saints, and his incomparably great power for us who
believe" (1:18–19a). Here Paul prays for power more directly: "I
pray . . . that he may strengthen you with power" (3:16).

The nature of this power is carefully circumscribed. The power
for which Paul prays is mediated through God's Spirit: "I pray . . .
that he may strengthen you with power through his Spirit" (1:16).

No less important, the sphere in which this power operates is what Paul calls the "inner being": "I pray . . . that he may strengthen you with power through his Spirit in your inner being [lit., the inner man]" (1:16). Exactly what does Paul mean by that?

We gain the clearest picture of what Paul means when we consider another passage he wrote where he uses exactly the same expression. In 2 Corinthians 4:16–18, Paul writes, "Though outwardly [lit., in "the outer man"] we are wasting away, yet inwardly [lit., in "the inner man"—exactly the same expression as in Eph. 3:16] we are being renewed day by day. For our light and momentary troubles are achieving for us an eternal glory that far outweighs them all. So we fix our eyes not on what is seen, but on what is unseen. For what is seen is temporal, but what is unseen is eternal." Paul's body, his "outer man," is wearing away under the onslaught of years and of persecution; the "inner man" is what is left when the outer man has wasted completely away.

Most of us in the West have not suffered great persecution, but all of us are getting older. In fact, sometimes we can see in elderly folk something of the process that Paul has in mind. We all know senior saints who, as their physical strength is reduced, nevertheless become more and more steadfast and radiant. Their memories may be fading; their arthritis may be nearly unbearable; their ventures beyond their small rooms or apartments may be severely curtailed. But somehow they live as if they already have one foot in heaven. As their outer being weakens, their inner being runs from strength to strength. Conversely, we know elderly folk who, so far as we can tell, are not suffering from any serious organic decay, yet as old age weighs down on them they nevertheless become more and more bitter, caustic, demanding, spiteful, and introverted. It is almost as if the civilizing restraints imposed on them by cultural expectations are no longer adequate. In their youth, they had sufficient physical stamina to keep their inner being somewhat capped. Now, with reserves of energy diminishing, what they really are in their inner being is coming out.

Even for those of us who are still some distance from being senior citizens, the restrictions and increasing limitations of the outer being make themselves felt. My body is not what it was twenty years ago. Every time I take a shower, a few more hairs disappear down the drain never to be seen again. I have arthritis in two or three joints; I have to watch my intake of calories; my reaction times are a little slower than they used to be; in a couple years I shall need reading glasses. And some day, if this old world lasts long enough, I shall waste away, and my outer man will be laid to rest in a hole six feet deep. Yet inwardly, Paul insists, in the inner man, we Christians "are being renewed day by day."

The Christian's ultimate hope is for the resurrection body. But until we receive that gift, it is our inner being that is being strengthened by God's power. In a culture where so many people are desperate for good health, but not demonstrably hungry for the transformation of the inner being, Christians are in urgent need of following Paul's example and praying for displays of God's power in the inner being. In short, Paul's primary concern is to pray for a display of God's mighty power in the domain of our being that controls our character and prepares us for heaven.

We must ask two important questions about Paul's first petition.

What purpose does it have? After all, many people pursue power. Simon the sorcerer wanted the power of the Spirit so that he could manipulate people and maintain his position in the community. Most of us know Christians whose talk about the power of God in their lives seems dangerously close to a perpetual game of one-upmanship. Their chase after power in some triumphalistic sense is a long way removed from the stance of the apostle. After all, the Paul who wanted to experience more of the power of Christ's resurrection also wanted to share more deeply in Christ's sufferings (Phil. 3:10), a balance almost unknown in the West. Exactly why, then, does Paul pray that Christians might know more of God's power?

We shall better grasp the nature and focus of this power for which Paul prays if we observe its purpose. "I pray," Paul writes, "that out of his glorious riches [God] may strengthen you with power through his Spirit in your inner being, so that Christ may dwell in your hearts through faith" (3:16–17a).

One cannot help but notice the trinitarian character of the prayer. Paul asks the *Father* (v. 14) that we might be strengthened through his *Spirit* (v. 16) so that *Christ* (v. 17) might dwell in our hearts through faith. Even so, on first reading this expressed purpose strikes the Christian reader as a bit strange. Do we not hold that Christ by his Spirit takes up residence in us when we become Christians (see John 14)? Why then does Paul say that the purpose of his prayer is that Christ may dwell in our hearts through faith? Isn't he already doing that?

It helps to recognize that the verb here rendered "to dwell" is a strong one. Paul's hope is that Christ will truly take up his residence in the hearts of believers, as they trust him (that's what "through faith" means), so as to make their hearts his home.

The picture becomes clearer if we think of an analogy. Picture a couple carefully marshaling enough resources to put together a down-payment. They buy their house, recognizing full well that it needs a fair bit of work. They can't stand the black and silver wallpaper in the master bedroom. There are mounds of trash in the basement. The kitchen was designed for the convenience of the plumber, not the cook. The roof leaks in a couple of places, and the insulation barely meets minimum standards. The electrical box is too small, the lighting in the bathroom is poor, the heat exchanger in the furnace is corroded. But still, it is this young couple's first home, and they are grateful.

The months slip past, then the years. The black and silver wallpaper has been replaced with tasteful pastel patterns. The couple has remodeled their kitchen, doing much of the work themselves. The roof no longer leaks, and the furnace has been replaced with a more powerful unit that also includes a central air conditioner. Better yet, as the family grows, this couple completes a couple of extra rooms in the basement and adds a small wing to serve as a study and sewing room. The grounds are neatly trimmed and boast a dazzling rock garden. Twenty-five years after the purchase, the husband one day remarks to his wife, "You know, I really like it here. This place suits us. Everywhere we look we see the results of our own labor. This house has been shaped to our needs and taste, and I really feel comfortable."

When Christ by his Spirit takes up residence within us, he finds the moral equivalent of mounds of trash, black and silver wallpaper, and a leaking roof. He sets about turning this residence into a place appropriate for him, a home in which he is comfortable. There will be a lot of cleaning to do, quite a few repairs, and some much-needed expansion. But his aim is clear: he wants to take up residence in our hearts, as we exercise faith in him.

When people take up long-term residence somewhere, their presence eventually characterizes that dwelling. The point was well understood by Jean Sophia Pigott when in 1876 she wrote a poem addressed to Jesus. The first verse expresses the joy of faith:

> Thou whose name is called Jesus,
> Risen Lord of life and power,
> O what joy it is to trust Thee,
> Every day and every hour!
> Of Thy wondrous grace I sing,
> Saviour, Counsellor, and King.

But it is the third stanza that captures just what Paul means when he prays that Christ might dwell in our hearts through faith:

> Make my life a bright outshining
> Of Thy life, that all may see
> Thine own resurrection power
> Mightily put forth in me.
> Ever let my heart become
> Yet more consciously Thy home.

Although the language is different, the notion is deeply akin to a much-loved emphasis among the Puritans. Adopting the language of Galatians 4:19, they were profoundly concerned that Christ might be *formed* in believers.

Make no mistake: when Christ first moves into our lives, he finds us in very bad repair. It takes a great deal of power to change us; and that is why Paul prays for power. He asks that God may so strengthen us by his power in our inner being that Christ may genuinely take up residence within us, transforming us into a house that pervasively reflects his own character.

The idea of getting rid of the old and dirty, and adopting the new and clean, of putting off the old and soiled and taking on the

Praying for Power

188

new and radiant, occurs in Paul's writings in many forms. For
instance, these verses from Colossians ought to be read slowly,
meditatively, and with frank self-examination:

> Put to death, therefore, whatever belongs to your earthly
> nature: sexual immorality, impurity, lust, evil desires and greed,
> which is idolatry. Because of these, the wrath of God is coming.
> You used to walk in these ways, in the life you once lived. But
> now you must rid yourselves of all such things as these: anger,
> rage, malice, slander, and filthy language from your lips. Do not
> lie to each other, since you have taken off your old self with its
> practices and have put on the new self, which is being renewed
> in knowledge in the image of its Creator. Here there is no Greek
> or Jew, circumcised or uncircumcised, barbarian, Scythian, slave
> or free, but Christ is all, and is in all.
>
> Therefore, as God's chosen people, holy and dearly loved,
> clothe yourselves with compassion, kindness, humility, gentleness
> and patience. Bear with each other and forgive whatever
> grievances you may have against one another. Forgive as the
> Lord forgave you. And over all these virtues put on love, which
> binds them all together in perfect unity.
>
> Let the peace of Christ rule in your hearts, since as members of
> one body you were called to peace. And be thankful. Let the
> word of Christ dwell in you richly as you teach and admonish
> one another with all wisdom, and as you sing psalms, hymns and
> spiritual songs with gratitude in your hearts to God. And
> whatever you do, whether in word or deed, do it all in the name
> of the Lord Jesus, giving thanks to God the Father through him.
> [Col. 3:5–17]

This passage is both powerful and practical. In concrete terms it
spells out the changes Paul expects to take place in the lives of
believers—or, to maintain the language of his prayer in Ephesians
3, it spells out the changes Paul envisages as he prays that God's
power will so operate in our inner being that we become suitable
residences for the risen Christ. This is the kind of purpose Paul
has in mind when he prays for power.

We may ask a second important question about this petition:
With what measure of resources is the prayer to be answered? It is one
thing to ask, what of the supply? The text answers our question. "I

pray," Paul writes, "that *out of his glorious riches* [God] may strengthen you with power through his Spirit in your inner being, so that Christ may dwell in your hearts through faith" (3:16–17). What are these "glorious riches" on which Paul is prepared to rely?

For Paul, the expression refers to what God has already secured for us on account of Christ. This is clear from another and perhaps better-known passage: "And my God will meet all your needs according to his glorious riches in Christ Jesus" (Phil. 4:19). From Paul's perspective, everything that is coming to us from God comes through Christ Jesus. Christ Jesus has won our pardon; he has reconciled us to God; he has canceled our sin; he has secured the gift of the Spirit for us; he has granted eternal life to us and promises us the life of the consummation; he has made us children of the new covenant; his righteousness has been accounted as ours; he has risen from the dead, and all of God's sovereignty is mediated through him and directed to our good and to God's glory. This is the Son whom God sent to redeem us. In God's all-wise plan and all-powerful action, all these blessings have been won by his son's odious death and triumphant resurrection. All the blessings God has for us are tied up with the work of Christ.

So the supply of God's "glorious riches in Christ Jesus" is as lavish as the benefits secured by Christ. To depreciate the supply is to depreciate Jesus; to doubt the provision God has made for us is to doubt the provision God has secured in his Son. It is far wiser to understand and believe that the God who has already so lavishly blessed us in his Son has no less lavish reserves of power to pour out on us as he brings us to Christian maturity. That is one reason why Paul petitions God for this transforming power: he is persuaded that the supply is as extensive as the benefits secured by Jesus Christ at Golgotha.

This first petition, then, is a plea for power—power to be holy, power to think, act, and talk in ways utterly pleasing to Christ, power to strengthen moral resolve, power to walk in transparent gratitude to God, power to be humble, power to be discerning, power to be obedient and trusting, power to grow in conformity to Jesus Christ. Here is no merely credal Christianity. Biblical Christianity, of course, insists that certain truths be believed and

190

openly threatens all those who refuse to believe: it is, in short, profoundly credal. But it is not merely credal. The devil himself can recite the Apostles' Creed, and doubtless confesses its truth, yet he has personally experienced nothing of its transforming power. But God's purpose for the men and women he redeems is not simply to have them believe certain truths but to transform them in a lifelong process that stretches toward heaven. And so Paul prays along just such lines: he asks his heavenly Father that out of his glorious riches he might strengthen believers with power through his Spirit in their inner being, so that Christ may dwell in their hearts through faith.

That brings us to the second petition:[1] that we might have power to grasp the limitless dimensions of the love of Christ. Here too, the point emerges directly from the text: "And I pray that you, being rooted and established in love, may have power, together with all the saints, to grasp how wide and long and high and deep is the love of Christ, and to know this love that surpasses knowledge" (3:17b–19).

Like the first petition, this one is a prayer for power. Here, however, the power of God in our lives, given in response to this prayer, operates a little differently. Its purpose is to enable us to grasp the limitless dimensions of Christ's love.

Paul does not mean to suggest that his readers have never before known God's love for them in Christ Jesus. Far from it: he knows they are Christians, and therefore acknowledges that they have been "rooted and established in love" (v. 17). He cannot think of their salvation without reminding himself that it utterly depends on God's sovereign love. Even in the first chapter of this epistle, Paul has devoted himself to the praise of "the God and Father of our Lord Jesus Christ," on the ground that "he chose us in him before the creation of the world to be holy and blameless in his sight. In love he predestined us to be adopted as his sons through Jesus Christ, in accordance with his pleasure and will—to the praise of his glorious grace, which he has freely given us in the One he loves" (Eph. 1:3–6). Small wonder, then, that he thinks of Christians as those who have been "rooted and grounded in love."

The remarkable fact about this petition, however, is that Paul clearly assumes that his readers, Christians though they are, do not adequately appreciate the love of Christ. He now wants them to have the power to grasp just how great the love of Christ is. This is not a prayer that we might love Christ more (though that is a good thing to pray for); rather, it is a prayer that we might better grasp his love for us.

This cannot be merely an intellectual exercise. Paul is not asking that his readers might become more able to articulate the greatness of God's love in Christ Jesus or to grasp with the intellect alone how significant God's love is in the plan of redemption. He is asking God that they might have the power to grasp the dimensions of that love in their experience. Doubtless that includes intellectual reflection, but it cannot be reduced to that alone.

Because some wings of the church have appealed to experience over against revelation, or have talked glibly about an ill-defined "spirituality" that is fundamentally divorced from the gospel, some of us have overreacted and begun to view all mention of experience as suspicious at best, perverse at worst. This overreaction must cease. The Scriptures themselves demand that we allow more place for experience than that. In the midst of extraordinary despair, the psalmist learns the secret of deepest contentment: "Whom have I in heaven but you? And earth has nothing I desire besides you. My flesh and my heart may fail, but God is the strength of my heart and my portion forever" (Ps. 73:25–26). Paul reminds us that "the kingdom of God is not a matter of eating and drinking, but of righteousness, peace and joy in the Holy Spirit" (Rom. 14:17). One of his prayers asks for a certain kind of experience: "May the God of hope fill you with all joy and peace as you trust in him, so that you may overflow with hope by the power of the Holy Spirit" (Rom. 15:13). So precious is the love of Christ to him that he needs only to come near the theme and he bursts into a spontaneous line of adoring praise: "I live by faith in the Son of God," he writes and then adds, "who loved me and gave himself for me" (Gal. 2:20). Peter tells his readers, "Though you have not seen him, you love him; and even though you do not see him now, you believe in him and are filled with an inexpressible and glorious joy, for you are receiving the goal of your faith, the salvation of your souls" (1 Pet. 1:8–9). The fact that they "have tasted that the Lord is good" (1 Pet. 2:3) becomes an incentive to purity. It cannot possibly be reduced to mean only that they have found Christianity to be intellectually satisfying.

Even in the epistle before us, Paul will go on to make a rather stunning contrast: "Do not get drunk on wine, which leads to debauchery. Instead, be filled with the Spirit" (Eph. 5:18). The assumption is that whereas wine offers a kind of high, it is treacherous, for it leads to debauchery. By contrast, the "high" engendered by the Holy Spirit brings no debauchery, no hangovers, but purity, right relationships, and the joy of the Lord (the next verse goes on to speak of making "music in your heart to the Lord").

So when Paul asks God that Christians might have the power to grasp the limitless dimensions of Christ's love, he does not use the language of merely intellectual comprehension. How do we appreciate love? How do we measure it? Can we speak of forty buckets of love? Of three-and-a-half acres of love? Paul resorts to metaphor, and then to paradox. His metaphor is linear measure: "to grasp how wide and long and high and deep is the love of Christ." His paradox is more stunning yet: "and to know this love that surpasses knowledge"—that is, to know what is beyond mere knowledge.

What we must understand is "that those biblical documents in which the writers give their teaching by telling of their experience must set standards of spiritual experience, just as they do of divine truth, and must be expounded in a way that brings out and enforces the one as much as the other."[2]

We must not think that Paul is appealing for uncontrolled mysticism. For him, the love of Christ is not merely something to be privately experienced. Christ's love was supremely displayed in history on a hideous cross outside Jerusalem some years before Paul wrote. That love was a wonderfully rich redemptive plan God himself had graciously disclosed across the centuries, and then brought to fulfillment in the death and resurrection and exaltation of his Son. Paul is not fostering some experience of love outside the constraints of the gospel. He is certainly not hinting that any "spiritual" experience whatsoever is valid and important. What he presupposes, rather, is that apart from the power of God Christians will have too little appreciation for the love of Christ. They need the power of God to appreciate the limitless dimensions of that love. And so Paul prays for power.

We may sing about these things more fluently than we talk about them. For a century and a half, the church has sung:

> Loved with everlasting love,
> Led by grace that love to know;
> Spirit, breathing from above,
> Thou hast taught me it is so.
> O this full and perfect peace!
> O this transport all divine!
> In a love which cannot cease
> I am His, and He is mine.
>
> Heaven above is softer blue,
> Earth around is sweeter green;
> Something lives in every hue
> Christless eyes have never seen.
> Birds with gladder songs o'erflow,
> Flowers with deeper beauties shine,
> Since I know, as now I know,
> I am His and He is mine.
>
> His for ever, only His:
> Who the Lord and me shall part?
> Ah, with what a rest of bliss
> Christ can fill the loving heart!
> Heaven and earth may fade and flee,
> First-born light in gloom decline;
> But, while God and I shall be,
> I am His, and He is mine.
> —George Wade Robinson (1838–1877)

Those who read Christian biographies know that many men and women of God have reveled in a deep experience of the love of God. It is said that R. A. Torrey earnestly sought God's face, and

Praying for Power

194

one day while he was reading the Scriptures and praying he was so overwhelmed with a profound consciousness of God's love for him that he began to weep and weep. Eventually he asked God to show him no more: he could not bear it.

A genuine and deep perception of the love of Christ rarely comes to the person who is not spending much time in the Scriptures. Even so, such perception may be triggered by tragedy—a terrible bereavement, for example, or prolonged suffering. As a boy of about ten years I experienced something somewhat analogous to this. I had been very ill and had spent several weeks in hospital. The threat to my life was removed, and I returned home for a slow convalescence of several months. One afternoon I awoke from sleep to find my mother sitting beside my bed, quietly crying. As only a ten-year-old could, I blurted out, "Why Mum, you *do* love me!"

Of course, that finished her off, and she rushed from the room. But as I think about that afternoon, I understand a little better why I spoke as I did. If you had asked me the day before whether or not my parents loved me, I would have answered unhesitatingly that they did. But the illness gave me an opportunity to witness my mother's tears, and that gave me cause to reflect. Instead of delivering the party line, "Of course my parents love me," I self-consciously analyzed what was going on and articulated my conclusion. If the result was neither well put nor well timed, the reflection itself was right and good and marked a step in growing up.

In a not dissimilar way, sometimes it is when we suffer, when we observe the universality of death's decree, when we are debilitated, when we observe an extraordinarily barbaric bit of cruelty, when we are sidelined by a chronic illness, that we are impelled to pause and reflect on the love of God to sinners and rebels such as we are. We serve the Lord Christ, who suffered in our place, who learned obedience through the things that he suffered. The trinkets and baubles that otherwise capture so much of our attention fade away, and the eternal things assume their rightful place. Then we know what it means to confess that God's love is "as shoreless and as endless as eternity."

Paul wants us to grasp something of the limitless dimensions of the love of Christ, to know this love that surpasses knowledge, so he prays that we might have God's power so as to be able to take this step. But why? Why does he think it so important? He tells us: he wants his readers "to know this love that surpasses knowledge—that you may be filled to the measure of all the fullness of God" (3:19b).

To put the matter simply, Paul wants us to have the power to grasp the love of God in Christ Jesus, to the end that we might be mature. To be "filled to the measure of all the fullness of God" is simply a Pauline way of saying "to be all that God wants you to be," or "to be spiritually mature." A similar expression is found in the next chapter of this epistle, where Paul tells us how various people in the church are to serve "so that the body of Christ may be built up until we all reach unity in the faith and in the knowledge of the Son of God and become mature, attaining to the whole measure of the fullness of Christ" (4:12–13). God himself, Christ himself, is the standard. God elsewhere says, "Be perfect, for I am perfect," and "Be holy, for I am holy"; now he says here, in effect, "Be mature, be complete, as I am mature, complete."

Do you see the stunning implication? Paul assumes that we cannot be as spiritually mature as we ought to be unless we receive power from God to enable us to grasp the limitless dimensions of the love of Christ. We may think we are peculiarly mature Christians because of our theology, our education, our years of experience, our traditions; but Paul knows better. He knows we cannot be as mature as we ought to be until we "know this love that surpasses knowledge." That is why he prays as he does: he wants us to grow in our grasp of Christ's love so that we will become mature, "filled to the measure of all the fullness of God."

We can intuitively understand how this works from our experiences in the natural realm. Perry Downs, a colleague at the institution where I teach, and his wife, Sandy, have for years served as foster parents. Most of the children they have helped, now well over twenty, have been newborns and have stayed with them until adopted. But some years ago, the agency with whom they are connected asked them to take in twin eighteen-month-old boys. Perry

Praying for Power

and Sandy hesitated but agreed to accept them when the agency assured them that the boys would be with them only for about six weeks.

The first night in the Downs's home, the boys were put to bed, and not a peep came from their bedroom. Curious, Perry crept into their room a half hour later. He found both boys wide awake, their pillows wet with tears, but neither was making a sound. It transpired that they had been beaten for crying in several of the homes in which they had been placed before coming to Perry's and Sandy's. This was their ninth home. Testing suggested that the twins were irremediably damaged emotionally and intellectually.

As it happened, the twins stayed with Perry and Sandy for close to two years. By the time they were adopted, they were judged within the "normal" range of intellectual and emotional capacity.

Of course, this is only one story out of millions. We need only read our newspapers to be reminded that, all things being equal, unless a child is reared in a home where love and discipline surround every step, that child will not attain emotional maturity. Countless studies have shown, for instance, that a girl reared without a strong and loving father rarely learns how to give and receive love. Inevitably, that will breed trouble in her own marriage. With the massive breakdown of the nuclear family, we have only begun to reap the whirlwind.

Not for a moment would I suggest that emotional scars are beyond repair. The grace of God reaches into every kind of environment and powerfully transforms broken people. But all things being equal, apart from the intervention of the grace of God, all of us know that for a human being to grow to full emotional and interpersonal maturity, the stability of a loving and disciplined home is an indispensable ingredient.

The same thing is true in the spiritual arena. Just as a human being cannot enjoy normal maturation and develop into a mature person without the structure of disciplined love in the home, so also a Christian who does not grow in the experience of the love of God in Christ does not grow to full maturity. That is what Paul presupposes in his prayer. He prays that Christians might have power to grasp the limitless dimensions of the love of God, so that they will be filled to the measure of all the fullness of God.

Like all analogies, this one is not perfect. In the case of the twin boys, they had been deprived of love and the structures of discipline; in our case, we run from such love, we deprive ourselves of such love—much like the prodigal son. But the result is the same: wretched immaturity, impoverished relationships, destroyed trust, a bankrupt sense of spiritual reality.

It takes nothing less than the power of God to enable us to grasp the love of Christ. Part of our deep "me-ism" is manifested in such independence that we do not really want to get so close to God that we feel dependent upon him, swamped by his love. Just as in a marriage a spouse may flee relationships that are too intimate, judging them to be a kind of invasion of privacy when in reality such a reaction is a sign of intense immaturity and selfishness, so also in the spiritual arena: when we are drawn a little closer to the living God, many of us want to back off and stake out our own turf. We want to experience power so that we can be in control; Paul prays for power so that we will be controlled by God himself. Our deep and pathetic self-centeredness is precisely why it takes the power of God to transform us, if we are to know the love of Christ that surpasses knowledge and grow to the maturity the Scriptures hold out before us.

It is wonderful to revel in the love of God. Truly to experience that love, to live in the warmth of its glow, invests all of life with new meaning and purpose. The brotherhood of the saints takes on new depth; "fellowship" becomes precious, not the artificially arranged shaking of hands in a service or the shared pot of tea or coffee. Forgiving others becomes almost natural, because we ourselves, thanks to God's immeasurably rich love, have been forgiven so much. Others may despise us, but that makes little difference if God loves us. How shall trouble or sorrow or bereavement drive us into macabre despair, when we can say, with Paul, "Who shall separate us from the love of Christ?" (Rom. 8:35). Our speech, our thoughts, our actions, our reactions, our relationships, our goals, our values—all are transformed if only we live in the self-conscious enjoyment of the love of Christ. Our testimony is then no longer

198

dry and merely correct; it is living and vital as well. We are, in short, growing up spiritually.

We should not think that Paul is advocating some kind of Lone Ranger Christianity, as if he is interested only in the maturation of the individual Christian. Far from it. He writes, "I pray that you, being rooted and established in love, may have power, *together with all the saints*, to grasp how wide and long and high and deep is the love of Christ, and to know this love that surpasses knowledge— that you may be filled to the measure of all the fullness of God" (3:17–19). "It needs the whole people of God to understand the whole love of God," writes John Stott.[3] In fact, it is hard to imagine any individual Christian genuinely growing in this regard yet unconcerned about fellow believers. It is inconceivable that a genuine, deepening grasp of the love of Jesus Christ could remain entirely privatized. Paul wants the entire church to grow in this way; and he prays to this end.

> To grasp how wide and long and high and deep
> The love of Christ, experience it when
> Mere knowledge bursts its categories, then
> Escape the fragile frame of language, reap
> The richest crop salvation brings, and heap
> Up mem'ries of a sea of love, again
> And yet again cascading o'er us—men
> Can know no other bliss so rich and deep.
>   Lord God, in love you have established us
>   And rooted us in soil no less fine—
>   Not single plants exposed to every gust
>   Of wind, but all the saints drink love sublime.
> Make me to know—a creature hewn from sod—
> The measure of all fullness found in God.

Is this not what you want? When was the last time you prayed along these lines? Do you not want to make it your goal to do so? Why not incorporate this sort of petition into your daily praying for the next six months? Can we perhaps hear God whispering, "You do not have, because you do not ask God" (James 4:2)?

Two Grounds for Paul's Petitions

1. Paul's petitions are in line with God's purposes. For this reason (v. 14), Paul says, he kneels before the Father and prays. For what reason? Clearly, the words *for this reason* point to something in the preceding verses. But when we read 3:1–13, we immediately notice something rather remarkable. The first verse of this section, 3:1, also begins with the words *for this reason*, and then the sentence trails off: "For this reason I, Paul, the prisoner of Christ Jesus for the sake of you Gentiles—." At a guess, Paul was heading toward his prayer for the Ephesians when he paused and decided it was necessary to say more about the nature of the apostolic ministry and its relationship to the gospel and the church. That means the words *for this reason* in verse 14 harken back to verse 1, and from there refer to Ephesians 1 and 2.

I do not intend in these pages to expound both of those chapters. Still, it is easy enough to summarize their principal thrusts, to identify the direction of Paul's argument. The apostle praises God for his sovereign grace in bringing lost Jews and lost Gentiles together into one new humanity, one new community. This God accomplished through the redemptive work of his Son on the cross. Addressing Gentile converts, Paul concludes, "Consequently, you are no longer foreigners and aliens, but fellow citizens with God's people and members of God's household, built on the foundation of the apostles and prophets, with Christ Jesus himself as the chief cornerstone. In him the whole building is joined together and rises to become a holy temple in the Lord. And in him you too are being built together to become a dwelling in which God lives by his Spirit" (2:19–22). Then Paul adds, "For this reason. . . . For this reason I kneel before the Father" (3:1, 14). For what reason? Paul prays for this reason, namely, that God's declared purpose in creating this new humanity is to bring the people in it to the kind of spiritual maturity portrayed in the extended metaphor of the "holy temple in the Lord . . . a dwelling in which God lives by his Spirit." In other words, Paul's prayers are entirely in line with God's purposes. Thus God's declared purposes become for Paul a reason for advancing these particular petitions to his heavenly Father. In short, Paul is praying in line with what he knows of God's will, just as he did in Ephesians 1 (see chap. 10 of this book).

We quickly learn that God is more interested in our holiness than in our comfort. He more greatly delights in the integrity and purity of his church than in the material well-being of its members. He shows himself more clearly to men and women who enjoy him and obey him than to men and women whose horizons revolve around good jobs, nice houses, and reasonable health. He is far more committed to building a corporate "temple" in which his Spirit dwells than he is in preserving our reputations. He is more vitally disposed to display his grace than to flatter our intelligence. He is more concerned for justice than for our ease. He is more deeply committed to stretching our faith than our popularity. He prefers that his people live in disciplined gratitude and holy joy rather than in pushy self-reliance and glitzy happiness. He wants us to pursue daily death, not self-fulfillment, for the latter leads to death, while the former leads to life.

These essential values of the gospel must shape our praying, as they shape Paul's. Indeed, they become the ground for our praying ("For this reason . . . I pray"): it is a wonderful comfort, a marvelous boost to faith, to know that you are praying in line with the declared will of almighty God.

2. Paul's petitions are addressed to the heavenly Father. "For this reason," Paul writes, "I kneel before the Father, from whom his whole family in heaven and on earth derives its name. I pray. . ." (3:14–16a). The expression that the New International Version renders "from whom his whole family in heaven and on earth derives its name" is extremely difficult to translate. It may simply mean that every notion of fatherhood—fatherhood of the nuclear family, of the clan, of the tribe—finds its ultimate archetype in God himself: God is the supreme Father, the model of all valid fatherhood. But it may mean that God is the heavenly Father of all his people, whether they be still in this world or already in heaven. Either way, God is the ultimate Father.

"Father" in Western thought does not have many overtones of dignity and authority. But in the ancient world, the father was not only the one who sought the good of his family, but the one who dispensed favors and ruled the clan or family unit. The God whom we approach in prayer is not simply the transcendent Other. He is the heavenly Father, and we are "members of God's household" (2:19). The God whom we approach is not only powerful, but he is related to us: he is our Father. Did not Jesus himself teach his disciples to pray, "Our Father . . ."?

Indeed, it is difficult not to see that Paul is alluding to Jesus' teaching: "So do not worry, saying, 'What shall we eat?' or 'What shall we drink?' or 'What shall we wear?' For the pagans run after all these things, and your heavenly Father knows that you need them. But seek first his kingdom and his righteousness, and all these things will be given to you as well" (Matt. 6:31–33). Or again: "Ask and it will be given to you; seek and you will find; knock and the door will be opened to you. . . . Which of you, if his son asks for bread, will give him a stone? Or if he asks for a fish, will give him a snake? If you, then, though you are evil, know how to give good gifts to your children, how much more will your Father in heaven give good gifts to those who ask him!" (Matt. 7:7–11).

So as Paul approaches God with his petitions, he reminds himself that the God he addresses is his heavenly Father, the archetypal Father, the Father of all who are truly his people in heaven and on earth. He is a good God; he knows how to give good gifts. Paul dares to approach this God with these requests because he knows God to be a good God, a heavenly Father. Thus the nature and character of God become for Paul a fundamental ground for intercessory prayer.

The more we reflect on the kind of God who is there, the kind of God who has disclosed himself in Scripture and supremely in Jesus Christ, the kind of God who has revealed his plans and purposes for his own "household," the kind of God who hears and answers prayer—the more we shall be encouraged to pray. Prayerlessness is often an index to our ignorance of God. Real and vital knowledge of God not only teaches us what to pray, but gives us powerful incentive to pray.

Praying for Power

A Final Word of Praise (3:20–21)

Paul has been asking God for some blessings of extraordinary value; he has been petitioning the Almighty for blessings that are immeasurably great. Now in his closing doxology (his "word of praise"), he puts these petitions in perspective by stressing two themes.

1. The God whom he petitions is able to do immeasurably more than all we ask or imagine. That is a staggering thought. The sophisticated, over-confident reader, both in Paul's day and in ours, might well think that the petitions set a high tone but that it is a bit optimistic to hope that God will actually answer such prayers. But Paul will not back down. The God to whom he prays, the God to whom he addresses his final word of praise, is "able to do immeasurably more than all we ask or imagine, according to his power that is at work within us" (3:20).

Partly, of course, this confidence is nothing more than the entailment of belief that God is omnipotent. To an omnipotent God, there cannot be degrees of difficulty. But surely Paul is saying something more than that about God. God is able to do immeasurably more than all we ask or imagine, not only because he is powerful but also because he is generous. He loves to give good gifts to his children. To think of God in any other way is to demean him; to think of God in this way is itself tantamount to a call to pray.

We simply cannot ask for good things beyond God's power to give them; we cannot even imagine good things beyond God's power to give them. Paul's concluding word of praise thus becomes an immensely powerful incentive to pray.

2. The ultimate purpose of Paul's prayer is that there be glory to God, in the church and in Christ Jesus. It is sad to think that even this late in the prayer we might stumble rather badly. But that is the case. It is possible to ask for good things for bad reasons. We may desire the power of God so to operate in our lives that we may become more holy; we may ask for power to grasp the limitless dimensions of the love of God—and yet distort these good requests by envisaging their fulfillment within a framework in which the entire universe revolves around our improvement. The root sin is the kind of self-centeredness that wants to usurp God's place. How tragic then if our prayers for good things leave us still thinking of ourselves first, still thinking of God's will primarily in terms of its immediate effect on ourselves, still longing for blessings simply so that we will be blessed.

We may have improved a little on the quality of what we ask for, but the deeper question is this: Do we bring these petitions before God both with a proximate goal (that we might receive what we ask for) and with an ultimate goal—that God might be glorified?

For that, surely, is the deepest test: Has God become so central to all our thought and pursuits, and thus to our praying, that we cannot easily imagine asking for anything without consciously longing that the answer bring glory to God?

That is Paul's vision in his concluding word of praise. He prays that there might be glory to God, both in the church, as the church progressively obeys God and pleases him and makes him the center of its existence, and also in Christ Jesus, presumably as Christ Jesus is lifted up by the church in thought, word, and deed.

Here, then, is how we shall reform our praying. We shall learn to pray with the apostle not only in his petitions, but in his words of praise, in his ultimate goal, in his profound God-centeredness.

Questions for Review and Reflection

1. How did you learn to pray? What have been the dominant influences on your prayer life?
2. Summarize the two petitions of Paul's prayer in Ephesians 3:14–21.
3. What are the purposes of these two petitions?
4. To what extent have you incorporated either or both of these petitions (not necessarily in exactly the same words) into your praying?
5. What are the two grounds for Paul's prayer, as Paul reports them?
6. What grounds or reasons lurk behind your prayers? How can you improve on these?
7. What steps can you take to make the glory of God the central concern of your life?

Praying for Power

12

Prayer for Ministry

(Romans 15:14–33)

Consistency, they say, is the hobgoblin of little minds. Applied to theology, this maxim eschews systems that are neat and tidy. A little mystery, a little inconsistency, leaves room for a sovereign and transcendent God.

On the other hand, few of us are prepared to think that inconsistency is a great virtue. The word conjures up fickleness, instability, even falsehood. Those who take the God of truth seriously cannot help but conclude, for instance, that the various parts of Scripture, this God's own self-disclosure, must cohere at some level. The Scriptures reflect the one God, the God of truth. We would not like to think that in this case inconsistency is the hobgoblin of a little Mind!

Even so, that does not mean the Bible is like a jigsaw puzzle that guarantees all the pieces have been provided. It is rather more like a jigsaw puzzle whose Maker has guaranteed that all the pieces he has provided belong to the same puzzle, even though for various good reasons he has not given us all of them. "The secret things

> ## Paul's Prayer for the Romans
>
> [14]I myself am convinced, my brothers, that you yourselves are full of goodness, complete in knowledge and competent to instruct one another. [15]I have written you quite boldly on some points, as if to remind you of them again, because of the grace God gave me [16]to be a minister of Christ Jesus to the Gentiles with the priestly duty of proclaiming the gospel of God, so that the Gentiles might become an offering acceptable to God, sanctified by the Holy Spirit. [17]Therefore I glory in Christ Jesus in my service to God. [18]I will not venture to speak of anything except what Christ has accomplished through me in leading the Gentiles to obey God by what I have said and done—[19]by the power of signs and miracles, through the power of the Spirit. So from Jerusalem all the way around to Illyricum, I have fully proclaimed the gospel of Christ. [20]It has always been my ambition to preach the gospel where Christ was not known, so that I would not be building on someone else's foundation. [21]Rather, as it is written:
> Those who were not told about him will see,
> and those who have not heard will understand.
> [22]This is why I have often been hindered from coming to you.
> [23]But now that there is no more place for me to work in these regions, and since I have been longing for many years to see you,

belong to the LORD," Moses tells us, "but the things revealed belong to us and to our children forever" (Deut. 29:29). That means that we will always have gaps as we construct the puzzle; it means that clumsy players will try to force some pieces into slots where they do not belong and may be tempted to leave some pieces out because they cannot see where they fit in.

So we must beware of those kinds of consistency that wittingly or unwittingly eliminate part of the Scriptures' witness, or that force the pieces of the puzzle together with such violence that we construct a warped picture, one without gaps, and fail to see that we have denied the existence of the secret things. God himself becomes domesticated, neat, controllable.

A CALL TO SPIRITUAL REFORMATION

²⁴I plan to do so when I go to Spain. I hope to visit you while passing through and to have you assist me on my journey there, after I have enjoyed your company for a while. ²⁵Now, however, I am on my way to Jerusalem in the service of the saints there. ²⁶For Macedonia and Achaia were pleased to make a contribution for the poor among the saints in Jerusalem. ²⁷They were pleased to do it, and indeed they owe it to them. For if the Gentiles have shared in the Jews' spiritual blessings, they owe it to the Jews to share with them their material blessings. ²⁸So after I have completed this task and have made sure that they have received this fruit, I will go to Spain and visit you on the way. ²⁹I know that when I come to you, I will come in the full measure of the blessing of Christ.

³⁰I urge you, brothers, by our Lord Jesus Christ and by the love of the Spirit, to join me in my struggle by praying to God for me. ³¹Pray that I may be rescued from the unbelievers in Judea and that my service in Jerusalem may be acceptable to the saints there, ³²so that by God's will I may come to you with joy and together with you be refreshed. ³³The God of peace be with you all. Amen.

(Rom. 15:14–33)

These reflections are important to the matter of prayer. At one level, I might argue, the prayers of Scripture are wonderfully consistent. Whether we consider the prayers of Moses, Paul, Peter, or John, they are addressed to the same God. Whatever differences these prayers have, they also disclose remarkable similarities in emphasis, tone, kinds of argument, and the like. For instance, does Paul tie much of his praying to his vision of the end, to his eager anticipation of Christ's return, and to the utter importance of living in the light of that cataclysmic event? So also does John of the Apocalypse; so also does Peter, when he writes, "The end of all things is near. Therefore be clear minded and self-controlled so that you can pray" (1 Pet. 4:7).

Prayer for Ministry

208

Even within the corpus of his letters, Paul's recorded prayers tend, as we have seen, to congregate around a number of themes. This does not mean they are formulaic: Paul's prayers are fresh, and some of their freshness is achieved because the apostle ties many of his prayers to his thanksgivings and to the themes of the letter he is then writing.[1]

Still, I am aware how little of the biblical material on prayer this short book has covered. For example, this book has not probed any of the psalms, and many of the psalms are prayers. Indeed, the prayers preserved in the psalms reflect the entire sweep of human experience—hope, fear, rage, doubt, faith, despair, betrayal, love, discouragement, loneliness, and much more. One of the reasons why elderly people appreciate the psalms more than young people is because they have lived longer and experienced more, and therefore they can resonate with the wide range of experiences reflected there. Yet all these valuable prayers remain untouched in these pages.

That's not all. There are many other prayers in the Bible. There are themes connected with praying that we have barely touched. For example, what do we make of "unanswered" prayer? What about those specific petitions that we are told to offer, such as, "The harvest is plentiful but the workers are few. Ask the Lord of the harvest, therefore, to send out workers into his harvest field" (Matt. 9:37–38)?

My only reason for mentioning these matters is that I would not want someone to treat this book as if it were a "how to" manual on prayer. I would not want to give the impression that if you simply repeat Paul's prayers, like magic incantations, you will transform your life. Prayer is not like a good recipe: simply follow a set of mechanical directions and everything turns out right in the end. That is why this book has tried to stress the relationship we must nurture as we pray to the living God; and in the ninth chapter we worked our way through some of the mysteries of praying, acknowledging, so to speak, the areas where there are large numbers of puzzle pieces missing. But some people love a kind of consistency in their spiritual disciplines that the Bible itself will not allow. I would therefore be remiss if I did not include a chap-

A CALL TO SPIRITUAL REFORMATION

ter on a prayer of Paul that is rather unlike the ones we have been looking at. In fact, this is a prayer that was not answered the way Paul wanted. Deep internal consistencies in all of Paul's praying are still plentiful, but they are not formal, shallow, mechanical.

In the prayer before us (Rom. 15:30–33), we do not find Paul telling others what he prays for, but asking prayer for himself and for his ministry. These are not petitions for holiness (whether of the individual believer or of the church), petitions for an increased grasp of the love of God, petitions for power to transform one's inner being. This prayer is a prayer for ministry, in particular for Paul's ministry. We may draw four important lessons from it.

1. Paul wants this prayer to be offered with earnestness, urgency, and persistence. Paul begins with a series of strongly emotive expressions. "I urge you . . . to join me . . . by praying to God for me" (15:30). The apostle does not lay a distant recommendation on these Roman believers he has not yet met, but passionately beseeches them. He reminds them of their union with him: "I urge you, brothers." This is the same language Paul uses in Romans 12:1, and with the same intensity: "Therefore I urge you, brothers, in view of God's mercy, to offer your bodies as living sacrifices, holy and pleasing to God."

But the strongest element of the appeal lies in what he says next: "I urge you, brothers, by our Lord Jesus Christ and by the love of the Spirit, to join me . . . by praying to God for me." The logic of the appeal runs something like this: If you truly confess Jesus the Messiah as Lord, I urge you in his name to pray for me. If you participate in the salvation he has gained for you, if you submit to him who has taught us to pray, if you have tasted his redemption and long to see his kingdom extended in the world, then I urge you to pray for me and my ministry. If you know anything of "the love of the Spirit" (which in this context does not refer to our love for the Spirit but to the love with which the Spirit fills us and empowers us), then demonstrate that love in this ministry of intercession to which I am urging you. If the Spirit is working in you, how can you not love? If you love me, how can you not pray for me? For you must always remember that your prayers reflect your grasp of who Christ is, and how well you love.

This is a frank appeal to Christian experience. Nor is it the only place in Paul's letters where Paul appeals to the experience of his readers. Consider this argument: "If you have any encouragement from being united with Christ, if any comfort from his love, if any fellowship with the Spirit, if any tenderness and compassion, then make my joy complete by being like-minded, having the same love, being one in spirit and purpose" (Phil. 2:1–2). Here, of course, Paul is not inciting his readers to pray. Nevertheless, the form of the argument is the same: if you have tasted of the blessings of the gospel, then surely you will do this thing that I ask of you. So also in Romans 15: if you belong to Jesus Christ and have experienced the powerful love of the Spirit operating through you, then surely toward an apostle of Jesus Christ you will gladly display that love by praying for him.

There is yet another expression that powerfully depicts the kind of prayer Paul wants offered on his own behalf. He writes, "I urge you, brothers, by our Lord Jesus Christ and by the love of the Spirit, *to join me in my struggle* by praying to God for me" (15:30, emphasis added). The italicized words represent one verb in the Greek original, a verb used only here in the New Testament. Nevertheless, other forms of the same word-group occur in the New Testament, sometimes in connection with prayer. For example, Paul writes to the Colossians and tells them this of Epaphras: "He is always *wrestling* in prayer for you, that you may stand firm in all the will of God, mature and fully assured" (Col. 4:12b, emphasis added). Elsewhere he writes, "I want you to know how much *I am struggling* for you [he is referring to his prayer life] and for those at Laodicea, and for all who have not met me personally" (Col. 2:1, emphasis added).

Clearly, Paul saw prayer as part of the Christian's struggle. The word-group is often associated with the strenuous discipline of the athlete who struggles to prevail. That is why Samuel Zwemer, ground-breaking missionary to Muslim lands, could utter his famous saying, "Prayer is the gymnasium of the soul." The idea is not that prayer becomes intrinsically superior and potentially more effective when it is offered up in a frenzy of sweat. Nor is there likely any direct allusion to the account of Jacob wrestling with

God (Gen. 32:22–32).[2] The idea, rather, is that Paul understands real praying to include an element of struggle, discipline, work, spiritual agonizing against the dark powers of evil. Insofar as the Roman Christians pray this way for Paul, they are joining him in his apostolic struggle.

To view prayer in this way is consistent with the picture of spiritual conflict painted in Ephesians 6. There Paul warns his readers that they need to put on the whole armor of God if they are to "stand against the devil's schemes" (6:11). Then, after telling them to dress themselves with the belt of truth, the breastplate of righteousness, the helmet of salvation, and all the other necessary pieces, Paul adds, "And pray in the Spirit on all occasions with all kinds of prayers and requests. With this in mind, be alert and always keep on praying for all the saints. Pray also for me, that whenever I open my mouth, words may be given me so that I will fearlessly make known the mystery of the gospel, for which I am an ambassador in chains. Pray that I may declare it fearlessly, as I should" (6:18–20).

In many parts of the world this business of spiritual warfare is taken a lot more seriously than many of us take it in the West. To live and serve in tribes whose culture is deeply embedded in animism, for instance, is startling. The shallowness of spiritual conflict in the West owes something, no doubt, to centuries of Christian influence and the relentless exposure of superstition. But, less honorably, it also owes something, nowadays, to raw secularism, and a pervasive world view that thinks of all reality on a naturalistic plane. In other words, our failure to perceive more of what is going on in the demonic realm may sometimes owe less to our Christian heritage than to our deep indebtedness to a culture that assigns sociological, psychological, and economic reasons for everything.

For good or ill, this state of affairs is changing. Most cities of any size in the Western world are now homes to witches' covens. The rise in a general interest in the occult sometimes explodes into a horrible media account of satanic rituals, even murder. Demonic powers may also unload massive doses of guilt and despair and shame upon us. Sadly, because we are so insensitive to the possibility that these bouts of depression may be related to our calling as Christians, we may foolishly try to overcome them and cheer ourselves up by going shopping, going out with a friend, reading a book. How seldom do we think of Paul's first recourse—his immediate desire to seek the face of the Lord Jesus in prayer.

Paul understands that this business of praying, of struggling in prayer, is no more than the entailment of the fact that we are engaged in supernatural conflict. We are not out on the streets simply trying to convince people intellectually. Our aim is not to impress people with our musical taste, fiery eloquence, or emotional power. We are out to win people to Jesus Christ; new birth is required, a demonstration of the power of God in conversion and transformation. Satan himself stands against us; for "our struggle is not against flesh and blood, but against the rulers, against the authorities, against the power of this dark world and against the spiritual forces of evil in the heavenly realms" (Eph. 6:12). But even if all of this dark power is against us, none less than Jesus is for us. Our struggle is a deep one, spiritual and supernatural. In such a conflict, we must learn to deploy appropriate weapons. And among the chief of these is this kind of earnest, urgent, persistent prayer.

2. Paul solicits prayer for himself, in connection with his own ministry. This is the first time in this book that we have focused attention on a passage where Paul solicits prayer for himself. On the other hand, if you go back to the list of Paul's prayers in chapter 4 of this book, you will discover that such passages are not unusual. It is worth pondering some of these texts. One was cited above (Eph. 6:12, 18–20). Here are three more:

> May God himself, the God of peace, sanctify you through and through. May your whole spirit, soul and body be kept blameless at the coming of our Lord Jesus Christ. The one who calls you is faithful, and he will do it. *Brothers, pray for us.* [1 Thess. 5:23–25, emphasis added]

> We do not want you to be uninformed, brothers, about the hardships we suffered in the province of Asia. We were under great pressure, far beyond our ability to endure, so that we

despaired even of life. Indeed, in our hearts we felt the sentence of death. But this happened that we might not rely on ourselves but on God, who raises the dead. He has delivered us from such a deadly peril, and he will deliver us. On him we have set our hope that he will continue to deliver us, *as you help us by your prayers*. Then many will give thanks on our behalf for the gracious favor granted us *in answer to the prayers of many*. [2 Cor. 1:8–11, emphases added]

And one thing more: Prepare a guest room for me, because I hope to be restored to you *in answer to your prayers*. [Philem. 22, emphasis added]

Paul would have uttered his "Amen!" to these lines from Joseph Hart:

> If pain afflict, or wrongs oppress,
> If cares distract, or fears dismay,
> If guilt deject, or sin distress,
> The remedy's before you: Pray.

Although in some sense all of these requests for prayer are tied to Paul's ministry, it is important to pause and ask exactly what he is asking prayer for here in Romans, and how these requests are tied to his vision of what he is called to do. In Romans 15, he asks for prayer for two things.

Paul asks for prayer that he might be rescued from unbelievers in Judea. The point is drawn from Paul's own words: "Pray that I may be rescued from the unbelievers in Judea" (15:31a). Paul had already explained that he was on his way to Judea, carrying with him a substantial amount of money collected by the churches in Macedonia and Achaia as a gift to believers in Jerusalem (15:26). But he knew he might not be accepted all that well in Judea, despite the fact that he was bearing a gift for some of its people.

The reason was both theological and cultural. There were many conservative, unconverted Jews in Jerusalem who not only thought of Paul as a turncoat, but perceived him to be an extremely dangerous character who was in serious danger of destroying the very foundations of God's biblical revelation in the Mosaic covenant.

214

From their perspective, his indifference to circumcision was tampering with God's law. His emphasis on Jesus and his death and resurrection ultimately diminished the temple as the meeting place between God and sinners. The Jewish identity and cultural heritage was tied to observance of rites and taboos; here was Paul trying to foster a new community made up of both Jews and Gentiles. From the perspective of his opponents, Paul was not only attempting the impossible, but the unthinkable, even the blasphemous.

The Book of Acts is full of brief reports of the animus directed against Paul by some members of the Jewish community. After his conversion, Paul's first trip to Jerusalem found him talking and debating "with the Grecian Jews, but they tried to kill him" (Acts 9:29). After his powerful address in Pisidian Antioch, on "the next Sabbath almost the whole city gathered to hear the word of the Lord. When the Jews saw the crowds, they were filled with jealousy and talked abusively against what Paul was saying" (Acts 13:44–45). As the "word of the Lord" spread throughout the region, "the Jews incited the God-fearing women of high standing and the leading men of the city. They stirred up persecution against Paul and Barnabas, and expelled them from their region" (Acts 13:50). In Lystra, after some initial success, "some Jews came from Antioch and Iconium and won the crowd over. They stoned Paul and dragged him outside the city, thinking he was dead" (Acts 14:19). There is more trouble, stirred up by Jews in Thessalonica (Acts 17:5–8), Berea (Acts 17:13), Corinth (18:12–17), Ephesus (19:8–9), and Macedonia (20:3). All this occurred before Romans was written.

Two things need to be emphasized. First, these descriptions are not the product of profound antisemitism. God knows, to our deep shame, how many people calling themselves Christians have done horrible things to the Jews. But at the beginning of the church's life, it was not so. Typically, it is the people in power who do the persecuting, and in the early days of the church's expansion, when the church was comparatively small and so many of the converts were coming from the synagogues, the synagogue authorities constituted some of the most virulent opposition to the gospel. In any case, so many of the first converts were Jews or proselytes that to speak of the "antisemitic" character of the church would be to abuse the term. Besides, Paul and others sometimes faced opposition from Gentile sources as well, and these incidents, too, are faithfully recorded (e.g., the beating and imprisonment Paul and Silas suffered in Philippi, Acts 16:16ff.; the riot in Ephesus, Acts 19:23ff.). If both Paul and Luke (in Acts) record some of the opposition the apostles suffered (read 2 Cor. 11:22ff.!), their record is motivated not by racial prejudice but by their understanding that the gospel divides human beings, whatever their race.

That leads us to the second factor that must be emphasized. The New International Version speaks of "the unbelievers in Judea" from whom Paul wishes to be rescued. The Greek is stronger: they are "the disobedient in Judea" or "the rebels of Judea." The distinction is important, especially today. We are inclined to buy into the modern view that "belief" is simply a matter of opinion. Whether or not you are a believer is a private matter. It has to do with your disposition and conditioning; no matters of ultimate truth are at stake. The New Testament writers, however, including Paul, never see things that way. They hold that God has objectively revealed himself—not only in the distant past, but now decisively in his Son, Jesus Christ, whom he raised from the dead. Not to trust him totally is not merely a question of religious preference, not a matter of "unbelief" in the modern sense, but willful disobedience, moral rebellion. It is the sinful elevation of personal opinion and preference and priorities above the centrality of God, who has with matchless kindness, forbearance, and love powerfully revealed himself to us. Not to believe that kind of God and that kind of revelation owes everything to utter self-idolatry, to sinful worship of self and all its myopic opinions. It is, in short, flagrant rebellion.

Small wonder, then, that Paul asks for prayer that he might be rescued from such people in his impending visit to Jerusalem.

Paul asks for prayer that his service in Jerusalem might be acceptable to the saints there. That, too, is nothing other than Paul's language: "Pray . . . that my service in Jerusalem may be acceptable to the saints there" (Rom. 15:31).

Prayer for Ministry

This plea for prayer reflects Paul's pastoral sensitivities to the situation in Jerusalem. Virtually all the believers in Jerusalem were Jews. Naturally, some of them were likely to be affected by those unconverted Jews who thought Paul's conduct despicable. Christians, after all, are often influenced by the views of unbelievers around them. Paul is a realist: he does not expect all the Christians in Jerusalem to understand, let alone approve, all that he has done.

There may be another factor in his concern. He is bringing money from the churches in Macedonia and Achaia to help poor believers in the Jerusalem area. He ardently desires that this gift will not only supply the needs of God's people, but also issue in an "overflowing in many expressions of thanks to God" (2 Cor. 9:12). But some people are not very good at receiving things—especially from those who are regarded as inferior. It takes grace to receive gifts in the right spirit, every bit as much as it takes grace to give them in the right spirit. If the Jerusalem saints come through with the right attitude, there will be not only thanks to God but also a rich infusion of a spirit of unity in the church scattered throughout the Roman Empire and beyond. That is why Paul asks for prayer for his service in Jerusalem.

These, then, are the two matters Paul specifically raises with his readers, asking for prayers on his behalf. Clearly, today we cannot ask for prayers along exactly the same lines. Nevertheless, it is not difficult to find legitimate application to somewhat similar needs today.

When we pray for missionaries, church planters, pastors, and other spiritual leaders, there are many needs we should keep in mind. We noted earlier in this chapter, for instance, that Paul asks for prayer that he might speak the gospel boldly, as he should: that sort of prayer should constantly be on our lips, offered to God on behalf of those whose task is so constantly the heralding of the gospel to others. But from the two petitions Paul asks for here, we may draw the following extensions:

We should pray that Christian leaders might be rescued from the opposition of outsiders who try to destroy their ministry. Nowadays this sort of trouble is unlikely to spring from a synagogue. In much of the Western world, the most destructive challenges will proba-

A CALL TO SPIRITUAL REFORMATION

bly not take the form of persecution that is physically dangerous—though Christians working in certain urban ghettos or with some cultists, occultists, and drug addicts face a measure of physical danger. The fact remains that there are many other threats to the vitality and fruitfulness of Christian leaders, and some of these threats come from outsiders.

Occasionally there are people who actively campaign to bring down a Christian leader. Once in a while a prominent Christian becomes the target of really nasty media attacks. I have seen local governments, led by some virulent antichrist (to use the language of 1 John 2:18), passing laws and exercising the civil bureaucracy to harass, limit, and if possible, destroy Christian ministry and its leaders. Again, although ministers are too often careless in relations with the opposite sex, and those who fall are not guiltless and are in fact frequently the instigators, nevertheless I have known two or three women who assigned themselves the job of seducing ministers and bringing them down, one of them with notable success. In some denominations the power politics are so ruthless and unprincipled that the kindest judgment is that some of the ecclesiastical politicians, despite their clerical robes, are "outsiders" in any biblical sense. These, too, can ruin Christian leaders whom they dismiss as too "conservative" or "biblicist" or "fundamentalist."

More commonly in our society the Christian leader incurs danger from outsiders not because the outsiders overtly plot to destroy the church but because their values and influence frequently become a snare. Sad to say, many ministers of the gospel, not to mention other leaders, are not immune to the blandishments of money and power. To be invited to join this club or that board may increase the leader's Christian influence and contacts. Indeed, probably most Christians will accept such invitations for precisely that reason. But in many cases accepting the invitation also serves to muzzle the Christian: there are now too many social conventions and obligations to make prophetic witness possible. The minister becomes domesticated, restrained by the leash of social prominence.

Prayer for Ministry

218

Fill in your own examples. It does not take long for the thoughtful observer to spot areas where Christian leaders are constantly in danger from outsiders and therefore need the prayers of God's people in their defense.

We should pray that Christian leaders might find that their Christian service is acceptable to those to whom they minister. Sometimes, of course, it is the leader who goes wrong, and the church shaped by biblical constraints will feel obligated to exercise discipline. That is an important issue, but not one I wish to deal with here. But for one reason or another, Christian leaders will frequently discover that their ministry is simply not acceptable to some of those they seek to serve, and this opposition can be extraordinarily destructive.

In some ways the problem is getting worse at the moment. The "baby-boomers" have come to power; the "baby-busters" are right behind them. In different ways, both groups tend to focus on one or two issues that are of enormous significance to them. These single-issue Christians, whether the issue is home schooling, the King James Version, a particular style of worship, the altar call as a test for orthodoxy, a particular model for outreach, a certain view of prophecy, become so fixated on their vision that they lose perspective and judge the ministry of others by twisted and reductionistic criteria.

Worse, many in this generation attend church to find peace and happiness, not pardon and holiness. They want to be fulfilled, not discover how Christ is the fulfillment of earlier revelation. They prefer entertainment to worship, oratory to truth, and programs to piety. If such people exercise a dominant voice in a church whose leaders earnestly seek to be faithful to Scripture (however contemporary the modes of expression), the leaders are in for a rough time.

We need to pray that God will send us undershepherds who are wise, spiritual, godly, disciplined, informed, prayerful, faithful to Scripture. But we also need to pray that their ministry will be acceptable to the saints. It is an enormous tragedy when there are too few faithful, anointed, visionary leaders; it is a terrible indictment on the church when those the Lord sends are treated like dirt. These things happen, and frequently. Perhaps they would not happen so often if more of us prayed that God would make the ministry of his most faithful and spiritually minded leaders widely acceptable among the saints.

3. For Paul, prayer for his ministry envisions further ministry. That is the conclusion that must be drawn from the "long-range" features in Paul's prayer. "Pray," he writes, "that I may be rescued from the unbelievers in Judea and that my service in Jerusalem may be acceptable to the saints there, so that by God's will I may come to you with joy and together with you be refreshed" (15:31–32). This must be understood against the background of the verses that immediately precede this request for prayer. Paul is not simply asking that he may get to Rome and have a much-needed holiday. Paul has explained that it has always been his ambition to preach the gospel on virgin turf, where the gospel is simply unknown (15:20). That is why he feels there is no more place for him to work in the eastern end of the Mediterranean (15:23). His plan, then, is to stop in Rome and visit his readers on his way to Spain (15:24), where he hopes to preach the gospel and extend his ministry to new fields. But first he must make the trip to Jerusalem and deliver the money that was carefully collected in Macedonia and Achaia to be given to poor believers in the mother church.

So when Paul asks for prayer in connection with his trip to Jerusalem, he cannot think of that trip without also thinking of ministry that he envisages beyond Jerusalem. First he plans on going to Rome to share in ministry there (Rom. 1:11–13), and then, using that as a base, he wants to go to Spain and to preach the gospel there. Who knows where he would have gone after that, if his plans had worked out? Thus "being refreshed" in Rome is meant to convey not only his joy in ministering there and being ministered to, but also his hope that he would pick up some support there to help him on his way to Spain.

This is a large, visionary view of prayer. Although it articulates the details of immediate concerns to God, it also keeps in mind the broad picture, and envisages further outreach. It does not simply ask God for enough grace to get us through the current mess;

it keeps asking where we are going, how we are reaching out, how triumph in this small scale may fit into the next stage of expansion.

It appears that Paul thinks several steps ahead of the service in which he is currently engaged. That is why this request for prayer not only takes in the immediate challenges, but places them within the larger stream and direction of ministry. Paul is a man who dreams dreams, who envisages new needs and opportunities, and these are carefully tied to his own prayer life and to the prayers he solicits from others.

Paul's prayer is not the same sort of prayer as the sweeping generalizations that sometimes ape it. We have all heard prayers of the sort, "Lord, pour your Spirit on everybody in the whole world. Lord, save everybody." This sort of prayer reflects one aspect of the character of God: the Lord takes no pleasure in the death of the wicked, and he himself cries out, "Turn, turn, why will you die?" Nevertheless, it is a prayer that will not receive a positive response, as the Bible itself makes plain, so there is little point praying it, at least in this form. But my impression is that for every believer who offers this sort of sweeping, generalizing petition, there are several more who get so bogged down on relatively picky points related to their health, prosperity, or better, the challenges of the next Vacation Bible School or the fickleness of a teenaged son, that they utterly lose any sense of the sweep and direction of ministry. They do not dream dreams; they never really pray for revival; they never envisage the potential next phase of ministry and the steps that could be taken to get from here to there.

Suppose you are a missionary working in a small tribe in central Africa. What do you pray for? In addition to the obvious—adequate health, village evangelism, the training of nationals—do you tie your requests to a larger vision? Do you think in terms of helping to set up indigenous and properly contextualized churches? Do you envisage outreach from this tribe to the next one? Is a Bible college necessary? If so, on what lines should it be established? What preparations are you making to work yourself out of a job? Do these dreams affect your prayer life?

I would not want to give the impression that everyone is called to expansive and immediately fruitful ministry. Some of us are called to situations where the work is slow and difficult. Even so, if we do not dream dreams and envisage what might be, it is unlikely we shall ever pray for them or work toward them. We shall spend our lives simply getting through each day's work as it comes up. How much better it is, wherever possible, to tie our immediate concerns to the larger possibilities of expanding ministry.

Furthermore, it is vitally important to recognize that Paul's prayer is nothing other than a concern for the gospel itself, and for its extension in a needy world. Here we do well to remember the frequently quoted words of E. M. Bounds: "One of the constitutional enforcements of the gospel is prayer. Without prayer, the gospel can neither be preached effectively, promulgated faithfully, experienced in the heart, nor be practiced in the life. And for the very simple reason that by leaving prayer out of the catalogue of religious duties, we leave God out, and His work cannot progress without Him."[3]

That is what is so attractive about Paul's prayer. He does not want his service to be acceptable to the saints in Jerusalem and to be tolerated by Jews there in order that his life might be a little easier or so that his reputation will be enhanced in the power blocs of the ecclesiastical hierarchy. He wants his way to be smoothed so that he can get on with the next phase of outreach. He cares about the gospel; he is passionately committed to its extension. That is what drives his prayers.

Is that what drives ours?

4. Finally, it is important to learn that some of Paul's prayers were not answered as he would have liked. Specifically, Paul requests prayer that he will be rescued from those in Judea who disobey the gospel, that his ministry will be acceptable to the saints in Jerusalem, and all of this so that he may be "refreshed" in Rome and sent on his way toward further outreach and church planting in Spain.

But we know how the story works out: we have the Book of Acts. Of these three requests, the second is granted, the first is

Prayer for Ministry

222

not (Paul was arrested in Jerusalem owing to the instigation of the "unbelievers in Judea"), and so far as we know, he never got to Spain. He did, of course, get to Rome, but not as he envisaged: after two years of incarceration in Caesarea, and a hearing before a demonstrably corrupt court, he appeals to Caesar and is shipped to Rome, experiencing another shipwreck (his fourth!) along the way. When Paul requested the prayers recorded in our passage, he certainly did not envisage these results.

Yet it is reassuring to recognize that some of Paul's prayers were not answered as he would have liked, for that is our experience as well. This is not the only "unanswered" prayer in Scripture, or the only prayer where some of the answers came in forms that the one who was praying would rather be without. In the Garden of Gethsemane, Jesus himself prayed, "Take this cup from me" and even though he added, "Nevertheless, not my will, but yours, be done," the fact remains that the initial request was not answered as Jesus would have liked.

In 2 Corinthians 12:1–10, Paul prays three times that the "messenger of Satan," his "thorn in the flesh," would be removed, and it wasn't. God answered by supplying more grace, and in time Paul came to see that this was a good and wise answer, but it certainly was not what Paul had in mind when he voiced his prayers in the first place.

Suppose, for argument's sake, that every time we asked God for anything and ended our prayers with some appropriate formula, such as "in Jesus' name," we immediately received what we asked for. How would we view prayer? How would we view God? Wouldn't prayer become a bit of clever magic? Wouldn't God himself become nothing more than an extraordinarily powerful genie, to be called up, not by rubbing Aladdin's lamp, but by praying? "Please give me the ideal spouse, today. In Jesus' name, Amen." "Please raise up eighty-two more missionaries for Zaire, complete with their support, by the end of the week. In Jesus' name, Amen." What an easy and domesticated religion.

But this is not true religion. This is magic, not worship; it is another power trip, not hearty submission to the lordship of

Christ. It is superstition, not a personal relation with the Father God who is wise, good, and patient.

He may give us what we ask for; he may make us wait; he may decline. He may give us the goal of what we ask for, but by quite another means, as when he provided Paul with more grace to cope with the suffering inflicted by the thorn in the flesh, rather than removing the thorn.

There are two poems, anonymous as far as I know, that sum up a great deal of profound theology in very practical terms:[4]

> I asked the Lord that I might grow
>   In faith, and love, and every grace;
> Might more of his salvation know,
>   And seek more earnestly his face.
>
> I thought that in some favoured hour
>   At once he'd answer my request;
> And, by his love's constraining power,
>   Subdue my sins and give me rest.
>
> Instead of this, he made me feel
>   The hidden evils of my heart,
> And let the angry power of hell
>   Assault my soul in every part.
>
> "Lord, why is this?" I trembling cried.
>   "Wilt thou pursue thy worm to death?"
> "'Tis in this way," the Lord replied,
>   "I answer prayer for grace and faith."
>
> "These inward trials I employ
>   From self and pride to set thee free,
> And break thy schemes of earthly joy,
>   That thou may'st seek thy all in me!"

Or again:

> He asked for strength that he might achieve;
>   he was made weak that he might obey.
> He asked for health that he might do greater things;

Prayer for Ministry

he was given infirmity that he might do better things.
He asked for riches that he might be happy;
    he was given poverty that he might be wise.
He asked for power that he might have the praise of men;
    he was given weakness that he might feel the need of God.
He asked for all things that he might enjoy life;
    he was given life that he might enjoy all things.
He has received nothing that he asked for, all that he hoped for;
    his prayer is answered.

There is a profound sense in which the sovereign, holy, loving, wise Father whom we address in Jesus' name is more interested in *us* than in our prayers. I do not mean to depreciate praying, only to say that God's response to our prayers cannot be abstracted from his treatment of us.

I do not know the end from the beginning. Only God does. But he is interested in me as his child, in the same way that he was interested in the life and ministry of the apostle Paul. Part of this business of prayer is getting to know God better; part of it is learning his mind and will; part of it is tied up with teaching me to wait, or teaching me that my requests are often skewed or my motives selfish.

Just as God's unexpected answer to Paul's prayers was the best possible answer (precisely because it was God's), so also his answers to our prayers will always be for his glory and his people's good.

Questions for Review and Reflection

  1. Are your prayers for others characterized by earnestness, urgency, and persistence? If not, why not?
  2. To what extent does love for the gospel and for gospel outreach drive your prayers? How can you improve in this area?
  3. Do you feel some of your prayers have not been answered? Have you received answers you did not expect? What light can you shed on your experience?
  4. Think through particular hurdles Christian leaders face in your church or group, and pray (preferably with others) for these leaders.

Afterword:
A Prayer for Spiritual Reformation

And now, Lord God, I ask your blessing on all who read this book, for without it there will be no real benefit. We may have education, but not compassion; we may have forms of praying, but no fruitful adoration and intercession; we may have oratory, but be lacking in unction; we may thrill your people, but not transform them; we may expand their minds, but display too little wisdom and understanding; we may amuse many, but find few who are solidly regenerated by your blessed Holy Spirit.

So we ask you for your blessing, for the power of the Spirit, that we may know you better and grow in our grasp of your incalculable love for us. Bless us, Lord God, not with ease or endless triumph, but with faithfulness. Bless us with the right number of tears, and with minds and hearts that hunger both to know and to do your Word. Bless us with a profound hunger and thirst for righteousness, a zeal for truth, a love of people. Bless us with the perspective that weighs all things from the vantage point of eternity. Bless us with a transparent love of holiness. Grant to us strength in weakness, joy in sorrow, calmness in conflict, patience when opposed or attacked, trustworthiness under temptation, love when we are hated, firmness and farsightedness when the climate prefers faddishness and drift.

We beg of you, holy and merciful God, that we may be used by you to extend your kingdom widely, to bring many to know and love you truly.

Grant above all that our lives will increasingly bring glory to your dear Son, our Lord and Savior Jesus Christ.

May the God of peace, who through the blood of the eternal covenant brought back from the dead our Lord Jesus, that great Shepherd of the sheep, equip us with everything good for doing his will, and may he work in us what is pleasing to him, through Jesus Christ, to whom be glory for ever and ever. Amen.

Endnotes

Preface

1. D. A. Carson, ed., *Teach Us to Pray: Prayer in the Bible and the World* (Grand Rapids: Baker/Exeter: Paternoster, 1990).

Introduction

1. J. I. Packer, in *My Path of Prayer*, David Hanes, ed. (Worthing, West Sussex: Henry E. Walter, 1981), 56.

Chapter 1: Lessons from the School of Prayer

1. There is a useful discussion of some of these matters in Thomas E. Schmidt, *Trying to Be Good* (Grand Rapids: Zondervan, 1990), chap. 3.

2. See David H. Adeney, "Personal Experience of Prayer," in *Teach Us to Pray: Prayer in the Bible and the World*, ed. D. A. Carson (Grand Rapids: Baker/Exeter: Paternoster, 1990), 309–15.

3. Bill Hybels, *Too Busy Not to Pray: Slowing Down to Be with God* (Downers Grove, Ill.: InterVarsity, 1988), esp. 101–6.

4. Patrick Johnstone, *Operation World: A day-to-day guide to praying for the world*, 4th ed. (Bromley, Kent: STL, 1986).

5. Stanley J. Grenz, *Prayer: The Cry for the Kingdom* (Peabody, Mass.: Hendrickson, 1988), 37.

6. See D. A. Carson, *The Farewell Discourse and Final Prayer of Jesus* (Grand Rapids: Baker, 1980), 109–10; British edition, *Jesus and His Friends* (Leicester: InterVarsity, 1986), 108–10.

7. For a defense of this interpretation, see Peter T. O'Brien, "Romans 8:26, 27: A Revolutionary Approach to Prayer?" *The Reformed Theological Review* 46 (1987): 65–73.

8. Quoted by C. S. Lewis in *Letters to Malcolm: Chiefly on Prayer* (New York: Harcourt, Brace and World, 1964), 67–68.

9. Ibid., 68.

10. In *My Path of Prayer*, ed. David Hanes (Worthing, West Sussex: Henry E. Walter, 1981), 57.

Chapter 2: The Framework of Prayer

1. The peculiar prepositional construction in the Greek text (*eis ho*) suggests that everything that precedes vv. 11–12 leads up to them; hence NIV's idiomatic rendering.

Chapter 3: Worthy Petitions

1. A slight ambiguity in the text prompts some interpreters to read this part of the verse a different way. Paul's prayer, literally rendered, is that God "may fulfill every good purpose and work of faith." It is possible to take "every good purpose" to refer to God's good purposes. But the "work of faith" is surely the believer's, and "every" most probably embraces both objects, so it is most natural to read the text as in NIV: that God "may fulfill every good purpose of yours and every act prompted by your faith."

Chapter 4: Praying for Others

1. The distinctions are to some extent artificial, of course. For instance, the group often labeled "Paul's prayers" are perhaps more immediate than the "reports" of Paul's prayers, but surely they too are merely reports, and partial ones at that: we have no transcript of a complete prayer of Paul.

2. Not included are passages such as Rom. 8:26–27, where Paul talks about prayer: "In the same way, the Spirit helps us in our weakness. We do not know what we ought to pray for, but the Spirit himself intercedes for us with groans that words cannot express. And he who searches our hearts knows the mind of the Spirit, because the Spirit intercedes for the saints in accordance with God's will."

Chapter 5: A Passion for People

1. See especially Peter T. O'Brien, "Thanksgiving within the Structure of Pauline Theology," in *Pauline Studies* (Festschrift for F. F. Bruce), ed. Donald A. Hagner and Murray J. Harris (Grand Rapids: Eerdmans, 1980), 50–66, esp. 56.

Chapter 6: The Content of a Challenging Prayer

1. An extraordinarily useful and perceptive article on the biblical theology of prayer is that by Edmund P. Clowney, "A Biblical Theology of Prayer," in *Teach Us to Pray: Prayer in the Bible and the World*, ed. D. A. Carson (Grand Rapids: Baker/Exeter: Paternoster, 1990), 136–73.

2. I.e., taking the preposition *en* epexegetically to "knowledge."

Chapter 7: Excuses for Not Praying

1. Lillian R. Guild, in *Ministry* (May 1985): 28.

2. The meaning of the Greek word is disputed. Literally, *anaideia* means "shamelessness," and some assign this shamelessness to the man at the door. He displays "sheer impudence" in demanding so much at so late an hour. Some extend this meaning to argue the word refers to this man's "unblushing persistence"; hence NIV's "persistence," referring of course to the perseverance of the man who is doing the knocking. This is almost certainly incorrect. The meaning of the word cannot easily be pushed so far, and the point of the parable turns not on

the attitude of the man doing the knocking, but on the attitude of the man inside the house. The way forward comes by recognizing that in Greek *anaideia* can mean "shamelessness" in a slightly different sense. Whereas in English "shameless" people are those who are potentially capable of any foul deed because they do not care if they incur shame, in Greek "shameless" people can be those whose conduct ensures that they will avoid shame: they act in such a way that they are literally "shame-less," utterly innocent of any shame. On this reading the word refers to the person inside the house. Because "shamelessness" in English does not readily carry this positive overtone, my rendering is paraphrastic: "desire to be without shame."

Chapter 8: Overcoming the Hurdles

1. Greek *dokimadzō*.
2. Greek *ta diapheronta*.
3. Viz., *dikaiosynē*.
4. I use the term *revival* in its historic sense, not in the modern usage found among such groups as the Southern Baptists, where revival is more or less equivalent to "evangelistic meeting." In this latter context, it is possible to speak of "holding a revival" or "planning a revival"; in the historic use of the term, such usage would be grotesque.

Chapter 9: A Sovereign and Personal God

1. The discussion that follows is a condensation of a longer treatment of God's sovereignty and human responsibility, drawn from my book *How Long, O Lord? Reflections on Suffering and Evil* (Grand Rapids: Baker, 1990/Leicester: InterVarsity, 1991), chaps. 11, 12.
2. Of course, he said "much people" instead of "many people," since at this period (in the late fifties) he was steeped in the King James Version!
3. Cf. J. Gresham Machen, *The New Testament: An Introduction to Its Literature and History* (repr. Edinburgh: Baner of Truth, 1976), p. 320, who, writing of believers at a slightly later stage, insightfully comments on the freedom of God: "That conception pervades all the prayers of the apostolic Church; in all of them man comes to God as one person to another. God is free; God can do what he will; through Christ he is our Father. He is not bound by his own works; he is independent of nature; he will overrule all things for the good of his children. Such is the God that can answer prayer."
4. Some readers may want to pursue this line of argument a little further. Cf. Paul Helm, "Asking God," *Themelios* 12 (1986–87): 22–24. A useful book is that by W. Bingham Hunter, *The God Who Hears* (Downers Grove, Ill.: InterVarsity, 1986), especially chap. 4.

Chapter 10: Praying to the Sovereign God

1. This language suggests that Paul has not personally met his readers, or at least most of them—much as in his letter to the Colossians (see chap. 6). If this letter was written by Paul to the church in Ephesus, the language in this verse is rather difficult to explain. In fact, the designation *to the saints in Ephesus* (1:1) is textually doubtful: in my judgment the words *in Ephesus* were not part of the original manuscript. It is quite plausible that this letter was a circular missive sent to believers throughout Asia Minor, from Ephesus to the head of the Lycus Valley (the same area covered by the "seven churches" of Revelation 2–3). If so, one can easily imagine how the words *in Ephesus* early became attached to the copy left in Ephesus, the first city at which such a letter would have been dropped off.

Endnotes

2. The last clause, which does not greatly concern us here, is rather difficult, and its meaning is disputed in the commentaries. I am inclined to take the Greek participle at the end of the verse not as active (NIV "who fills") but as passive ("which is being filled," referring to the church), with "fullness" in apposition to the general thought that precedes this last clause. The thought, then, is roughly this: Christ, who as sovereign head presides over the church, is also immanent within the church, filling it perfectly "as it attains to the maximum of its perfect plenitude" (the language is that of H. Chadwick). Christ is the one in whom the fullness of Deity resides (Col. 2:9), and out of that fullness constantly supplies the church with all it needs.

Chapter 11: Praying for Power

1. The structure of the clauses in these verses is rather complicated. As a result, commentators differ over their relationships, and therefore over the number of independent petitions. The exposition here results from my own reading of the structure of these verses.

2. J. I. Packer, A Quest for Godliness: The Puritan Vision of the Christian Life (Wheaton: Crossway, 1990), 69.

3. John R. W. Stott, God's New Society: The Message of Ephesians (Downers Grove, Ill: InterVarsity, 1979), 137.

Chapter 12: Prayer for Ministry

1. This is a major conclusion of the important studies by G. P. Wiles, Paul's Intercessory Prayers, SNTSMS 24 (Cambridge: Cambridge University Press, 1974), and Peter T. O'Brien, Introductory Thanksgivings in the Letters of Paul, SuppNovT 49 (Leiden: Brill, 1977).

2. The verbal similarities needed to bolster such a claim simply aren't there. See David G. Peterson, "Prayer in Paul's Writings," in Teach Us to Pray: Prayer in the Bible and the World, ed. D. A. Carson (Grand Rapids: Baker, 1990), 99, and the literature cited there.

3. E. M. Bounds, A Treasury of Prayer, compiled by Leonard Ravenhill (Minneapolis: Bethany Fellowship, 1961), 159.

4. Most recently they were cited by J. I. Packer, in My Path of Prayer, ed. David Hanes (Worthing, West Sussex: Henry E. Walter, 1981), 63–64.

Extended Note

In the preface I mentioned that the material in this book had originally been prepared as seven sermons. Some preachers who read these pages may be interested to learn how the material was originally configured. The more topical chapters were extended introductions to typically expository sermons. Aside from many editorial changes to prepare the material for the printed page, the seven sermons formed a series with the title "Praying with Paul," and the seven titles and passages were:

1. Foundations (2 Thess. 1:3–12) [material from the introduction, and chaps. 2 and 3 of this book]

2. People (1 Thess. 2:17–3:13, esp. 3:9–13) [material from chaps. 4 and 5]

3. Practice (Col. 1:1–14, esp. 1:9–14) [material from chaps. 1 and 6]

4. Excellence (Phil. 1:1–11, esp. 1:9–11) [material from chaps. 7 and 8]

5. Mystery (Eph. 1:3–23, esp. 1:15–23) [material from chaps. 9 and 10]

6. Power (Eph. 3:14–21) [material from chap. 11]

7. Ministry (Rom. 15:14–33, esp. 15:30–33) [material from chap. 12]